ALSO BY STEVE COLGATE

Fundamentals of Sailing, Cruising, and Racing (1978)

Steve Colgate
on Sailing

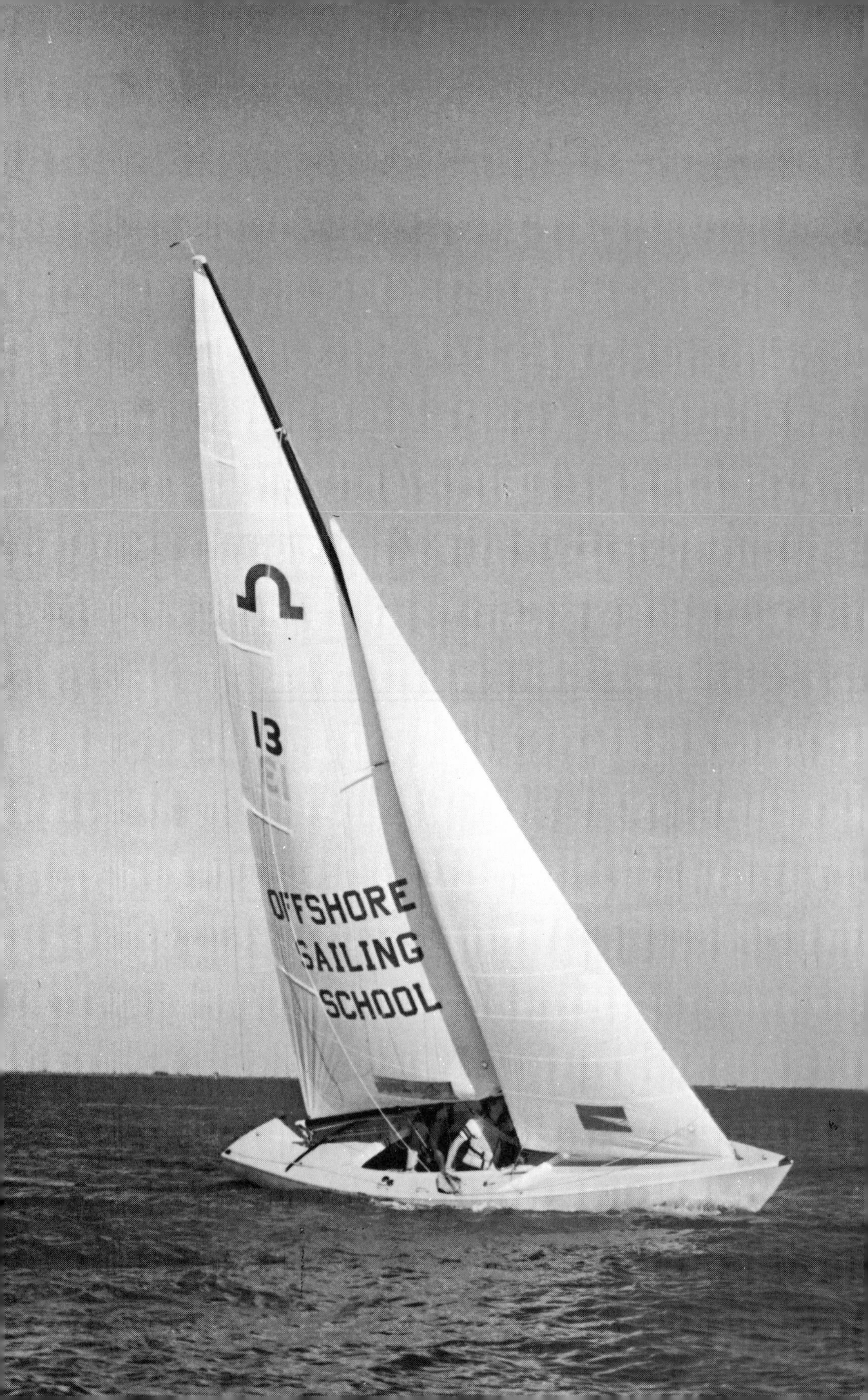
13
OFFSHORE
SAILING
SCHOOL

Steve Colgate on Sailing

STEVE COLGATE

Edited by Marcia Wiley
Drawings by Mike Dickey

W. W. Norton & Company
New York · London

Printed in the United States of America.

Composition by The Sarabande Press.
Manufacturing by Courier Westford.
First Edition

Library of Congress Cataloging-in-Publication Data
Colgate, Steve.
Steve Colgate on sailing / Steve Colgate; edited by Marcia Wiley;
drawings by Mike Dickey.
p.   cm.
Includes index.
1. Sailing.   I. Wiley, Marcia.   II. Title.
GV811.C564   1991
797.1'24—dc20   90-41977

ISBN 0-393-02903-4
W.W. Norton & Company, Inc. 500 Fifth Avenue, New York, N.Y. 10110
W.W. Norton & Company, Ltd., 37 Great Russell Street, London WC1B 3NU
2   3   4   5   6   7   8   9   0

CONTENTS

CHAPTER IV

SEAMANSHIP

LINES

BOATHANDLING

CHAPTER V

THE WIND

CHAPTER VI

NAVIGATION: PILOTING

CHAPTER VII

RACING TACTICS

CHAPTER VIII
MEDICAL PROBLEMS, ACCIDENTS, SAFETY

Special thanks for their contributions: the late Tom Blackaller, Chris Bouzaid, Peter Conrad, Harold Cudmore, Dick Stearns, Dick Tillman, and Stu Walker.

Steve Colgate

on Sailing

Chapter I

THE THEORY OF SAILING

WHY A BOAT SAILS

There's something magical about sailing . . . the way a sailboat ghosts along in the slightest breeze, her white sails reflecting in the calm, blue water; the way she blasts to windward in heavy seas seemingly impervious to the forces of nature trying to push her back whence she came, and the way she resists the wind's best efforts to blow her flat and sideways. Yet it isn't all that magical when you think about it. In my other books we've covered the basics of *how* a boat sails; now let's find out *why* she sails.

Just like airplane wings, the sails of a sailboat develop aerodynamic lift. This lift derives from the Center of Effort (CE) of all the sails on the boat. We locate it by finding the geometric center of each sail and then drawing a line between these centers; the CE is on this line based on the comparable sail areas. In Figure 1, the mainsail is 900 square feet. We bisect the angles made by the head, the foot, and the clew, which gives us the location of the CE of the mainsail. We do the same to the 300-sq.ft. jib to get its Center of Effort and connect the two CEs with a line. Since the jib is one-third the size of the main, the Center of Effort of the whole sail plan is at a point one-third the length of the connecting line.

The lift along the curved sail is in a direction perpendicular to a line tangential to the sail. It is greatest where the curvature is greatest and the

Figure 1

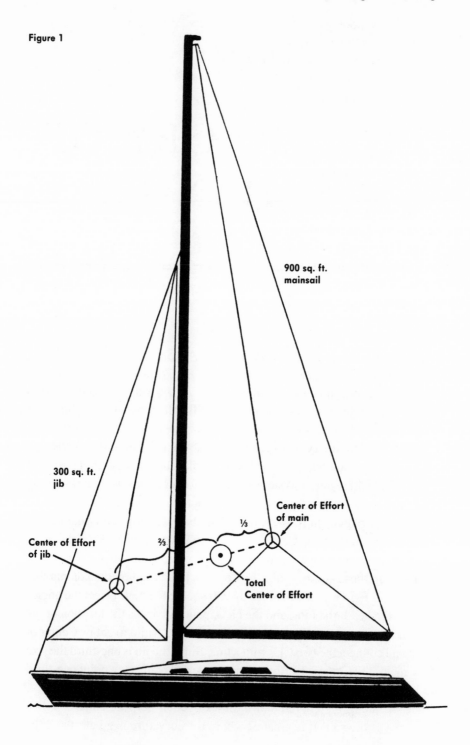

airflow is smoothest, which is in the forward third of the sail. Once the airflow starts to separate near the back of the sail, lift is reduced. We diagram the lift along the sail as a series of little arrows pointing in the direction of the lift, the length of which indicates the amount of lift; the more the lift, the longer they are, as in Figure 2. A resultant arrow that adds up the length and direction of all the little arrows is shown in Figure 3.

The lift of the sails is a factor in the final forward drive of a sailboat. At any particular point, forces creating forward drive are balanced by forces resisting drive called *drag forces*. If we increase the drive, the boat will sail faster, but the drag forces will also increase and a balance occurs. Although there is *aerodynamic* drag—the wind in the rigging, for example—the greatest drag comes from *hydrodynamic* drag; i.e., drag on every part of the boat under water.

The importance of hydrodynamic drag should not be underestimated. There are three types: Wavemaking Drag, Friction Drag and Induced Drag. The first two account for about 80 percent of the total hydrodynamic drag. As the boat moves through the water, she has to push the sea aside and down. This is Wavemaking Drag and is greater or less depending on the shape and displacement of the boat. Knife your hand through the water in the bathtub and it slices through fairly easily. If you turn it so your palm faces forward, you feel a great deal more resistance. Notice how the water is pushed out to the sides and there's tremendous turbulence at the back of your hand. This is Wavemaking Drag. Pushing your hand through the water slowly doesn't take too much effort, but trying to push it really fast takes a great deal of force. This is a pertinent factor in Wavemaking Drag. It's not as much of a problem in light winds and slow boatspeed as it is in high wind velocities when the boat is going near her maximum speed.

Friction Drag is the drag caused by the water flowing across the underwater surfaces of the boat. A boat bottom covered with seaweed and barnacles will create more friction as the water flows over it—and will therefore sail slower—than a smooth, clean bottom. Induced Drag is drag resulting from

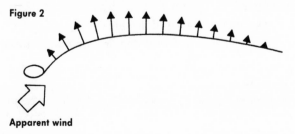

Figure 2

Apparent wind

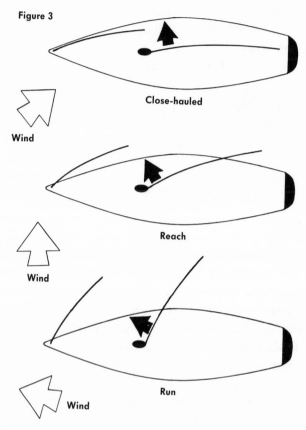

Figure 3

Close-hauled

Wind

Reach

Wind

Run

Wind

the forces that create lift. It's a small portion of the total drag, and since it depends upon the design of the sailboat, I don't consider it when I'm out sailing.

Do I consider the other drags? Indeed I do. How? In lots of little ways. Have you ever left a spare halyard attached near the bow pulpit? That halyard cannot be winched tight enough not to vibrate, even imperceptibly. This vibration creates aerodynamic drag many times the diameter of the wire. Even if it could be tightened enough to stop vibrating, it still disrupts the airflow meeting the jib, just where you want the flow to be clean. The halyard should be secured as tightly alongside the mast as possible. Aerodynamic drag is also produced by crew standing up when you're sailing to windward. Except when in action, crew should stay low to the deck, either sitting or lying down.

Hydrodynamic drag caused by even a small bit of slime on the bottom is discussed later. However, lines dangling in the water over the leeward rail also create hydrodynamic drag. When racing you are always thinking of

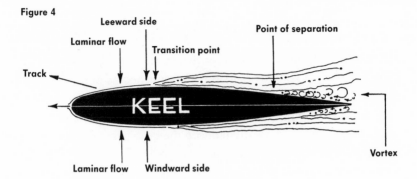

Figure 4

ways to reduce drag, so it behooves you to know a little about it.

As the boat's hull and keel pass through the water pushing it aside, water works just like other fluids, including air. Refer to Fig. 4. It illustrates a layer right next to the hull surface that has essentially no movement; it's called the "boundary layer." If you drive your car on a dusty road it will acquire a thin coat of dust. Then drive it on a highway, and even if you drive 80 m.p.h., that dust won't blow off. Each layer above the boundary layer moves a little faster, but as long as the flow is smooth and layered (it's called "laminar flow"), it creates very little drag.

As the thickness of the hull and keel increase farther aft, the water flow velocity increases because of the wedge effect. At a certain point, called the "transition point," the water can no longer retain laminar flow and turbulence starts. The drag coefficient is much greater for the turbulent flow than for laminar flow. As the flow continues aft along the underwater surfaces of the sailboat, the airfoil shape starts to decrease in thickness. The flow can follow the shape as the thickness decreases, but eventually it reaches a point, called the "separation point," where the flow breaks away into tiny little whirlpools called "vortices." A vortex is often caused by the difference in pressure from one side of the keel to the other. The flow of water over the keel and air over the sails is aft and downward. This "downwash" is enhanced by the swept-back design of many keels, the slope of the luff of the jib from the jibstay and the rake of the mast for the mainsail. Any fluid tends to flow from an area of greater pressure to an area of lesser pressure. When flow from the lifted side—the leeward side of the sails and the windward side of the underwater appendages—passes under the sails or keel, vortices are generated and greater drag results.

So, you say, how does this relate to me when I'm racing? It's long been known that these tip vortices can be reduced by "end-plating;" that is, by laying the foot of a genoa jib right along the deck so the flow of high pressure on the leeward side is directed aft instead of under the foot of the genoa. Just keep this in mind when you're tempted to raise the tack of the jib for some reason or other. Years ago, roller-reefing booms were very popular. I discovered I could end-plate the mainsail by rolling the boom to leeward a quarter turn. We didn't lower or reef the mainsail, we just changed the position of the boom and greatly reduced the crossover. We demonstrated the technique's effectiveness by attaching wool telltales to the sail.

As for hydrodynamic drag, we want to move the transition point from laminar to turbulent flow as far aft as possible. We do this with surface preparation, making sure that the bottom is absolutely smooth and clean. When you clean the boat in the water, work hardest on the leading edges and worry less about the after edges because there's not much you can do aft of the point of separation.

Figure 5 illustrates the various forces that affect the performance of a sailboat. We have discussed the lift, drive and Center of Effort (CE) of the sail. We must also consider heeling force, as in Figure 6. Heeling is generally detrimental. As a boat heels, less sail area is exposed to the wind. If a boat were blown flat, for instance, there would be no wind in the sails at all. Since the number of square feet of sail area is a very important factor in the speed of a sailboat, anything that reduces the effective sail area is harmful. When a boat heels, the underwater appendages lose their area in

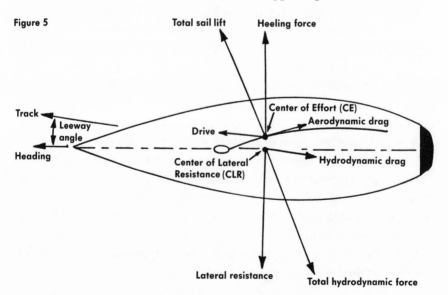

Figure 5

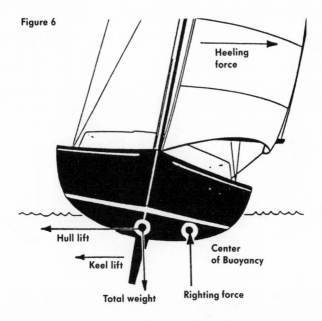

Figure 6

Heeling force

Hull lift

Keel lift

Center of Buoyancy

Total weight

Righting force

the same manner as the sails. If the boat is vertical, the surface areas of the keel and rudder help keep the boat from slipping sideways. If the boat were blown flat, the keel and rudder wouldn't be doing anything at all, so you can see that any angle less than vertical is detrimental.

One of the fundamental relationships of the proper balance of a sailboat is that between the CE of the sail plan and the Center of Lateral Resistance (CLR) of the hull shape.

The CLR is the center of the underwater surfaces of the hull. If you draw the underwater portion of a sailboat and cut the profile out of cardboard, the CLR is the point where the piece of cardboard will balance level on the head of a pin. The relationship between CE and CLR and their affect on the balance of a sailboat is best described in terms of a weather vane on a roof with the pivot point at the CLR. If the CE is directly above the pivot point the weather vane won't rotate, just like the perfectly balanced boat in Figure 7. Actually, this is an oversimplification since naval architects design a boat with the CE slightly forward of the CLR (a distance called "lead") in order to balance the boat. If we add a larger jib to our weather vane as in Figure 8, we move the CE forward. When the wind blows, the bow rotates to leeward. Conversely, if we add sail area near the stern of the boat (Figure 9), the CE will be moved aft of the CLR, the stern will be blown to leeward and weather helm develops.

There are ways to reduce heeling. For instance, keep crew weight on the

Figure 7

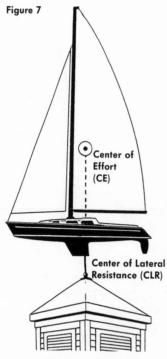

CE above CLR; boat is balanced

Figure 8

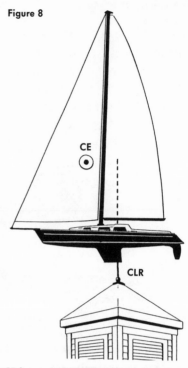

CE forward of CLR. Bow blows away from the wind, lee helm results.

Figure 9

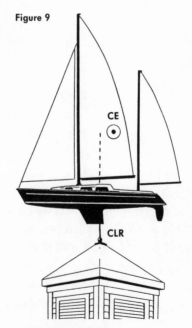

CE aft of CLR. Stern blows away from the wind, weather helm results.

windward side of the boat at the location of widest beam (some skippers go to great lengths to get heavy crew—I heard of an English boat with a 490-lb. wrestler as crew), stow sails and equipment in the lowest part of the boat and reduce weight aloft as much as possible.

Figure 10 diagrams the difference in stability between a keel-boat and a centerboarder. Stability is obtained from the "lever arm" between the Center of Buoyancy (CB) of the boat pushing upward (resisting any tendency to push the hull deeper in the water) and the Center of Gravity (CG) of the boat pushing downward. The CG is the center of the earth's gravitational effect on the boat. A boat suspended by a wire at its exact CG could be rotated in any direction yet remain motionless when released. The CB is

Figure 10

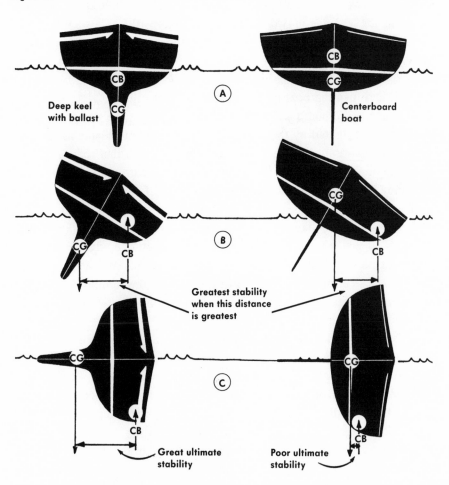

Deep keel with ballast

Centerboard boat

Ⓐ

Ⓑ

Greatest stability when this distance is greatest

Ⓒ

Great ultimate stability

Poor ultimate stability

really the CG of all the water that particular hull shape displaces. The CG remains in one position because the hull shape and weight position don't change (except for crew weight).

The CB moves in relation to the amount of hull that's submerged. As some of the boat lifts out of the water when heeled and the leeward side submerges deeper, the CB moves to leeward. Figure 10(A) shows that, at rest, the CB and CG are in vertical alignment in both the keel and centerboard boat. As they heel—Figure 10(B)—the CB of the center-boarder moves much farther to leeward than does that of the keelboat. However, the CG of the keelboat has swung out to windward because it's so low, whereas the CG of the centerboard boat has remained in the same spot. They are both developing a lever arm to resist heeling based on the lateral distance between the CB pushing up and the CG pushing down, but are attaining the leverage in two diverse ways. Figure 10(C) shows both boats on their side, an unusual situation. Note that the lever arm on the keelboat is now the greatest it has yet been, but on the centerboarder it is almost nonexistent. If the latter tips any farther, the CG will be on the other side of the CB and turn the boat upside down.

Because centerboard sailboats can capsize, they are designed small enough to be righted by the crew with a minimum of outside assistance. Some shallow-draft cruising boats have centerboards that reduce leeway (sideslipping) when sailing to windward, but they are really keelboats in that they have positive stability; i.e., they are self-righting.

There are at least three terms describing stability: Initial, Ultimate, and Positive. A flat raft (like a heavy centerboarder) may have excellent Initial Stability in that it takes several people standing on one edge to raise the other edge out of the water. However, once one edge is sunk and the raft is heeling at a steep angle, it takes very little additional weight to increase the angle until it finally flips over. This indicates that the raft has poor Ultimate Stability.

A keelboat will have the opposite qualities. It will heel the first few degrees very easily, yet will be practically impossible to capsize. Thus, it has poor Initial Stability and good Ultimate Stability. However, if it does capsize, which can only be due to a freak wave or a phenomenon of that sort, the keelboat should "turn turtle," i.e., roll through 360 degrees and come rightside up again. Thus, she has Positive Stability.

In theory, the easiest way to change the balance of the boat is to change the location of the whole rig. If you move the mast and sails aft, you increase weather helm; moving the mast forward reduces it. Since lee helm is highly unusual, we usually talk about adjusting to more or less weather helm. Anything in the latter direction, carried to extremes, will produce lee helm.

Although moving the whole rig forward or aft is possible on small boats, it's time-consuming. On larger yachts it's expensive. Another solution is to change the amount of sail area forward and aft (as on the weather vanes). Adding a bowsprit allows moving the headstay forward and using a larger jib. The CE will move forward and the weather helm will be reduced.

While on this subject of balance, we should also consider "pitching" force. Weight at the top of the mast is doubly harmful. It aggravates heeling, and at the same time increases pitching. If you go up to the top of an 80-ft. mast at sea while sailing to windward in waves, you'll know what pitching is all about. The bow of the boat may go down into a wave a few feet, but the top of the mast describes an arc like a pendulum. You are thrown forward until the mast stops abruptly, and then you are thrown aft. The forward pitch seems more violent and the momentum of the mast pitching forward drives the bows deeper into the seas and increases the arc it makes. Instead of slicing through the waves, the boat buries her bow and loses much of her forward momentum, and she's unable to pick it up again before hitting the next wave.

Every pound of weight at the top of the mast makes the pitching worse. I discovered just how much effect weight aloft has when I was racing Little America's Cup catamarans. The boat I was sailing was extremely light and accelerated very fast. But there's always a trade-off in sailing. A light boat has very little momentum, and this one was slowed by every little wave chop as her bow dug in. Between races we unstepped her mast and were able to find a pound of extraneous weight at the masthead to discard. The result was electrifying. The catamaran's performance improved immeasurably, and from only one pound of weight reduction!

BOAT SPEED

The theoretical maximum speed that a displacement boat can sail is 1.34 $\sqrt{\text{LWL}}$. In other words, a sailboat with a waterline length of 49 feet has a theoretical hull speed of 9.4 knots.

As a sailboat moves through the water, she creates a bow wave and a series of little transverse waves that move along the hull. The faster she goes, the more volume of water is pushed aside and the larger the bow wave becomes. The length of a wave is directly proportional to its height. As the bow wave gets higher, the distance from crest to crest lengthens. What begins as a series of small waves along the hull becomes a smaller number of larger waves until at last the distance between crests equals the waterline length of the boat. At this point a boat has an enormous bow wave followed by an equally large quarter wave near the stern, with a trough between the two.

The boat has reached her hull speed, because any greater speed causes the quarter wave to move even farther aft. Without a wave to support the stern, it will drop into the trough. A sailboat would never have enough power in her sails to exceed her hull speed. The formula is derived from the speed that a wave travels through the water, which is 1.34 times the square root of the distance between crests. Since the distance between the crest of the bow wave and that of the quarter wave can't be greater than the waterline length of the boat, the theoretical maximum speed of the boat becomes equal to the speed of the bow and quarter waves.

We hear of heavy displacement boats that are slow and light displacement boats that are fast. Actually, a 40-ft. sailboat that weighs 18,000 lbs. can be either light or heavy displacement. It all depends on its displacement/length ratio. The boat is "heavy" if the waterline length is short, and is considered "light displacement" if the waterline length is long. The displacement is measured in long tons (2,240 lbs.) and the length is measured as $\frac{1}{100}$ of the waterline length cubed. The displacement/length ratio for the 18,000-lb., 40-ft. boat with a 26-ft. LWL—the old-fashioned style of boat with long overhangs—would be:

$$\frac{18{,}000 \div 2{,}240}{(.01 \times 26)^3} = \frac{8.036}{.018} = 446.$$

If the waterline was three feet longer (29 ft.) the displacement/length ratio would be about 330, a fairly normal ratio. A 32-ft. waterline produces a 245 ratio—or moderately light weight; a 35-ft. waterline gives a ratio of 190, definitely a light-weight boat, and a 38-ft. waterline gives a displacement/length ratio of 145, which is in the range of ULDBs (Ultra Light Displacement Boats).

Note that the 18,000-lb. weight of this boat and its 40-foot overall length didn't change; only the waterline length changed.

This brings up the whole subject of safety and speed trade-offs. When you keep the waterline length constant and change the weight of the boat, the opposite of the above example, the heavy boat has a higher ratio and sails more slowly than the lighter boat. Weight presses the hull down, more weight makes a bigger "hole" in the water, and more volume of water has to be pushed aside as the hole moves forward. The advantage of a heavy boat is its momentum. Greater mass creates greater momentum, so it's not easily stopped by waves but, instead, plows through them.

The hull and equipment on such a boat have to be stronger and thereby heavier to withstand the force of the waves. It's a vicious circle: The boat has to be built heavier to withstand the seas; the weight sinks it deeper in the water and subjects it to greater wave force. At a certain point, however, the boat is powerful and strong enough to take any storm nature can throw at it and survive. Before the 1960s it was unheard of for an ocean-going sailboat to break apart at sea. Now, if not commonplace, it's certainly not rare, as sailboats are built lighter and lighter.

The advantage of ULDBs is their lack of wave-making drag. The hull speed is much slower for heavy-displacement boats and the bow and quarter waves much higher when sailing at maximum hull speed. A light-displacement boat will have much smaller bow and quarter waves because the distance from crest to crest is longer. That translates into less drive needed to reach hull speed. It's also the reason it's so much harder for smaller boats to pick up a "tow" on the quarter wave of larger boats nowadays. Furthermore, the light-displacement boat sits more on the surface of the water, and the part of the waves that hit it broadside are the upper part of the wave—more spray and foam than solid water. So the hull and equipment don't have to be built to withstand the wave pounding a heavier boat is subjected to.

The problem is that owners and designers don't limit themselves to a minimum displacement/length ratio of around 145. Sometimes they lighten up their structure so much to save weight that the ratio drops to around 70. It is then so light as to be unsafe. Moreover, they produce a boat that is superior on one point of sail, but extremely poor on another. With a displacement/length of about 100, a sailboat with a flattish hull shape can plane (skim the surface of the water like a flat stone that has been thrown) and reach speeds far exceeding the hull speed of the particular design. Such a sailboat can sail very fast downwind, but cannot get out of its own way upwind. This is useful on a race like the Transpac from San Francisco to Hawaii, which is mostly downwind. However, it limits the boat for other racing and cruising. A light boat accelerates quickly, which is an advantage for picking up a surf, but it stops quickly, such as when it plows into a wave when sailing upwind.

Everything is a compromise move and, being conservative, I would give up some speed for greater safety. For cruising, it's the only way to go, but even in racing, if you don't finish, you can't win. Repairs of breakdowns result in great losses of speed and distance during races. Consider the trade-offs carefully.

Attention to the little boat-speed items can pay great dividends. For instance, few sailors have a true picture of the importance of a clean, smooth bottom surface and its importance to boat speed.

Once, when I was racing 5.5-Meter sailboats in preparation for the Olympic trials, we tested two boats against each other. One had just been launched and the other had been in the water for about a week. We intended to test sails, and the boats had to be even in speed so that one could be used as a control while we changed sails and trim on the other. The boat that was newly launched was so much faster we had to drag lines behind it in order to keep the two boats even.

The next day we started a series of races, so after practice we hauled our 5.5-Meter, the slow one, and washed off the bottom. I was chagrined to see just the start of some slime. After all, the boat had only been in the water a week and was still quite clean. However, my concern that there was some other reason for our speed problems in practice was quickly dispelled the next day when racing. We had no problem at all beating the boat that had been so incredibly fast the day before.

That experience alerted me to the importance of having a clean racing bottom. Many racing sailors put the emphasis on bottom preparation, such as careful sanding and a smooth, hard finish, but a small amount of slime will negate all the previous work. There are those who believe the beginning of slime is a positive speed factor—such as the slime on a fish that in some way helps it move through the water. My opinion is that on a boat bottom, NO slime is good. Boats aren't fish.

Recently, I sailed in the International One Design class in Bermuda Race Week with Dr. Stuart Walker. This was a switch-boat series of 10 races. After each race the sailors rotated to another boat, so with 15 crews and 10 races, each crew had a chance to race most of the available boats. The boats had all been cleaned at the beginning of the week, and they were all quite equal in speed. By the last two days I was convinced we'd be faster if we took a rag to the bottom of each boat we sailed.

The last race was a light-weather race and we only had to beat the International One Design World Champion and keep him out of first place to win the series. We were buried at the start and split tacks with him. When we converged again we had him and sat firmly on top of him, luffing our sails and slowing him down past the layline to the windward mark. He jibed away twice, because of overstanding, but we still had him completely in our wind shadow. By the time we reached the weather mark, we were next to last by a large margin and he was last.

At this point we had completed our objective of keeping him out of first place. The lead boats were rounding the jibing mark and catching them seemed an impossible task. I said to Stuart, "Now, let's see how many we can pass." We started working up through the fleet and at the finish we were in second place. Quite literally, in the prevailing light airs, we had blinding speed.

One competitor who saw us pass about six boats on the run came up to me afterward and said, "How were you setting your chute? We were copying everything you were doing and you were still going faster. Did you have a streak of wind down there?"

I must admit that, knowing that we had won the series and would probably defend the win next year, I allowed as how we were just lucky. But you can bet that from now on, before each race I'll be checking our boat for a slimy bottom.

Chapter II

SAILS: HOW AND WHY THEY WORK

Having discussed in Chapter I the relationship of the CE of the sails to aerodynamic lift, we now take a closer look at the sails, their construction and why they function as they do.

SAIL SHAPE

In sailboat racing, there is no other speed determinant as important as a sailboat's sails, and the way they are set and trimmed. Sail material is constantly stretching as the forces on it change. The forces change not only when the wind strength changes, but also when the boat slows down, as when plowing into waves, or speeds up, as when surfing or sailing in smooth water. There are numerous devices to control this stretch and thereby the shape of the sail.

Sails power a sailboat much like an engine powers a car. When a car is moving slowly uphill or over bumpy terrain, you keep it in low (first) gear. As it picks up speed and the ground levels off, you shift to second gear. When the car is moving fast on a smooth road, you shift to high. With a sailboat, full sails are the low gear and flat sails are high. When seas are heavy and the boat is sailing slowly ("stop and go" as she hits each wave),

Figure 11

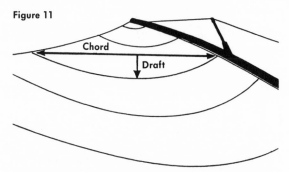

Draft is the maximum depth of the sail measured from the chord, an imaginary straight line drawn from luff to leech.

the sails need power. Full sails are the answer. In smooth water and high winds, when the sailboat is moving fastest, flat sails are desirable.

Draft. The mainsail is a versatile sail and can be made flat or full at will. But, what is a "full sail" or a "flat sail"? The terms are relative. A sail is flatter or fuller than another based on the relationship of the maximum depth of the curvature (the *draft*) to the distance from luff to leech (the *chord*). Figure 11 shows the cross section of a mainsail. An imaginary line drawn from luff to leech is the chord. A line drawn perpendicular to the chord at the point where the sail is the greatest distance from the chord is the "draft" or "camber." The "camber-to-chord" ratio is the relation of this distance to the chord, usually expressed as a percentage. If the chord is 120 inches, and the camber is 12 inches deep, the camber-to-chord ratio is 10 to 1 or 10%. Sails can be used effectively as flat as 5% or as full as 20% at the CE, depending on the class of boat and the sailing conditions. Draft varies at different heights up the sail.

Of great importance is the position of maximum draft in the sail. Figure 12 shows three sails with quite different locations of maximum draft. The draft of A is in the desirable location for a mainsail—40% to 50% aft from the leading edge (the luff). The draft in B has been blown aft because of inadequate luff tension or stretch near the leech. C shows the draft forward, near the mast. This can happen when a sail is designed to accept a certain amount of mast bend but the mast hasn't been bent enough.

The sailmaker puts draft into the sail in two ways: by a "luff and foot round" and by "broadseaming." If you laid a mainsail on the floor and "luff and foot round" was the only draft producer, it would look like the shaded sail in Figure 13. However, when it is put on a straight mast and boom, the excess material becomes draft, indicated by the dashed line in Figure 13. As

Figure 12

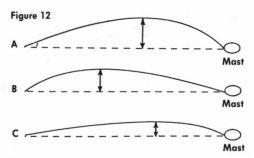

The maximum draft of a sail may be found in numerous locations in different sails.

Figure 13

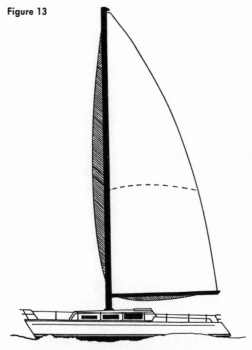

The extra material along the luff and foot of a mainsail become draft when on a straight mast and boom.

the material stretches in the wind, this draft moves aft toward the desired location in the middle of the sail. In light winds on a straight mast, the draft created by luff round will be forward, near the mast. If you bend the mast and boom to conform with the designed edge round, then the sail will be flat as a board.

Figure 15

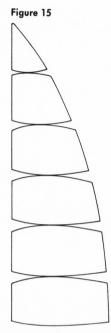

Figure 14

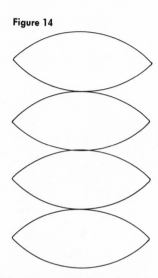

Before it's sewn together, a football
may look something like this.

A sailmaker also gets draft by curving the
panels and then sewing them together.

The other method of creating draft—broadseaming—is simply narrow-ing the panels of cloth before they are stitched together. To understand how this creates draft, imagine a football that has been taken apart at the seams. It looks somewhat like Figure 14. Sewn together, it becomes a football. The same method is practiced in sailmaking, as shown in Figure 15. Draft created in this manner is placed exactly where the sailmaker wants it and does not depend on mast bend or stretch to put it in the right place. A combination of both methods is used in the manufacture of all sails.

Figure 12B shows the maximum draft aft, near the leech of the mainsail. As the breeze freshens, sail material stretches and the draft tends to move aft toward the leech. This will cause the battens to cock to windward in the mainsail, which produces a less efficient airfoil. Increased tension on the luff can reduce this movement aft.

SAIL CONSTRUCTION

The threads that run across a panel of sailcloth are called the filling threads, or the "fill." The threads that run lengthwise are called the "warp." The warp stretches more than the fill, but the greatest stretch comes in a diagonal direction, called the "bias." Most sails are designed with this stretch in mind.

For example, the mainsheet will exert the greatest force on a mainsail,

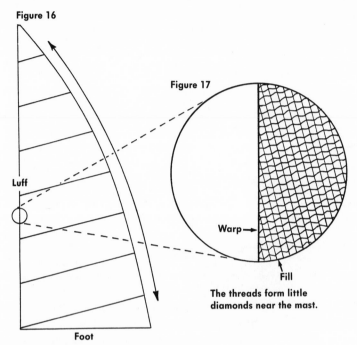

Figure 16

Figure 17

Luff

Warp→

Fill

The threads form little
diamonds near the mast.

Foot

Panels meet the mast
on a bias.

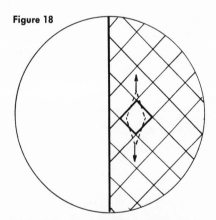

Figure 18

As the luff is tensioned and the top and
bottom of the diamonds are stretched,
material is pulled in from the middle of the sail.

Figure 19

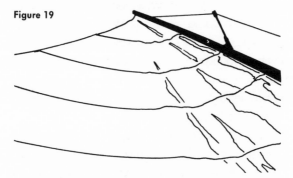

Excessive luff tension causes wrinkles near the mast.

Figure 20

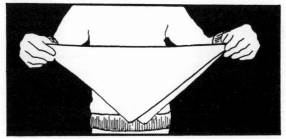

Hold a handkerchief at two corners on the bias.

Figure 21

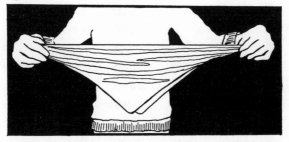

Pull out and creases appear as the bottom corner pulls up.

and most of it will fall on the leech. Consequently, the panels of cloth are sewn together so that the crosswise threads—or filling threads—lie along the leech of the sail (see Figures 16 and 17).

This means that all the panels along the luff of the sail must be cut on the bias, where stretch is greatest. If we were to blow up a small section of the sail along the mast, we would see that the threads look like a cluster of little diamonds at the bias (Figure 17). As we pull down on the luff and increase the tension, each diamond elongates (the dotted lines) and pulls material in from the center of the sail (see Figure 18). If we pull down hard on the luff when there is not enough wind to warrant it, vertical troughs or creases running parallel to the mast will appear (Figure 19).

You can simulate this effect by taking a handkerchief and pulling it at two diagonally opposite corners, as in Figure 20. The same trough will appear that appears when there is too much luff tension. Figure 21 shows that as the corners are stretched apart on the bias, the material moves upward. The lower corner that was even with the man's waist is now a few inches higher.

PROPER MAINSAIL ADJUSTMENT

Tensioning the luff. There are two ways to tension a mainsail's luff—with a downhaul and with a cunningham. In the days of cotton sails, you bought a sail that was actually too small in light air. This allowed you to stretch it to flatten the sail when the wind velocity increased. Of course, this meant that you automatically penalized yourself in light air by having reduced sail area.

To solve this dilemma, Briggs Cunningham, skipper of *Columbia,* the winner of the America's Cup in 1958, created the "cunningham." He placed a grommet above the mainsail tack fitting in a full-sized sail. Then, when he had pulled the sliding gooseneck on the masthead down as far as possible using the downhaul, stretching the luff of the sail as far as it could go, he put a hook attached to a block and tackle through the grommet. Tightening the tackle added further tension to the mainsail luff. Although some wrinkles do appear along the foot of the sail below the grommet when the system is in use, they don't seem to make an appreciable difference in the efficiency of the sail.

This grommeted hole in the mainsail became known as a cunningham in honor of its inventor and it is now commonplace in the sails of most classes of sailboats. With a cunningham, a sail can be used full-sized for light-air performance, yet be tensioned along the luff when the breeze increases, to keep the draft from moving aft.

A variation of the cunningham is also used on jibs. Many small boats have a cloth-tension device attached to the jib near the tack, and a wire that leads to the cockpit can be adjusted to increase or decrease the tension of the luff.

Large sailboats also have jib cunninghams, but they serve a dual purpose. One is to tension the luff when the halyard is two-blocked in order to keep the draft forward, and the second is to be able to release the tack attachment to make it easier for an "outside set." This is a set when the new jib is pulled up to leeward of the jib that is already up. By taking tension on the cunningham a few feet up the luff and releasing the tack of the original jib, you can feed the new jib under the foot of the original jib much more easily.

When using a cunningham, remember that a Dacron jib is more sensitive to luff tension than a Dacron main. Always watch for the results of winching on any line on a sailboat. Don't just "winch in" indiscriminately.

When sailing to windward, the point of maximum draft on a jib should be about 35 percent of the chord behind the luff, compared to about 50 percent of the chord in a mainsail. If the wind increases, it's far easier for the draft of a jib to work aft of its normal location, which means you must constantly change the jib luff tension for highest efficiency whenever the wind velocity changes. Luff tension must also be changed depending upon what point of sail the boat is on. When reaching or running, you want a very full sail with the draft well aft. You should ease off the downhaul and cunningham in this situation.

The newer sail materials—Mylar, Kevlar, and Spectra cloth—have very little stretch, so halyard and cunningham adjustment is negligible when using sails of these cloths.

The traveler. Important mainsail adjustments are made with the traveler—a track with a sliding mainsheet block that is placed athwartships beneath the main boom. Travelers with ball-bearing cars are preferable because they run more freely under the pressure of the mainsheet when the boat is close-hauled. The traveler's function is to permit adjustment of the angle of the boom relative to the centerline of the boat while keeping the boom from rising. If, instead of using a traveler, we ease the mainsheet, the force of the wind on the sail will lift the boom in the air and the top part of the leech will fall off to leeward.

Figure 22 shows the constant angle the apparent wind makes with the luff of the sail over its full length when the mainsheet is trimmed in tight. Figure 23 shows how this angle changes in the upper part of the sail when the mainsheet is eased. The upper part can actually be luffing even though the bottom part is full of air. This effect is called "twist" and is usually undesirable.

There are a couple of exceptions. The wind on the surface of the water is slowed down by friction, so the wind at the top of the mast has a greater velocity than at deck level. Thus, the top of the sail is continually in a puff relative to the bottom of the sail. Apparent wind comes aft in a puff. In order for the apparent wind to have the same angle to the luff all the way up and down, a slight twist at the head of the sail is necessary.

The other time a twist in a sail is desirable is in very heavy air. The upper part of the sail greatly affects a boat's heeling, just as weight at the top of the mast does. If you want to reduce heeling, simply reduce the effectiveness of the upper part of the sail by inducing twist. Instead of easing the traveler, ease the mainsheet.

The traveler is also used to help control heeling. We all know that as a

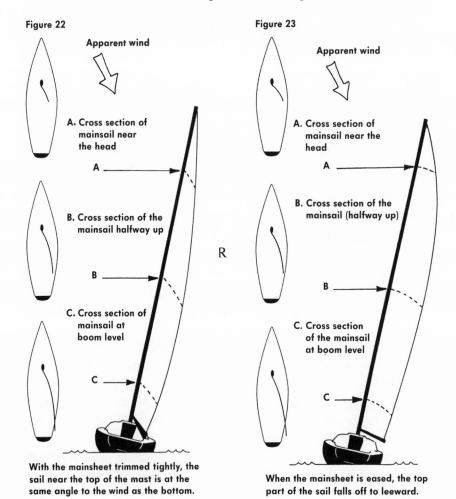

Figure 22

Apparent wind

A. Cross section of mainsail near the head

A

B. Cross section of the mainsail halfway up

B

C. Cross section of mainsail at boom level

C

R

With the mainsheet trimmed tightly, the sail near the top of the mast is at the same angle to the wind as the bottom.

Figure 23

Apparent wind

A. Cross section of mainsail near the head

A

B. Cross section of the mainsail (halfway up)

B

C. Cross section of the mainsail at boom level

C

When the mainsheet is eased, the top part of the sail falls off to leeward.

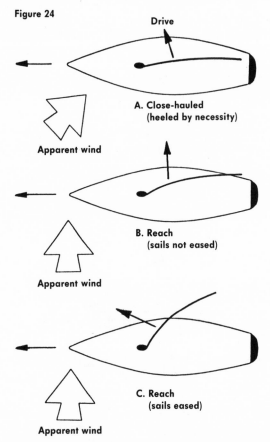

Figure 24

Drive

Apparent wind

A. Close-hauled
(heeled by necessity)

Apparent wind

B. Reach
(sails not eased)

Apparent wind

C. Reach
(sails eased)

Apparent wind

Heeling is reduced when drive and heading line up together.

sailboat turns from close-hauled to a reach, the sails should be eased (see Figure 24). If we are heeling excessively when close-hauled, we can reduce the heeling by easing the traveler. Many good small-boat sailors use the traveler rather than the mainsheet to adjust to changes in wind velocity. Every novice has learned that when you are hit by a puff, you ease the mainsheet and head up into the wind to reduce heeling and avoid a capsize. The advanced sailor does much the same thing, but eases the traveler instead, although this depends to an extent on the type of sailboat. Since the apparent wind comes aft in a puff, easing the traveler maintains the angle the apparent wind makes with the luff of the sail.

As you fall off to a true reach, easing the traveler acts like a boom vang, keeping the boom from rising and preventing twist. However, its effectiveness ends when the traveler car reaches the outboard end of the track and the

Figure 25

No vang tension; mainsail twisted so top part is useless

mainsail must go out still farther. Now the mainsheet, instead of pulling down, is angled out over the water and a boom vang has to do the work of keeping twist out of the sail. In Figure 25 the vang is not in use and the sail is badly twisted. Figure 26 shows the difference in the leech when the boom vang is pulled tight. The farther forward in the boat the traveler is located, the farther out the boom can go before the traveler car reaches the end of the track and the vang must take over. The undesirable aspect of having the traveler forward is that the mainsheet pull is from the middle of the boom rather than the end of the boom where it will counteract the force of the leech. This gives the skipper far less control over the leech of the sail.

The closer the traveler is to the boom, the more positive is its control. If the traveler is mounted down on the cockpit sole several feet beneath the boom, a puff may cause the mainsheet to stretch, and the boom will lift and move outboard, negating some of the traveler's usefulness. On some IOR boats, the traveler is forward of the cockpit and just aft of the companion-way. This creates a potentially dangerous situation. If a person comes up the steps from below just as the boat is jibing, the traveler can whip across the boat and knock him over the side. It's preferable to have the traveler in a

Figure 26

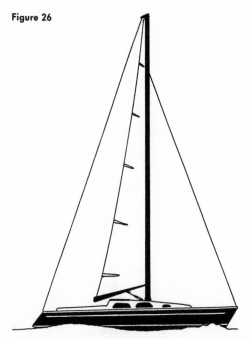

Vang tight; mainsail presents its full area to the wind.

location where it can do the least damage to crew members in case of an accidental jibe in heavy winds.

There is still another use of the traveler. It permits you to trim the main boom up to the centerline of the boat without having to pull down hard on the mainsheet. Theoretically, the closer the boom comes to the center of the boat, the higher you can point. On a light day, however, trimming the main in tight can result in a very tight leech. The solution is to leave the mainsheet lightly trimmed and pull the traveler car up to windward, bringing the boom toward the middle of the boat without pulling it down at the same time, as in Figure 27. This procedure is standard on all boats from dinghies to maxis.

One of the most important uses of a traveler is for accelerating after a start. With the traveler eased, the boat can luff along the starting line with the mainsheet relatively tight. At the gun, trimming the traveler gives instant acceleration and—as long as it's done in concert with the turn to windward—reduces leeway. The force on the sail is more in the direction of the boat's heading. If, on the other hand, you set the traveler in the middle of the boat, have not set the boom vang, and depend on trimming the mainsheet to fill the sail, a number of things happen. The bottom of the sail fills first and it will be near the middle of the boat when it does. The side force on

Figure 27

Traveler car

**Pull the traveler car to windward to get
the boom near the centerline of the boat
without pulling down hard on the mainsheet.**

the boat will be strong, just when the boat is moving slowly through the
water and unable to resist such side force. The result is leeway rather than
forward motion.

The backstay. The adjustable backstay is a mast-bending device. On
small boats, a block and tackle attached to the lower end of the backstay
produces the leverage for bending the mast with a minimum of effort. On
larger sailboats the backstay is usually hydraulic. Such systems are extremely powerful, yet can be controlled by one person pumping a handle.
Normally, there's a control panel with a hydraulic release valve for each item
that is hydraulic. A boat may have a hydraulic backstay, baby stay, boom
vang, flattening reef, and even a hydraulic first reef (at the clew). Whenever
one needs to be eased, a crew member turns the valve for that item and
releases the pressure; when more hydraulic pressure is needed, he closes
the valve and pumps.

Other factors are involved in mast bend—leech tension, angle and length
of the spreaders, placement of the partners where the mast goes through the
deck (if any), tension on the jumpers (if any), location of the mainsheet

Figure 28

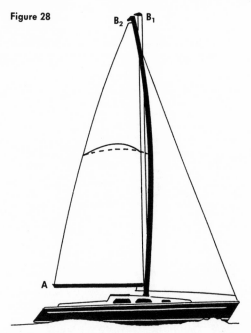

Bending the mast changes the camber-to-chord ratio
and flattens the sail.

blocks along the boom, etc. But for now, we'll focus on the backstay.
Tightening the backstay bends the mast and flattens the mainsail.

When the backstay is tensioned, the middle of the mast bows forward,
lengthening the chord—as the dotted lines in Figure 28 indicate—and
decreasing the draft. With a longer chord distance and the same amount of
sailcloth as before, the draft has to be less as the excess material built into
the sail along the luff is stretched out and the sail flattened. But also note the
action at the top of the mast. It is pulled back and down, which effectively
shortens the distance between the top of the mast and the end of the boom.
The distance A to B2 is shorter than the distance A to B1. This frees the
leech of the sail because the material sags off rather than tightens. The end
result is indicated by the solid lines in Figure 29. Even if the chord length
remains the same, a free leech creates a flatter sail since the draft is less.
Figure 29 also shows that the drive will be in a more forward direction,
which reduces heeling.

Weather helm is reduced as the leech is freed. With a tight leech, airflow
on the windward side of the sail bends around until it exits off the leech in a
windward direction. The tight leech acts like a rudder, forcing the stern to
leeward and creating weather helm. But when the leech is freed, the air can

Figure 29

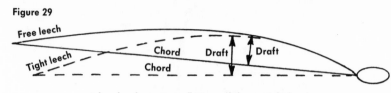

A free leech creates a flatter sail than a tight leech.

Figure 30

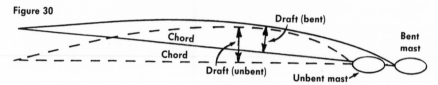

The combination of moving the mast forward and freeing the leech really flattens the sail.

flow straight aft or slightly to leeward, which minimizes the turning effect of the leech. Figure 30 shows how the combination of the mast moving forward and a freer leech creates a much flatter sail.

Running backstays. Running backstays (called "runners") are wires attached to the mast on either side at two levels and are stretched tight on the windward side of the boat by means of a block and tackle. They control the bend of the mast and thereby control the fullness of the mainsail. A running backstay is invariably attached to the deck at a point where the main boom will fetch up on it in an accidental jibe. If it were led farther aft the boom could swing through under the running backstay, but the mainsail would hang up on it and rip.

Many racing boat masts will bend excessively and break unless one running backstay is always set up when it's blowing. So, as the main is trimmed in for a controlled jibe, the leeward backstay is cranked in tight before the windward one is released. Thus, it's important to let the boom hit the runner in an accidental jibe. It's better to round up than lose the mast by releasing the runner.

Just because it's blowing hard on a beat, you don't necessarily want the runner in farther than on a light day. As the breeze freshens, easing the runner allows the mast to bow forward, which flattens the mainsail and eases the leech. On most boats that depend heavily on runners for mast control, a "baby stay" forward of the mast counteracts the pull of the backstays and helps keep the mast in a fixed position. Think of a mast as a paper straw. If you press down on the straw when it's vertical, it takes quite a bit of force to break it. But press down on top while bending it sideways with another finger, and the straw will collapse easily. A mast is not round like a straw, but elliptical, so it can take much more bending out of column. Still, there are limits, particularly when the boat is beating in heavy seas and "falling off the tops of waves." Such pounding causes the mast to compress and bend forward. The backstays and baby stay help stabilize the bend and keep it from going too far and breaking.

On a run, to get fullness in the mainsail and to make the boat track better, we ease the permanent backstay. A sailboat sails faster on a run when there is forward mast rake (the mast leans forward). Yet, the mast should be straight and not have a reverse bend. Most rigs have a certain amount of "pre-bend." In other words, letting off the permanent backstay allows the mast to straighten somewhat, but not completely. By cranking the runners in tightly, you can make the mast almost perfectly straight, and the baby stay will prevent a reverse bend. A reverse bend can be very dangerous, because a mast is not engineered to bend in that direction (i.e., aft in the middle). The compression of the spinnaker pole pushes the mast toward a reverse bend, and both a broach or letting the spinnaker collapse and fill with a "bang" can pump the mast dangerously. During a jibe, the baby stay must be released, thrown over the spinnaker pole, and set up on the other side, and in heavy air this is a vulnerable moment for the mast. Thus, the runners must be set up tight on the windward side of the boat during this procedure.

The mainsheet. Mainsheet tension, particularly on light days, will harden up the leech and cock the battens to windward. The sail will look much like the unbent mast position in Figure 31 which shows a cocked leech on the boat to the left caused by over-trimming the mainsheet. Because this is a fuller shape, we can say that mainsheet tension makes any cross section of the sail fuller, whereas an eased mainsheet, and the corresponding twist in the sail as the boom rises, makes the cross section of the sail flatter.

The outhaul. The outhaul mainly affects the draft in the lower part of the sail near the boom. Figure 32 shows the outhaul eased, and it is obvious that it creates a greater draft in the sail. Even if the actual draft remains the same, the shortening of the chord makes the camber-to-chord ratio larger, thereby making the sail fuller. Easing the outhaul excessively will cause wrinkles along the foot of the mainsail and reduces the projected area of the sail while running.

The flattening reef. The flattening reef is a cringle a short distance up the leech of the mainsail that has a dual purpose. First, when sailing to windward, tightening the flattening reef using the hydraulic system elimi-

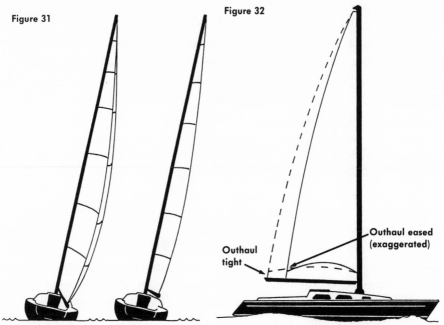

Figure 31

Figure 32

Outhaul
tight

Outhaul eased
(exaggerated)

On the left, too much mainsheet tension cups   An eased outhaul creates a fuller sail.
the leech of the mainsail.

nates the foot shelf of the sail and greatly flattens the lower portion. The sail has no reef points at this level because not enough material is taken out to be tied. The flattening reef creates a new foot from the original tack to a point a short distance up the leech. The second purpose of the flattening reef is to raise the outboard end of the boom up a foot or so to avoid dipping it in the sea on a tight reach. When the boom dips the forces are tremendous. If the boom vang is tight, the boom can break. The force of the water pushes the boom toward the stern of the boat, which is the same as trimming the mainsail. That's the last thing you want to do under broaching conditions — the main should be eased, to allow the boat to straighten up. Therefore, a crew member should tend the vang and ease whenever the boom hits the water. This luffs the upper part of the sail, which affects the heeling of the boat the most and allows the boom to lift out of the water. Because it also reduces the drive force of the mainsail considerably, it's undesirable to release the boom vang very often. Using the flattening reef to raise the end of the boom makes it unnecessary to release the boom vang as often and more drive is maintained for longer periods of time.

HOW TO "SEE" SAIL SHAPE

Because it's difficult for many sailors to see fine adjustments in sail shape, visual aids are helpful. When you order a sail from your sailmaker, pay a little extra for "fast stripes," which are stripes made of tape applied to either side of the sail which run from luff to leech at two or three levels up the sail. They are invaluable for showing the shape of the sail and also help you to see hard spots that may develop as the sail ages.

To determine how much mast bend there is, with an indelible pen draw short vertical lines on the mainsail at spreader height, evenly spaced about three inches apart. Sight up from under the gooseneck to the masthead and determine where an imaginary straight line would fall, or attach a line to the main halyard and pull it tight to the tack of the sail. Using this method we can determine that the mast in Figure 33 has about 17 inches of mast bend.

To see how much twist the mainsail has, sight up the sail from under the boom and line up the second batten from the head with the boom. It should be parallel or falling off a little, but it should not be cocked to weather. If there is room to stand on the afterdeck behind the main boom, you can get a

Figure 33

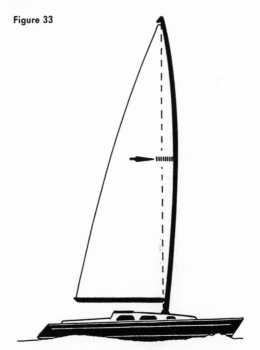

The amount of mast bend can be determined by sighting up the mast past marks spaced at known intervals.

good overall perspective of the mainsail from that position. Better yet, get in a chase boat and follow directly behind your sailboat. Then you'll really be able to see what your main looks like.

In a small boat, colored tape can be placed on the backstay to correspond with a certain amount of mast bend. If the backstay enters the deck aft, put a foot of PVC tubing around it. The tape will disappear inside the tubing and not get rubbed off going through the deck. Colored marks on the mainsheet can serve as a guide as to how much twist there is in the mainsail leech for given wind conditions. Marks next to the traveler at 1-inch increments can help you duplicate a traveler car position. Also, a mark on the jib halyard against a series of marks spaced at equal intervals on the mast can be helpful in duplicating luff tension if your jib is Dacron. The shape of a Kevlar jib can't really be changed by luff tension, so a mark is useful only to avoid overstressing the cloth.

Jib trim is a little harder to judge than the main. When setting a genoa, which overlaps the spreader, use the spreader tip as a guideline. Depending on the type of genoa, the lateral jib lead placement, the wind and sea conditions, and the luff tension, the sail should be trimmed anywhere from a point a few inches off the spreader tip to just touching it. If the jib does not overlap the spreaders the leech will probably point right at them. Place a piece of tape on the spreaders as a guideline and trim the sail until the leech points at the tape.

One way of determining whether the jib is trimmed in too tight or the draft is too far aft is to observe the amount of backwind in the mainsail. If the backwind extends farther back than usual, it is probably caused by an overtrimmed jib or lack of jib halyard tension.

Last, for an overall look at jib shape, go to the bow and look at the leeward side. This can help you see if the draft has been blown aft. If the jib stay sags to leeward excessively, the draft in the sail will appear to have been blown aft and the boat will not sail to windward well. Make sure there is enough permanent backstay tension to cure the problem.

All of the above will help you to duplicate the same shape at another time, but only testing alongside another boat will tell you which shape or what sail is fastest. Sailmakers do this all the time when testing sails, and it can help you, too, if you can find a willing collaborator with a boat equal to yours.

Sail side by side close-hauled, both with clear air, keeping one boat as a "control" (don't change anything on it) and changing only one variable (such as the mainsheet tension or mast bend) on the other at any one time. The position of the boats is very important. If the leeward boat is too far

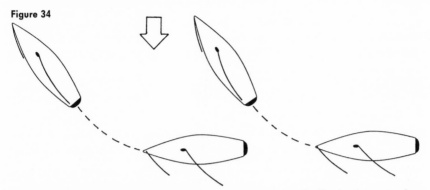

Figure 34

To get into a good speed testing position, follow on a beam reach, then harden up to close-hauled simultaneously.

forward and too close to the windward boat, she'll have a safe leeward position and be hurting the other. If she's too close and not far enough forward, she'll be hurt by the blanket zone of the windward boat. One way of getting into the proper position for testing is for one boat to follow the other on a beam reach. Then, at a predetermined signal, both harden up to close-hauled as in Figure 34. Both will have clear air and neither will be hurting the other until one or the other sails faster. One crew member should be calling the compass bearing of the mast of the other boat to determine whether she's gaining or losing. You can't do it by eyeball because any slight header or lift will make it appear that one is gaining or losing when that may not be the case.

PROPER JIB ADJUSTMENT

Twist in the mainsail results when the top part of the sail falls off to leeward because of inadequate leech tension. The same problem exists with the jib. Two things determine how much twist a jib will have when beating—jib sheet tension and the fore-and-aft placement of the jib leads. If the lead is too far aft, the jib sheet will pull along the foot of the sail, but there won't be enough downward tension on the leech. The result is that the top part of the sail will tend to luff first.

However, other things can have the same effect as moving the jib lead block forward or aft. For instance, raking the mast aft by lengthening the jibstay (see Figure 35) effectively moves the head of the sail aft and lowers the clew. If the jib lead remains in the same place, raking the mast frees the leech of the jib.

Figure 35

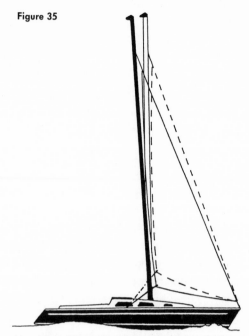

Raking the mast aft frees the leech of the jib. Move the jib lead forward to maintain leech tension.

A good rule of thumb is that the opening (slot) between the jib leech and the body of the mainsail should remain parallel. This means that if we induce twist in the mainsail in heavy weather to reduce drive in the upper part of the main, thereby reducing heeling, we must do the same to the jib.

In light air, the fullness should be down low in the jib. You can accomplish this by easing the jib sheet. This has the same effect as easing the outhaul on the main along the boom. Easing the jib sheet increases draft by shortening the distance between the tack and the clew, and this gives you greater drive in light air and lumpy seas. However, there is one detrimental side effect to easing the sheet. As the clew goes out, the angle of the jib sheet is lowered and frees the leech. Therefore, to regain the proper leech tension, you must move the jib lead forward.

The jib tack, jib halyard tension, and jib downhaul, or cunningham, also affect the location of the clew and the jib lead. With Dacron sails, one usually increases the tension on the luff of the sail to control the jib's shape as the wind increases. As the jib stretches under the force of the increased wind velocity, the draft tends to move aft in the sail, and more luff tension is required to keep the draft in the same location. But when the luff tension is increased by tightening the jib halyard, pulling the head of the sail higher, the clew is lifted higher also, and the lead will need to be placed farther aft. In heavy air you may even want a little twist in the sail, and the lead may need to come back even farther.

However, if you get your luff tension by pulling down the luff downhaul or jib cunningham, the clew will be lowered and the lead will appear to be aft of its previous location. Since the wind is blowing relatively hard when this is done, you may not want to change the jib lead position. It is now effectively aft of where it had been and may produce the desired twist.

Observe what jib halyard tension does to the leech of the sail. As draft is pulled forward, the leech should become free and flatter. On high-aspect sails (those that are tall and narrow rather than wide and squat), the opposite can sometimes happen. The halyard pulls on the leech almost as much as on the luff because the angle is about the same, so luff tension cups the leech instead of freeing it.

As a boat falls off onto a reach, the jib sheet is eased and a great deal of twist can develop. To correct this, the lead must go forward again. In the old days, sailboats did not have effective boom vangs for their mains and the top part of the mainsail twisted off to leeward when reaching. To make the jib leech match the curve of the main, the jib lead was moved aft.

Not so today. Effective boom vangs keep twist in the main to a minimum; therefore, little twist is needed in the jib. So, in most cases, the lead when on a reach should go forward, not aft, to pull down on the leech and reduce twist.

One other sensitive adjustment for the jib lead is its correct distance outboard from the centerline of the boat. To find this point, first draw a line from the tack of the jib to the jib lead and measure the angle it makes with the centerline of the boat. This is called the "jib lead angle," and it will vary greatly from boat to boat.

On a narrow keelboat the jib leads may be fairly well inboard and she will still maintain speed while pointing high. On a beamy centerboarder, however, the jib leads must be placed farther outboard for her to develop enough drive to go through the seas.

Think of the lateral placement of the jib lead in the same terms as the mainsheet traveler. If the traveler needs to be eased, the jib lead should probably be led outboard, too. The best way to tell whether your jib lead angle is correct is to test your boat against another. Sail close-hauled alongside another boat of the same class and vary the lateral position in or out. The correct location will show up in increased speed.

Figure 36

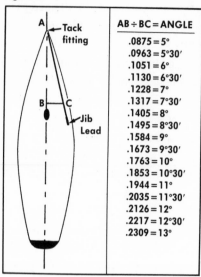

AB ÷ BC = ANGLE
.0875 = 5°
.0963 = 5°30'
.1051 = 6°
.1130 = 6°30'
.1228 = 7°
.1317 = 7°30'
.1405 = 8°
.1495 = 8°30'
.1584 = 9°
.1673 = 9°30'
.1763 = 10°
.1853 = 10°30'
.1944 = 11°
.2035 = 11°30'
.2126 = 12°
.2217 = 12°30'
.2309 = 13°

Divide BC by AB to determine jib-lead angle.

You can measure the angle by using the table and diagram in Figure 36. To do so, first measure in inches along the centerline from the tack fitting to any point just forward of the mast (distance AB on the diagram). From B, measure at right angles to the point that intersects a straight line running from the tack fitting to the jib lead (distance BC). Divide BC by AB and carry it to four places. Then consult the table for the jib lead angle in degrees. Example: AB is 59 inches and BC is 11 inches. Eleven divided by 59 is .1864, which is a hair over 10½ degrees in the table. Start with an angle of about 9 degrees and work in and out from there based on wind strength and sea conditions.

CARE AND HANDLING

Sails are the driving force of the boat and must be treated carefully during and after use to preserve both shape and fabric. Procedures for stowing and caring for sails on various sized boats differ according to hardware, size, and use, but in general, the following procedures are standard.

Furling, flaking. The mainsail of a larger yacht is usually left on the boom from one day to the next. It's difficult to remove it after each sailing session and if the sail is properly flaked down and secured and the sail cover is used, removal is not necessary. In general, a mainsail attaches to the mast in one of two ways: either the luff slides directly into a grooved track on or in the mast, or the luff of the sail is equipped at intervals with slides which fit the track of the mast. Lowering procedures for the above vary slightly.

When lowering and stowing a main with a luff that slides in a mast groove, the luff of the sail comes out of the groove as the sail is lowered and we flake the sail on the boom. When handling a very large sail—such as a maxi-yacht mainsail—after it is lowered, the part we want to flake over the boom first is usually at the bottom of the pile of sail because the head comes down last. Take a few moments to pass the head over to the other side of the boom and follow with the rest of the sail. This sorts the sail out for easy flaking, with the head now on the bottom of the pile and the foot area on top. Even with smaller boats, this little extra effort makes things easier in the long run.

It takes at least two persons to do a good flaking job: one is positioned at the luff of the sail and the other at the leech. Working as a team, they grab the luff and the leech, respectively, at a point 4 to 6 feet from the foot, and pull hard away from each other forming a fold, which they pass over the boom so that 2 to 3 feet of sail falls on one side of the boom and an equal amount on the other. Usually the reefing tack and clew cringles are good guides as to where to grab the sail. They are the right distance apart, provide good handholds, and are parallel to the boom. Next, the team repeats the process, grabbing luff and leech the same distance apart from the boom as before. This continues until there is about 6 to 8 feet of sail remaining near the head. At this point, it may be necessary to put a few sail ties (also known as sail stops) around the folds near the clew to keep the sail from flipping off the boom. At the head of the sail, instead of making a fold, the "flakers" pass the head under and around the boom once or twice and, holding all the folded sail on top of the boom, pull it tight (Figure 37). Next, they pass a sail tie with a bowline in one end through the eye of the headboard of the sail. Pulling on the sail tie helps tighten the furl. They then pass the tie around the boom, slip it through the bowline, pull it tight like a slipknot and tie it off with half-hitches. (Incidentally, whenever you use a sail tie, be sure there's a bowline in one end, which facilitates using the tie as a cinch). Always pass the sail tie around the boom away from you so that when you pass the end through the bowline, you can pull it toward you to tighten it.

When lowering a main with slides attached to the luff, the slides remain on the mast, piling one on top of the other at the boom as the sail comes

Figure 37

Use sail stops with a bowline tied in the end so it will cinch tight. Wrap the head around the sail and boom and pull tight with a sail stop through the headboard.

down. You flake the sail by starting at the clew and following up the leech, folding the sail over the boom as you go and securing the flaked sail with ties.

A "fast and dirty" alternative is to make a pocket along the foot of the sail by grabbing the leech 4 to 5 feet from the clew, dumping the rest of the sail in the pocket (or hammock) formed by this portion of the sail, and rolling it up on top of the boom. Secure it with sail ties, and the sail is furled.

Among other furling systems in use are "lazyjacks." These are lines that run from the top of the mast to the boom, at intervals along the boom, on either side of the sail. As the sail is lowered, these lines keep it from falling off the boom, and it flakes automatically on top. Lazyjacks are not new. They originated aboard schooners in the old days, to guide the sails and the large heavy gaff down on top of the boom. The modern twist is that many sailors using fully-battened mainsails find the lazyjacks particularly useful for lowering this type sail.

In a fully-battened mainsail, the battens run the full distance from leech to luff of the sail. They give the sail a better shape, support the leech and reduce flogging of the sail when luffing or when it's being raised or lowered, and thereby extend the sail's life. When the sail is lowered, the battens line up parallel to the boom and keep the leech stretched out, for a very neat and easy flaking job.

After the sail is flaked or furled and stopped on top of the boom, we protect it with an ultraviolet (UV) resistant sail cover. First, the cover should be secured around the mast and then stretched aft over the sail along the boom, with the clew end tied tightly. Then fasten the grommet snaps (or shock cord threaded through hooks and eyes) along the edges of the sailcover under the boom, starting at the gooseneck and working aft.

Sail fabric is highly susceptible to the deteriorating effects of the ultraviolet rays of the sun. There are sailcloth and thread available that resist UV rays, but they have not proved totally satisfactory. The only lasting solution so far has been to protect the sails with sail covers made out of "Sunbrella" cloth that filters out almost all such rays, or to remove the sails completely and store them out of the sun, which is often the practice on smaller boats.

When sails are put away after use, they are sometimes just stuffed into a sailbag. This practice breaks down the filler with which the cloth is treated to reduce porosity and stretch. Thus, the effective life of the sail is reduced. Furthermore, stuffing the sails wrinkles them. It may take as long as an hour of sailing to smooth out the wrinkles, and wrinkles make the sail smaller, thereby reducing sail area, which is a disadvantage particularly when racing. They also disrupt the airflow over the surface of the sail, which reduces it effectiveness as an airfoil.

For these reasons, it's best to fold or roll a small sail rather than stuff it into a bag after use. To fold, lay the foot of the sail on a flat surface, and, working with a crew-member at the other end, each places a hand a few feet up the luff and the leech of the sail and make a fold of the cloth over the lower hand. Repeat this, folding accordion-style, until you reach the head of the sail. Then roll the sail up and place it in the sailbag. When folding the mainsail, the clew should end up on the outside of the roll; when folding the jib, the tack should remain on the outside of the roll, because these corners are attached first when the sails are used next. A side benefit is that folding results in a smaller, neater package for stowing and saves space—which is scarce on a sailboat.

When the jib is set, it is either hanked onto a jibstay or run up a grooved headstay. When lowering a hanked jib, we have two choices: we can unhank the sail and bag it—i.e., fold it just as we do the mainsail on a small boat—or we can leave it hanked on and bag it right on the headstay. If doing the latter, when you finish you must make sure the neck of the bag is tied tightly around all the hanks so the jib can't work out of the bag and start up the headstay. Also, you should detach the jib halyard from the sail and snap it to the base of a stanchion. This is an easy way to stow a jib at night on a cruising boat when you plan to use it first thing the next day.

Rolling works best for smaller sails such as jibs. It's easier to roll from the foot first. But that means the edges of the leech and luff are exposed and catch on the bag as you slide it in. A plus is that the head is on the outside.

Just put it in the jibstay groove, attach the halyard and haul it up. A minus is that the tack can't be attached because it's rolled up inside the sail and it's easy to make the mistake of hoisting the sail too far so that the tack jams up in the groove.

A better way is to start at the middle of the sail, with one person at the luff and one at the leech and the head and tack together. Roll the folded sail so the upper half of the sail is inside the roll and the lower half outside. The rolling takes half the time because you are rolling double layers together; it is smooth on the outside and slides easily into the bag; both tack and head are exposed so both can be attached before hoisting next time; and when hoisted, the sail unrolls much more easily than it would if the whole sail were rolled in one direction, like a window shade.

When lowering a jib in a groove, be careful not to lose it over the side. The tack attachment should be the last to be removed and only when the sail is totally under control. Some sails have holes along the luff through which a line is passed to keep it flaked. If there is no line, flake the luff of the sail as it comes down and put a sail tie around it and through the head and the tack to keep it sorted out. Most such jibs are bagged in a long zippered tube that forms a flat rectangle when unzipped. Lay the bag along the weather rail first and then drag the jib aft to the bag. Lay the foot of the sail on the bag and follow up along the leech, flaking back and forth as you go. When the flaking is finished, zip the bag closed and stow it below. In some cases the bag is one-third the length of the foot. Just pick up the sail one-third of the foot length from the clew and carry the fold forward to the tack. The sail is now folded in thirds and the bag can be zipped.

On cruising yachts you will see roller-furling headstays. In this system, the jib is hoisted in a groove, but when not in use it is furled around the headstay rather than lowered. To furl the sail you simply pull on a line that leads from a drum at the base of the jib aft to a winch near the cockpit, which rotates the whole headstay, rolling up the jib. If you want to reduce sail area, you just roll it up halfway. The end result is not perfect because the middle of the stay lags behind the ends in rolling, and the middle of the sail becomes very full. Also, the clew rises higher in the air the more the jib is rolled up. This is fine when reaching in heavy air because there is less chance to scoop water, but it puts the CE high off the water and increases heeling. Sailmakers have attempted to solve the former problem by adding foam strips near the middle of the sail to flatten it as it rolls up. In another solution, a headstay manufacturer developed a roller-furling headstay that rotates from the middle first, which takes draft out of the middle of the sail before the top and bottom.

The sail, when rolled up, is still exposed to sunlight and subject to UV deterioration, so sailmakers add a panel of UV-resistant material along the leech. This panel is on the outside of the rolls as the jib is rolled up and protects the rest of the furled sail.

When using a roller-furling system, you generally sail on a reach to unroll the jib. This allows the sail to unroll without flailing against the mast and shrouds. It's best to control the line from a winch rather than let it fly. If you don't use a winch, when the jib is about half unrolled in a fresh breeze you won't be able to hold the line, and if you just let it fly, the line can become tangled in a turning block or twist and become jammed around the furling drum, making it very difficult to rewind.

To furl the jib, it's necessary to luff it completely. Free the sheet and head the boat up to reduce speed and heel angle, but don't flog the sail against the shrouds. This hurts the sail and increases friction, making the sail more difficult to furl. If there's any resistance, look aloft to see whether there's a line fouled in the jib.

In the case of a roller-furling mainsail, the roller is either inside the mast—in which case the sail disappears from view and is protected from sunlight, dirt, and rain—or it is parallel to and just aft of the mast. The advantage of the latter system is that the sail can be lowered if jammed, but it does leave the sail exposed to the elements. One disadvantage to the furl inside the mast when it was first put in use was that the slot opening in the mast created a whistle. The problem didn't occur at anchor or at a mooring because then the boat was lined up with the wind. However, at a slip, with the wind abeam, the slot whistled like someone blowing across the top of a bottle. This problem has been solved by the development of a slot insert which is hauled into place by an extra halyard. The invention of this type of sail-handling equipment, combined with electric self-tailing winches, has made it possible for two people to handle much larger sailboats than ever before. For instance, it is now possible for a couple to easily handle even a 70-foot yacht.

Reefing. At present, the most efficient method for reefing a sail is the "jiffy reef," sometimes called the "slab reef." The process is as follows: The mainsheet is eased and the main halyard lowered so the reef cringle on the luff can be hooked or tied down. Then, the clew cringle is winched tight, which creates a new foot of the sail along the boom. The main is trimmed in and the reefing job is almost complete. The excess sail at the bottom is cinched tight around the boom with sail stops. If the sail has reef points from which lines hang down on either side of the sail, a reef knot should be used. Otherwise, pass a sail stop through the grommet in the sail until the stop fetches up against the bowline tied in the end of it. Pass the stop around the boom and the reefed sail and cinch it tight. Tie a simple slipknot, so the end can be pulled to release it.

Mistakes can occur during this process. For instance, if the clew is pulled tight before the luff is, the sail will be pulled out of the mast groove and ripped. There must be heavy vertical pressure on the luff to keep this from happening, so always finish reefing the luff first. When the clew reefing line is led through the sail either before the mainsail is set or in preparation for reefing, it should first pass through the clew cringle from the same side of the sail on which it leaves the boom. It is then passed through a reinforced slit in the sail near the foot, around the boom and then tied to itself above the slit with a bowline as in Figure 38. After the clew has been pulled down tight, take a piece of line long enough to go around the boom two or three times, pass it through the cringle and around the boom twice and tie it tightly. This is a safety line in case the clew reefing line breaks. There's a terrific amount of strain on it from the mainsheet tension. If the clew line breaks, it will rip out all the sail stops you used to tie up the excess material after reefing and will rip the sail at each reef point. Once the safety line is tight and secured, ease the clew reefing line slightly to even the load

Figure 38

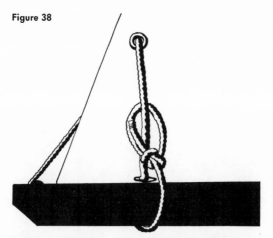

Pass the reefing line through the slit in the sail first, then pass it around the boom and tie a bowline slipknot.

between the two lines. This is done as a matter of course on a maxi-yacht, but is a good idea for 50-footers as well.

When you shake out the reef, the process is reversed. You untie the safety line, ease the mainsheet and release the clew reef line before releasing the luff and cranking up the halyard. If you don't, the sail will pull out of the groove as you tension the luff. A common mistake is to forget to untie the reef points before easing the clew. This, of course, causes the sail to rip at the reef points.

A variation on jiffy reefing has been developed by Garry Hoyt's fertile imagination using the Harken brothers' ball-bearing blocks. It's reefing using only one line. As the halyard is eased the reefing line is winched in, which takes care of both clew and tack reefing cringles at the same time.

SAILCLOTH: TYPES AND MANUFACTURING

There are three basic types of sailcloth: Woven, non-woven, and laminates. The most widely used woven sailcloth for mainsails and jibs in the U.S. is Dacron, a synthetic polyester fiber with high-tensile strength and great resistance to stretch. It was first produced in 1944 and licensed to various countries under different names. In England, for instance, it is called Terylene; in Russia, Lavsan. However, the material is exactly the same, only the weaves differ.

The woven sailcloth most used for spinnakers is nylon. It is a synthetic material originally developed in 1933 by a firm named Carothers, which had offices in New York and London, hence the derivation of the name nylon. Nylon has great strength, toughness and elasticity.

Kevlar is DuPont's name for high-strength aramid fibers that are also woven into cloth. Weight for weight, Kevlar is as much as 20 times stronger than steel. However, it is weakened by continual bending, as would be a wire coathanger that is bent back and forth until it breaks. Flogging a Kevlar sail has the same effect.

Cloth is woven on a loom. The long threads on the loom are called the warp threads. One warp thread (called an "end") is raised and the one next to it is lowered to allow a shuttle to pass through bearing the fill (called a "pick") thread that goes through the width of the cloth. Then the first warp thread is lowered and the one next to it is raised and the shuttle passes back through again with the fill thread. The resulting weave can have many different characteristics depending on the type of thread used for the warp or for the fill. If a warp end is a small thread, while a fill pick is a thicker thread, the cloth is "fill-oriented." The fill is the "primary yarn direction" of a fill-oriented cloth, because it is most stretch-resistant in that direction. The "secondary yarn direction" is 90 degrees to the primary; in this case, the warp.

As the cloth is woven, the smaller threads tend to pass up and down, over and under the thicker threads. This is called "crimp." It can contribute to the elongation of the fabric under load. When describing the thickness of threads, we count the number of warp ends per inch and then the number of filling picks per inch and the results are "count."

You may also hear the term "sett" used regarding cloth in general. A "low sett" cloth has a low number (a low count) of thicker threads. A "finer sett" cloth has a larger number of thinner threads woven closely together. These cloths can appear quite different, yet they may be the same weight.

The measurement of a sailcloth's weight in England makes more sense than it does here. It is measured in ounces per square yard, as if cloth were 36 inches wide (one yard is 1,296 sq. in.). In the U.S., we weigh cloth as if it were 28½ inches wide (so one yard is 1,026 sq. in.). Comparing a yard of each cloth, the English cloth weighs more, because it has almost two square feet more material. Our 6.5-oz. yard of cloth is an 8.2-oz. yard in England.

Other sailmaking terms it's useful to know include the following:

Tensile strength: This measurement indicates the load at which a sailcloth will break.

Yield strength: Sailcloth stretches under load and normally returns to its original shape in the absence of load. The yield strength is the load at which the material no longer returns to its original shape.

Tear strength: This is the sailcloth's resistance to tearing.

Porosity: If a sail is porous, air will be able to get through the material. The drive of the sail is derived from the difference in pressure on the two sides of the sail. If air passes through the sail from an area of greater pressure to one of lesser pressure, the pressure equalization will result in less drive. Spinnaker porosity can be tested by pressing a small section hard against your mouth and blowing. If the cloth is old and tired, you will be able to blow through it. There are also machines for testing sailcloth porosity.

Modulus of elasticity: This is the measure of stretch of elasticity of a fabric. A high modulus of elasticity means the fabric has low stretch.

In sailcloth manufacturing, the process from thread to finished cloth is a fairly simple progression on complicated-looking machines. Polyester thread arrives from DuPont on spools of various denier (thickness). The denier is the weight in grams of 9,000 meters of yarn.

A 250 × 440 cloth has warp threads of 250 denier and fill threads of 440. If the cloth is fill-oriented, the fill threads are thicker. The lighter warp threads will curve over and under the thicker fill threads. In other words, the warp will be crimped while the fill remains straight. This results in less stretch in the fill direction—the width of the cloth.

The greatest preparation goes into getting the warp yarn ready for the looms. First, a machine winds the yarn from the cardboard-cone rolls provided by DuPont onto plastic-cone rolls. At the same time, some additional twist may be added to the thread.

Twist tightens the multiple filaments that make up a strand of thread. Just as you twist the neck of a plastic garbage bag to make it small enough to tie, twist reduces the thickness of the thread and produces a tighter weave.

Next, a number of rolls are put on a larger machine that winds all the threads alongside one another on a large spool, at the same time treating them with a solution that toughens these warp threads against the beating they take on the loom.

Now the spool of warp threads is put on the loom and, as each is alternately raised and lowered, the shuttle containing the fill thread of the desired denier is passed back and forth the width of the cloth. A ram packs the filling thread tightly against the adjacent thread. The fill thread runs right off the roll provided by DuPont onto an automatic bobbin winder which then inserts the bobbin of yarn into the shuttle. A hot knife at each end cuts and fuses the filling threads.

After the cloth leaves the looms where it was woven, it is run through a machine that scours and cleans it. The residue of the solution that was used previously to treat the warp threads is washed off. On another machine, the cloth is passed over and under a number of large rollers that are heated by gas to a moderate temperature. This dries the cloth in preparation for the resin-impregnation machine. After the cloth has been thoroughly resinated with melamine resins to fill the voids in the cloth, it is clipped to a "tenter" frame and passed into an oven to dry the resin in the cloth. Basically, the tenter frame clips keep the fill threads perpendicular to the warp threads as the resin dries. Otherwise, the cloth could end up skewed. Up to this point, no machine has had enough heat to do anything but dry the cloth. Now it is passed through a "contact" heat-set machine (set to temperatures above

300° F) to catalyze and cure the resin and to heat-set the polyester threads. This shrinks the cloth for a tighter weave, brings it up to full tenacity and reduces stretch.

The next process is calendering. The cloth passes through two large rollers that press the cloth with tons of pressure much like a large, old-fashioned, laundry wringer. One roller is made of extremely hard metal and one of somewhat softer material. This stabilizes the cloth and makes it very smooth. A smooth surface reduces friction drag of the air passing over the surface.

Some sailcloths are coated on one side with a resin that makes the cloth extremely stiff and hard to handle, but reduces stretching to a minimum. This type of cloth might be used for a racing mainsail on a sailboat with a very stiff rig. Since you are unable to bend the mast to flatten the main and depower the rig, you need a sail that will maintain its original shape longer. Such cloth also allows the racing sailor to keep the sail up over a wider range of wind strengths.

The finishes of the cloth range from "soft" to "medium firm" to "firm" to "super firm," yet these terms are very subjective and based on your comparisons with sailcloth you've used before. Soft cloth is more difficult for a sailmaker to sew well and results in a sail that may not look so good when it is initially set. It may have to go back for a number of adjustments and recuts, but once it is right, it should last longer and is ideal, therefore, for cruising sails. Since it is soft, it is easy to handle and does not crease much.

Only two sailcloth manufacturing steps remain. The first is a machine with electrically heated knives that trims the selvage (the raw, untrimmed edges of the cloth), and cuts it into manageable lengths for sailmaker rolls. This same machine can cut the cloth into numerous rolls of cloth tape just by setting a number of the cutting knives a few inches apart. The last step is to pass the cloth over a light box so any defects can be detected. It is amazing how imperfections that cannot be seen in normal sunlight conditions show up in the backlighting of a light box.

After making the cloth, most manufacturers will test it to make sure that it has the desired durability. A flutter test, which mimics in a short amount of time the amount of abuse caused by a sail luffing under normal use for a period of years, is done on a small sample of the sailcloth.

Chapter III

THE SPINNAKER

Setting the spinnaker adds immense sail area and power to any sized boat, but can be difficult—even dangerous—to handle if not done correctly. Smooth, trouble-free spinnaker work comes from understanding the procedures from setting to takedown thoroughly through long experience under all conditions. Let's start by getting to know the parts and characteristics of this exciting sail.

The spinnaker is a triangular sail, with a head, tack, and clew. The tack of the spinnaker is in a fixed position—at the end of the spinnaker pole. As with other sails, the edge of the spinnaker from the tack to the head is the "luff," from the clew to the head is the "leech," and from the clew to the tack is the "foot." When the spinnaker is not in use, the two edges are identical, so we call each a leech (and each corner a clew) until the sail is set and the luff is established by whichever corner (now called the tack) is attached to the spinnaker pole.

The spinnaker is hoisted by the spinnaker halyard, and the tack is held in place by the pole, which is always set to windward (i.e., on the opposite side of the boat from the main boom). Actually, the jaws of the pole fitting snap over the line attached to the tack of the spinnaker. This line is the "afterguy" or, more commonly, the "guy" (Figure 39). The guy leads aft outside of everything to a turning block on the rail and thence to a winch. The free corner (now the clew) of the spinnaker is attached to a sheet that leads aft to turning block and winch on the other side of the boat. When you jibe the spinnaker, the tack becomes the "new" clew and the "old" clew becomes the "new" tack at the pole.

Two lines hold the pole in position: the topping lift, which keeps it from

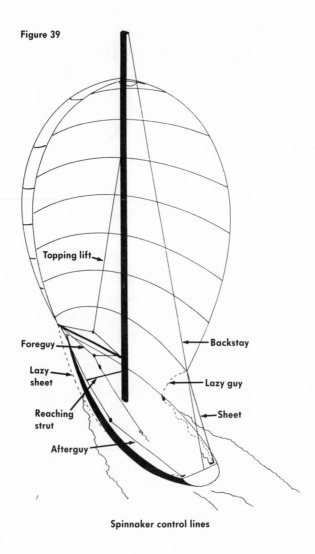

Figure 39

Topping lift

Foreguy

Backstay

Lazy sheet

Lazy guy

Reaching strut

Sheet

Afterguy

Spinnaker control lines

falling when the spinnaker isn't full of wind, and the foreguy (also called the downhaul), which keeps the pole from "skying" (pointing up in the air) when the spinnaker is full and from coming aft when the guy is trimmed. On large cruising and racing boats, two additional lines—the lazy guy and the lazy sheet—are sometimes added to facilitate jibing the spinnaker.

Also essential in spinnaker control is the reaching strut, as shown in Figure 39. This is a short pole set perpendicular to the mast and through which the spinnaker guy is led. It is used when close-reaching (when the spinnaker pole is near the headstay). Without the strut, the guy rests against the shrouds and when you try to square the pole (by pulling it aft), there is so little angle outboard that it takes a tremendous amount of winching of the guy to pull the pole aft. This results in so much compression on the pole that either the pole or the guy may break.

I thought about this problem and in the fall of 1957 came up with the "reaching strut" solution. At that time no such "outrigger" was permitted under the racing rules. As soon as it became legal, however, struts flourished. Over the years they have become more and more sophisticated, to the extent that some maxis have a hydraulic telescoping strut to handle the strain. On large yachts, when the pole is well forward and the guy is lying against the shrouds, it takes 10 men and a boy to push the strut out against the heavily loaded guy and hook it on the mast. If you find yourself in this position, it helps to take the strain temporarily on the lazy sheet, which will permit enough slack in the guy so that it can easily be slipped into the fitting on the end of the reaching strut.

TYPES OF SPINNAKERS

There are various cloth weights used in spinnakers for light or heavy air and variously shaped spinnakers for use in different conditions.

Weights of cloth range from extremely light ½-oz. material up to tough, 2.2-oz. nylon cloth. Common intermediate weights in ounces are ¾, 1.2, and 1.5. A spinnaker made from ½-oz. cloth is used in very light air and up to a maximum apparent wind of 7 to 8 knots. Spinnakers made of ¾-oz. cloth are carried up to 12 to 14 knots of apparent wind and are probably used more than any other weight chute. It's a popular standard weight for many classes of small sailboats and has a wide wind range for larger yachts. Spinnakers of 1.2-oz. cloth are fairly rare; 1.5-oz. is more common and offers a better range for upper wind levels.

Most boats have to douse the spinnaker for other reasons before the upper wind range of a 1.5-oz. chute is reached. They may be broaching, rolling badly, or otherwise out of control, and either a smaller chute or none at all is indicated. If they go to a smaller chute, it will normally be about 85 percent of full size and made of 2.2-oz. material, since it will be used in even higher apparent-wind speeds. This weight is generally regarded as the maximum weight needed. A storm chute is made of at least 2.2-oz. cloth, and usually something else will break—halyard, pole, guy, or sheet—before the spinnaker goes, unless it is flogged to death luffing (rather than being kept full).

A spinnaker of any weight cloth that is allowed to collapse and then fill with a "bang" time after time in heavy air will fatigue and eventually blow out.

The need for a heavier weight spinnaker does not necessarily increase with wind strength or boat size. There are other factors involved. For instance, when I first started steering the 81-foot maxi-yacht *Nirvana,* my closest frame of reference was our 54-foot ocean racer *Sleuth.* On *Sleuth,* I knew when we had to change from a ½-oz. spinnaker to a ¾-oz. spinnaker to avoid blowing out the lighter chute. At first glance, *Nirvana'*s 5,000-sq. ft. chute seemed incredibly huge, maybe triple the size of *Sleuth'*s, and the equipment was equally impressive, with heavy wire guys, massive Kevlar sheets and powerful coffee-grinder winches to control the forces involved in flying such a spinnaker. Even the spinnaker pole was over 30 feet long— longer than many cruising boats I've sailed.

With such a huge sail pulling the boat along at 10 to 15 knots, surely the cloth had to be heavier and stronger than that on a smaller boat such as *Sleuth* in the same wind conditions. So I thought, until we carried a ¾-oz. chute easily in whitecap weather. Then I realized that just because the forces were tremendous at the three points of attachment—head, tack and clew (and the corners had been heavily reinforced)—the wind pressure on any particular square foot of sail wasn't any greater than on *Sleuth.* In fact, it was less, much less. Why? Because, when the boat is broad-reaching or running in a given wind strength, the apparent wind is reduced the faster the boat sails.

Because a maxi sails so fast downwind, the apparent wind strength is greatly reduced. For example, a boat sailing 8 knots dead downwind in a 16-knot true wind will have an 8-knot apparent wind blowing across the deck. A larger boat with a longer waterline length is capable of much higher speeds in the same wind strength—let's say 12 knots. Thus, the apparent wind over the deck of the larger boat is only 4 knots.

A square foot of spinnaker cloth on the smaller boat is going to be stressed much more at 8 knots than on the larger boat at 4 knots. In fact, the forces quadruple as the wind strength doubles. The relationship is to the square of the wind strength. The square of 8 is 64 and the square of 4 is 16. So the forces are four times greater ($64 \div 16 = 4$) on the smaller boat with the slower boat speed and the stronger apparent wind.

The result was that we were carrying spinnakers made of lighter sail cloth in much higher wind velocities on *Nirvana* than were carried on any other boat I've ever sailed.

Another important factor to remember when carrying a chute is that the apparent wind increases quickly when you go from a run to a reach. This was demonstrated to me very graphically during the 1985 Fastnet Race on *Nirvana*. We were nearing the finish line on our way to setting a course record as long as we could beat *Atlantic Privateer* across the line. *Privateer* was a fast light-air boat and was closing rapidly even though we were flying our ½-oz. chute. Our navigator called for a 10-degree course change to get around a point of land before the finish. Small as this was, it generated a large change in apparent wind direction because of the light air and the speed of the boat. We went from a broad reach at close to maximum apparent wind speed for the sail to a beam reach beyond maximum. Since we were only about a mile from the finish we held our breath, but it didn't help. The sail blew out after only a few moments. Having anticipated the problem, we had the ¾-oz. chute going up practically before the ½-oz. finished tearing apart. The quick recovery held off *Atlantic Privateer* and we finished 38 seconds ahead of her to break the 605-mile course elapsed time record by half a day.

Even if a spinnaker doesn't tear when carried beyond its maximum wind speed, it will distort. It will stretch beyond any elastic memory inherent in the cloth and will end up baggy, so it's a good idea to remain within the wind ranges recommended by the sailmaker.

Spinnaker shapes vary with their purpose. The fullness of a spinnaker is measured in the same manner as a mainsail or jib. Draw an imaginary line from luff to leech (the chord) and measure the distance from it to the maximum depth of the sail (the draft). If three persons each take a corner of the spinnaker and pull out so that three edges are tight, the draft remaining is that which is built into the sail by the sailmaker. If the persons at the clews come closer together, thereby letting the foot droop, we will get increased draft caused by the clew position. Easing the spinnaker pole forward has the same effect. If the person at the head of the sail walks toward the persons at the clews, the luffs will droop. This lets the middle of the sail sag and, although the whole sail may seem fuller, a cross section at the middle of the sail will show that it's flatter there. The drooping luffs make the distance to the deepest part of the sail less in the middle than at other locations. Raising the spinnaker pole or easing the halyard has the same effect. It frees the luff and flattens the middle of the spinnaker.

Although we can control some of the spinnaker shape when it's set, we rely on the sailmaker to give us its basic shape. Running and general purpose spinnakers tend to be full because they are less dependent upon airflow around the outside of the sail for their drive. They need to catch a lot

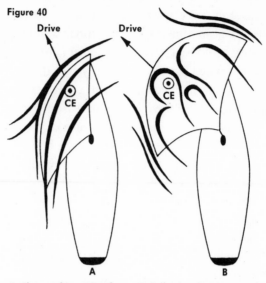

Figure 40

A. Flat reaching spinnaker:
1. CE in close to boat
2. Airflow more smooth
3. Drive more forward
4. Flow exits leech easily

B. Full spinnaker on a reach:
1. CE out over water
2. Airflow more turbulent
3. Drive more sideways
4. Leech cupped

of air—like a parachute—to drag the boat downwind. Spinnakers designed for reaching are flatter, for a couple of reasons. First, they act much like a genoa jib and the longer the airflow remains attached to the backside of the sail before it breaks away to turbulent flow, the more drive will be generated by the sail. Second, on a reach the spinnaker will be on the leeward side of the boat with the pole near the headstay. A full sail would be like a jib with a tight leech or a main with battens cocked to windward. The after part of the sail will be generating lift in a backward direction. With a flat spinnaker, the after part of the sail will be close to parallel with the centerline of the boat and most of the drive will be forward. Third, the center of effort (CE) of a full spinnaker will be farther away from the boat as she heels. Compare the flat and full spinnakers in Figure 40. The greater the distance the drive is separated from the drag, the more the tendency to broach.

Imagine a 30-foot spinnaker pole set to leeward and tied to the shrouds at right angles to the boat. Come along in an outboard and give the end of the pole a good shove in the direction the boat is sailing. What will happen? Of course, the boat will tend to round up to windward. This is called "turning moment." If the pole were only 10 feet long it would take much more of a shove to have the same effect. There would be less turning moment.

Figure 41

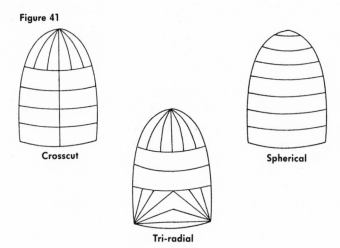

Crosscut

Tri-radial

Spherical

The other way a spinnaker is shaped is in plane form as viewed from aft. Running chutes have high shoulders in order to gain the greatest projected area—the square-foot area that the wind "sees." This puts the CE up high in the sail, but it doesn't matter because the direction of the drive is in line with the drag of the boat. Also, high shoulders (carrying the girth or width of the spinnaker up high) put more sail area up high when the wind is stronger. A reaching chute or a storm chute should have the CE as low as possible without losing too much sail area for the reasons mentioned above. Such spinnakers have little or no shoulders.

There are three common types of spinnakers made by sailmakers: the crosscut, the spherical, and the tri-radial. Probably the most widely used is the crosscut as shown in Figure 41. The threads in a crosscut chute are aligned so that the fill is parallel to the leeches. The center seam is along the bias of the cloth. The result is that the leeches are very stable and don't stretch much, and therefore the sail doesn't develop undesirable leech fluttering. Since the center of the sail is along the bias of the cloth, however, the sail will become much fuller as the cloth stretches there. If a cloth is used that has a lot of bias stretch, the crosscut spinnaker can become too full when used on a reach. The stiff leeches and full center make the crosscut a good running chute, especially in rough conditions.

The threadline relationship of the spherical spinnaker is different. There is no center seam and the filling threads in the center of the sail are vertical, resulting in the leeches being along the bias. Thus, the leeches stretch more than the middle of the sail. When the sail gets older, the leeches will stretch and not return to the pre-stretch position. The leeches will become fuller and cup, which is undesirable for reaching. Generally, the spherical cut is better for reaching than running because it doesn't stretch in the center. It's a compromise between the full crosscut for running and shock-absorption, and the flat tri-radial designed for reaching. The spherical ends up flatter than the former and fuller than the latter.

The third common type is the tri-radial. The warp threads align with the direction of greatest stress from the corners of the sail toward the center. The tri-radial is excellent for reaching and for heavy air because it doesn't distort. The stretch is in the same direction as the threadline. Also, the sail doesn't get fuller along the center or the leeches when gusts hit, so any puff turns directly into driving force for the boat rather than being absorbed by stretching.

Of the three sails, the tri-radial is easiest to recognize because of the panels emanating from the corners of the sail. Like the crosscut, it has a center seam. And, like the crosscut, the leeches don't stretch, which makes it sensitive to pole height. Lowering the pole pulls the luff down and makes the sail fuller in both these cuts.

WHEN TO FLY IT

The first big spinnaker decision is whether or not to fly. Is the crew experienced enough? Is the wind too heavy or too light? Is the wind too far forward?

The wind strength and direction weigh heavily on the choice of chute as described above. Once, in a 5.5-Meter boat, I set a running chute in light air with the wind well aft, only to find that the increased boat speed brought the apparent wind so far forward that a reaching chute was called for. Shortly thereafter, on rounding the weather mark and anticipating the same true-wind angle, but in a heavy breeze, I set a reaching spinnaker only to find that the increased boat speed failed to bring the apparent wind forward much. That day we should have set the running spinnaker. On a larger boat, the navigator would have calculated the anticipated strength and angle of the new apparent wind and the proper chute for the conditions would have been selected.

On a light-to-medium day, some spinnakers can be carried to advantage when the apparent wind is well forward (as close as 55 to 60 degrees relative from the bow), but they could cause a broach and a bad weather helm at the same apparent wind angle in heavier air. Learning to read wind conditions relative to the spinnaker comes with practice; it's part of the challenge.

Another factor in your decision to set or not is the relative sail areas of spinnaker and jib. On a boat with a large jib, if the wind is too far forward or heavy enough to cause a broach, you may find the boat will go faster under the jib. On other boats, the spinnaker has so much more area than the jib, that even if you are broaching you will probably net out with a faster speed through the water with the spinnaker than without. When racing, go by the old axiom, "If in doubt, set."

On very heavy days it almost always pays to carry a spinnaker if you're racing. I've often heard the argument on large racing boats that if the boat is already at hull speed, setting a spinnaker won't improve it. That's a fallacy. When sailing in a trough of a wave and up the other side, the boat is rarely going near hull speed, and needs the extra power that a spinnaker provides. Furthermore, under surfing conditions there is no such thing as hull speed; all sailboats can surpass it. The spinnaker will give just enough more power to start the surf earlier and make it last longer.

Always remember the importance of the apparent wind angle. I've often heard the argument when we're beam-reaching with an 85 percent flat spinnaker that we'd go faster with a full-sized spinnaker because the breeze had died a little. Experience dictates that the full-sized spinnaker increases weather helm for the reasons mentioned earlier. The increased rudder drag often offsets the greater size of the spinnaker.

On very light days a chute will fill well if the spinnaker cloth is light enough and the apparent wind relatively far forward. But with the wind way aft, particularly with leftover slop rolling the boat around, a jib may do just as well. The spinnaker will just flop back and forth, wrapping around the jibstay and catching on the spreaders. You're usually better off without it in such conditions.

THE SET

Now that you are familiar with the sail and its equipment, let's go through a set. The same procedures are involved in both large and small boats; each, respectively, just requires more or fewer people to do the job.

Careful preparation always precedes a spinnaker set, racing or cruising, and that begins with the last time the spinnaker was put away or "bagged."

To bag a spinnaker properly, first find the head of the sail (it will have a swivel attached to it and may even be marked). Follow one leech down from the head, making accordion pleats of large segments of sail and holding on to them as you gather them all the way to the clew (see Figure 42). Change hands and repeat on the other leech to its clew. Next, while one person holds the folded leeches and all three corners (head and two clews) together, another stuffs the spinnaker belly into the bag. The leeches go in last and the clews and head are left on top of the bag and should be tied together with the head between the clews. Leaving them outside the bag facilitates attaching halyard, sheet, and guy the next time the sail is set.

Since the spinnaker is triangular, if two edges are untangled, the third must also be, and the above packing system will work 99 percent of the time.

When getting ready to set, first attach the sheets to the shroud, lifeline, or stanchion on the foredeck and lead them aft, one on each side, outside of everything, to the turning blocks at the stern or quarter, as shown in Figure 39, thence to the proper winches. Next, with the packed bag on deck or readily available, set the spinnaker pole by attaching the topping lift and downhaul and lifting the pole off the deck to the fitting on the mast. Snap the fitting on the pole's other end over the guy before lifting. The pole should be resting against the windward side of the headstay. If you are using a lazy sheet, it should be over the top of the pole and lightly taped to the wire guy so it doesn't come off before or during the set. Then it's ready for the first jibe. Next, attach the guy, sheet, and halyard to the respective corners of the spinnaker. Be sure the bag is secured to the boat so that it will not fly overboard as the sail goes up. Finally, check to be sure that the halyard leads correctly and is clear all the way up. You are now ready for the hoist, and the spinnaker should come out of the bag without a twist.

Figure 42

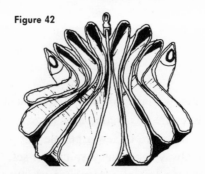

**Fold each edge of the spinnaker from the head
to the clew so it can be hoisted without twists.**

Alternate methods of preparing the spinnaker to avoid twists include "stopping," the bucket system, and a spinnaker sleeve. Stopping consists of furling the spinnaker with the two vertical edges together on the outside of the furl and tying it at intervals with easily breakable twine. Racing crews often "stop" storm spinnakers or heavy-duty spinnakers used in high winds. The sail is hoisted in stops, and breaks out when the sheet is pulled, breaking the lower stops. Then the wind fills the lower part of the spinnaker and breaks out all the stops farther up. An advantage of this method is that the sail can't fill when it's only half hoisted, which can be disastrous in heavy air.

The bucket system was developed by sailors who felt "stopping" was too time-consuming. Their system is to cut the bottom off a plastic bucket, stretch rubber bands around it and pass the spinnaker through head first, keeping the leeches together and sliding the rubber bands onto the sail at desired intervals.

Spinnaker sleeves—called "snakes" or "turtles"—are used on large racing yachts. Starting at the head with the vertical edges lying parallel on top, tapered nylon cloth is zipped around the spinnaker about three-fourths of the way down. The bottom part of the chute is dog-legged and stopped with wool stops so that one leg leads to the pole and the other to the sheet. One of the zippered edges is longer than the other, so that when the spinnaker is set, the crew just pulls the zipper farther down, it comes off the shorter edge and separates all the way up to the head. The sleeve falls in the water and is pulled aboard by a retrieving line attached to the boat.

This is a tried and true system used on many ocean racing yachts. Problems can arise if the spinnaker is allowed to twist inside the sleeve. As long as the sleeve is carefully zipped directly over the two vertical edges, this is unlikely to happen. Sometimes the spinnaker is sleeved at dockside by hoisting it aloft on a halyard and zipping the sleeve closed as the sail goes up. This facilitates aligning the leeches, and gravity keeps the sail from bunching up. However, since you are pulling down on the zipper, the Velcro at the top of the sleeve that keeps it from sliding away from the head of the sail can pop off, causing the zipper to open from the top down accidentally. It can be very embarrassing to have your spinnaker fill at dockside, knocking off other boats' masthead antennas and causing other damage. It's imperative, therefore, to tie a sail stop tightly around the top of the sleeve and the sail as a precautionary measure as you sleeve the sail. Remember to take off the stop when you bag the sail for stowing.

For the hoist of an unstopped, unsleeved spinnaker, the boat must be on a reach or a run, and a small amount of the sail pulled out of the bag ready to go. Then, with one crew in the cockpit tending the guy on the windward winch and another to leeward to tend the sheet, a third crew on the halyard hoists away. As the sail goes up, the guy is trimmed so that the "tack" meets the pole and the pole comes aft. The sheet is also trimmed moderately to further separate the corners of the sail.

To avoid a premature fill, the crewman on the halyard should hand-over-hand it rapidly until the sail is halfway up, then quickly wrap the halyard around the winch for the rest of the hoist. He must avoid having the spinnaker fill before the turns are on the winch. But if he puts turns on too soon, the friction of the winch slows the process and increases the possibility of the sail filling too soon. If that happens, the sail will be pulled from the bag too quickly and end up in the water, where it may rip or the boat may sail into it. On the other hand, if the sail fills with wind before the wraps are put on the winch, the halyard will burn the skin off the crewman's hands as it zings out, and it will be a long, laborious process to get the sail up. Any boat with enough crew members will have the halyard already wrapped around a winch so that it can't possibly get away. As one crew member tails the winch, one or two others pull down on the halyard as it exits the mast. This is called "bouncing" the halyard. As long as the halyard is two-blocked before the spinnaker fills, a winch handle is not needed for even the largest spinnaker.

Once the sail is all the way up, the halyard should be secured firmly and the jib lowered immediately so the wind can get at the spinnaker and fill it.

Although most boats benefit from lowering the jib right away, there are some that sail faster under certain conditions with both jib and spinnaker set. Those boats with high-aspect ratio, non-overlapping jibs can often keep the jib flying with the spinnaker on a reach in moderate wind conditions. When the wind is heavy, the jib will tend to create more heeling force than desirable with a resulting tendency to broach. When the wind is light, flow over the jib will tend to suck the spinnaker in toward the jib, making it collapse more easily and fill with difficulty. If the jib on your boat resembles a spinnaker staysail, you may be able to fly it with the spinnaker. A spinnaker staysail is usually a high, narrow sail that trims to the center of the foredeck when the wind is abeam and toward the rail when the wind is aft. It may increase boat speed as much as two-tenths of a knot.

THE RIGHT TRIM

The spinnaker is a restless sail and it takes concentration and long practice to become good at trimming it, but following certain general principles will help you get there.

When running (as opposed to reaching), the spinnaker is fairly well stalled; it is dragging the boat downwind. True, there's a little flow around the back side of the luff (from a crew member's vantage point), but that doesn't result in much drive. Therefore, we want the greatest projected area possible; the more area exposed to the wind, the greater the sail's effectiveness. Keeping the pole well squared (i.e., aft) and the sheet well trimmed does it. The dotted line spinnaker in Figure 43 shows the amount of area exposed to the wind with the pole forward; the solid line spinnaker shows the increased "projected area" from having the pole squared aft.

But there's a price to pay for having the pole well aft. As we square the pole aft, and also trim the sheet to keep the spinnaker from collapsing, it is drawn in closer and closer to the mainsail. Here the spinnaker is in the bad air of the main and loses efficiency, so we must ease the pole forward and ease the sheet to get the chute away from the sail plan. Somewhere there is a

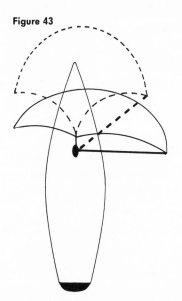

Figure 43

Moving the pole forward gets the spinnaker into clearer air but reduces its projected area.

Pulling the pole aft increases projected area, but brings the spinnaker into the mainsail's turbulent lee.

64 Steve Colgate on Sailing

happy medium between starving the spinnaker behind the main and losing projected area through too much ease. This is where experience comes in.

The second general principle of spinnaker trimming to remember is that a spinnaker is a symmetrical sail and should look symmetrical when flying. Although there are a few exceptions to this, such as when close reaching or in light air, it is generally true. If the spinnaker is misshapen because the pole is too high or too low, it will lose much of its effectiveness.

Thus, pole position is important. A good starting point is to set the pole square to the apparent wind. The masthead fly is in undisturbed air and is a good guide. Set the pole at right angles to it. As the boat sails farther downwind, however, air over the mainsail tends to flow forward and around the mast, so that the spinnaker is almost sailing by the lee. This means that the pole needs to be squared aft, past perpendicular to the masthead fly. Actually, it will be perpendicular to the shroud telltales. I would use the masthead fly as a guide until the wind is well aft and then switch to shroud telltales.

There are some unusual instances where the masthead fly is not very accurate for spinnaker trimming, such as on a 12-Meter yacht. Because of a Twelve's ¾ rig, the head of the spinnaker is considerably lower than the masthead fly and the apparent wind at the top of the mast is noticeably farther aft than that at pole height, due to increased wind velocity aloft. Another exception to setting the pole perpendicular to the apparent wind occurs when you are using a very short-footed spinnaker. In that case, squaring the pole brings the clew near the jibstay and much of the projected area is lost.

Generally, the pole should be level, not parallel to the water but perpendicular to the mast. This means that if you raise or lower the outboard end of the pole, you should raise or lower the inboard end (the end attached to the mast) correspondingly. The idea is to get the spinnaker as far away from the sail plan as possible; but to insist on keeping the pole level to achieve this is overkill. A pole has to be cocked 25 degrees from level to decrease its effective length 10 percent, and during the first 20 degrees, only 5 percent is lost, so a few degrees off of level really doesn't make much difference. Probably more speed is lost by fussing around with the inboard pole height than is gained by having the pole exactly level. Also, a slight cock upward will put the pole in line with the guy and reduce the bending strain on the pole.

More important is the height at which the whole pole is set. The general rule is to keep the tack and clew of the spinnaker level with the plane of the deck (not the water). But this really goes back to keeping the spinnaker symmetrical. When the two corners are level, the spinnaker is symmetrical, looks good, and sets well.

The exceptions to this occur mainly while reaching, and in either high or low wind velocities. While reaching, particularly when flying the spinnaker with the jib set, the tack of a normal reaching spinnaker on a class boat can be set higher than the clew. This opens the slot between the spinnaker and the jib. It also eases the luff of the spinnaker and flattens the chute.

Once the pole is set correctly, it's fairly simple to play the spinnaker. The sheet should be eased until there is a slight curl along the luff, and then trimmed to make the curl disappear. This must be done constantly and is where concentration plays its biggest part. The novice often overtrims the spinnaker, which then is in the disturbed air behind the mainsail where it collapses. To correct it he trims harder, which makes matters worse. This is called a "starve." Pull the pole aft to correct the problem and ease the sheet . . . "When in doubt, let it out."

The spinnaker guy should also be played, particularly if the boat is small or if you are running in a slop. As the boat rolls to windward, the pole must be squared and the sheet eased. As it rolls to leeward, the pole should be eased forward and the sheet trimmed.

All changes in apparent wind direction necessitate changes in pole position and sheet trim. If the boat starts surfing, falls off a plane, or if the wind velocity changes, the apparent wind direction will be affected and the spinnaker trimmer will have to make adjustments. Moreover, he must learn to anticipate these changes ahead of time.

Easing the halyard. There are times when the spinnaker halyard should be eased—but when, and how much?

The next time you are on a reach with the spinnaker set, look up behind the mainsail on the lee side. Then ease the spinnaker halyard six inches or so while looking at the leech of the sail, not the head. It will become obvious how much the slot between the spinnaker and the main will open up to allow free air passage.

When running downwind in a breeze, easing the halyard has two effects. First, it gets the spinnaker away from the disturbed air of the mainsail; second, it allows the spinnaker to be more vertical than it is when fully hoisted. In light air, however, the halyard should not be eased because then the spinnaker will just come straight down. Nor should it be eased on a reach in heavy air, because the sail's center of effort will go out farther over the water and possibly cause a broach. On a run in heavy air, an eased spinnaker will be more apt to roll from one side of the boat to the other (oscillate) than it would if fully hoisted. In short, easing the halyard is rarely done on a run and is really only beneficial on a medium-air reach, where it can be strikingly effective.

Spinnaker trimming in light air takes a great deal of patience. Lower the pole way down, but always keep the pole end a little higher than the clew. Then, when a puff fills the sail, the pole will be at the proper height. In other words, keep the pole at the proper height for the 10 percent of the time that the spinnaker is filled and doing the boat some good, not the 90 percent of the time that it is drooping and not producing any drive. Another reason to keep the pole a little higher than the clew in light air is that a low pole will stretch the luff and fold it over. When a puff comes, the spinnaker is unable to fill because of the shape of the luff.

The same thing can happen with some very full-shouldered running spinnakers. The luff can collapse from a starve and though you know you must pull the pole aft, first you have to overtrim the sheet to unfold the luff. Only then can you pull the pole back with the spinnaker full. In light air it is better to have the pole too low rather than too high. When the pole is too high, it causes the spinnaker to droop to leeward, to be partially blanketed by the main, and it will take a much stronger puff to fill it.

Another problem occurs in light air when also carrying a jib. On a reach, air flowing past the lee side of the jib causes a suction on a reach, and if the spinnaker collapses, it sucks into the jib and is very difficult to fill again. The natural tendency is to trim the jib to get it away from the spinnaker, but actually the opposite should be done. The first time the spinnaker collapses, free the jib sheet to break down the airflow over the jib. If it happens often, take the jib down.

An alternative to taking it down on a small keelboat is to roll it up. Take a short piece of line, a length of wool, or a piece of single-strand electrical conductor wire with you to the foredeck. Grab the jib slightly aft of midway between the luff and leech and roll it forward, pulling down as you roll. Tie the sail to the jibstay with the line or wool or twist-tie the wire. The beauty of the wool or the twist tie is that you don't have to go back on the foredeck when you want to unroll the jib. Just pull on the jib sheet to break the wool or pop the wire.

JIBING TECHNIQUES

There are two basic jibing techniques: the end-for-end jibe, used most often on small boats; and the dip-pole jibe used on larger racing and cruising boats.

In the end-for-end system, as the boat heads down from, for example, a starboard tack reach in order to jibe, the pole should come aft and the sheet should be eased. The boat is on a dead run at the instant of jibing and the spinnaker should be trimmed for that point of sailing. The main boom and spinnaker pole should then be jibed over and the boat should head up to the new port tack reach. The pole should be forward near the jibstay and the sheet trimmed in.

During the jibe, the foredeck crewman on a boat such as the Soling stands against the mast facing forward. From this position he has the best leverage for controlling the pole and getting it off the mast. Also, he can see the spinnaker and help keep it full. On a reach-to-reach jibe, he should take the pole off the mast and then off the "old" guy. This makes the spinnaker freewheeling and the mid-cockpit crew can pull the spinnaker around the boat without the pole's restricting it in any way. The foredeck crew then connects the end of the pole that was previously at the mast to the "new" guy and snaps the other end of the pole into the mast fitting. This is called "end-for-ending" the pole.

Usually the skipper will turn the boat through the jibe smoothly and evenly, keeping the spinnaker full. The one exception to this is in doing very-light-air, reach-to-reach jibes. On the initial reach, the apparent wind is forward and the boatspeed greater than it possibly could be downwind. As the boat turns into the jibe, the spinnaker collapses because the momentum of the boat overruns the spinnaker. This makes it very difficult to ease the sheet to get the spinnaker around to the other side of the boat because there's no wind in the sail and no pull on the sheet. The solution takes timing, but is worth practicing. Just as the boat arrives at the mark to be rounded, while the spinnaker is still full on the reach, release the sheet and square the pole. At the same instant turn the boat fast to the new reaching course. The spinnaker collapses (as it would anyway), but it is around the jibstay to the new leeward side. Quickly shift the pole to the new windward side, and you begin sailing with the spinnaker full on the new reach having hardly even slowed down.

A running jibe is much easier. The boat's heading changes only slightly, so all we are doing is changing the pole from one side to the other while keeping the spinnaker full. Again, the foredeck crew braces his back against the mast, with feet spread apart for balance while handling the pole. He should grab (or be handed) the old sheet and bring the sheet in to the mast, so that the pole remains out to windward as long as the wind is on that side of the boat. Snapping the pole off the mast and into the new guy, he then pushes the pole out to the new windward side (tripping the old guy out in the same motion) past the mast, if possible, to help the spinnaker over to the new weather side of the boat before bringing the pole end back to snap into the mast. Thus, the foredeck crew can help keep the spinnaker full during a jibe. In light winds the skipper should hold the main boom in the middle of the boat briefly to keep the spinnaker full while the pole is transferred to the other side.

On larger sailboats, the spinnaker pole is too heavy to take completely off the mast and end-for-end, so a dip-pole technique, in which the pole remains attached at the mast, is used. In this system, the mast end of the pole is raised up on its mast slide to enable the other end of the pole, which has been detached from the spinnaker guy, to dip down sufficiently to clear the headstay. Then it is attached to the new guy and hoisted again, and the topping lift and downhaul are secured when the pole is at the proper height.

On ocean racers, the spinnaker is sometimes equipped with double guys and sheets. The secondary lines are called the "lazy guy" and "lazy sheet," because they are not used until jibing. In the jibe, the lazy guy and sheet are trimmed so that they take the full pull of the spinnaker. A crew member then pulls the lanyard that opens the jaw of the pole and releases it from the afterguy. This is called "tripping the guy." The topping lift is eased and the pole swings down. The foreguy is trimmed to bring the pole to the center of the boat where another crew member waits with a loop of the new guy to snap into the jaw of the pole as it swings down inside the headstay. When the new guy has been snapped into the pole end, the foredeck crew yells, "Made," which is the signal for the topping lift to be pulled to lift the pole back to a level position, the foreguy eased and the new guy trimmed, pulling the pole end out to the tack of the spinnaker. The coordination of the crew on the topping lift and foreguy keep the pole under control at all times during the jibe. With the strain now on the new guy and sheet, the lazy guy and sheet are relaxed to wait for the next jibe. With this method, properly executed, the spinnaker never collapses during a jibe, so no speed is lost.

When you don't have the benefit of time for the jibe and conditions are howling, change the timing of the jibe. Let's say you're in an around-the-buoys race, running in 25- to 35-knot winds and rolling madly. Jibe the mainsail first. Get it over, vanged down, with a preventer holding it forward and your running backstay set and tight *before* you jibe the spinnaker. Then jibe the spinnaker pole over. You'll find this a much better system than jibing both main and spinnaker at the same time or even jibing the spinnaker first followed by the main. Even though they're all hairy, this system will provide more control than the others.

One other jibing method should be kept in mind for use under vicious wind conditions—the twin-pole jibe. With this system, you set a second pole to leeward so that the spinnaker is completely stabilized before you jibe the mainsail. After jibing, you take down the original pole, which is now to leeward. This type of jibe is commonly used in larger boats that can afford to carry the weight of a spare spinnaker pole. The wind would probably be in excess of 30 knots and/or the crew shorthanded to need to use this system. And, lastly, time must not be a factor. An ocean race, where a strategic jibe is called for but doesn't have to be done quickly, is made to order for a twin-pole jibe.

Occasionally pandemonium reigns on the foredeck during a spinnaker jibe, and often the foredeck crew, who is all wrapped up in spinnaker cloth, lines, etc., is the butt of abuse when actually the fault lies with the helmsman. The skipper who turns the boat too sharply and who gives the crew inadequate directions or time to react will almost certainly cause a bad jibe. In heavy air, the helmsman must be sure to counteract the tendency for the boat to round up into the wind right after the jibe. The boom swings over with great force and, when it reaches the end of the mainsheet, it stops abruptly and the sail presents a wall to the wind. Something has to give until an equilibrium is found, so the boat heels over and a strong weather helm results. The forces in the sail out over the water turn the bow of the boat toward the wind. This combination will cause a broach in heavy air unless the helmsman heads the boat off decisively to meet the anticipated turning moment. However, if the jibe is done properly, the boat, although being steered as if to jibe back again, sails straight ahead. Nothing can make a crew look worse than bad helmsmanship.

SPINNAKER PEELS

Most of us were racing simply and happily dousing one spinnaker before setting the next until the America's Cup 12-Meter crews changed the rules of the game. They invented the spinnaker "peel," in which the new spinnaker is set inside the one that's set. When both are full, you release the tack of the original outside spinnaker and it "peels" off like the skin of an orange; hence the origin of the term. The only problems arise with crossing halyards and the transfer of the tack of the new chute to the pole. As for the former, you must be careful that the halyards are not fouled aloft as you hoist the new spinnaker. As for the latter, there are two solutions. One is to attach a "changing strap" to the tack of the new spinnaker before hoisting. It's snapped to a tack shackle or eye at the base of the headstay and to the headstay itself about 6 to 8 feet up. When the new spinnaker is hoisted, the tack is held in place at a reasonable level to allow the foredeck crew to attach the original guy shackle to the corner of the sail. After the guy is attached and the slack is taken out of it, the changing-strap shackle holding the tack of the spinnaker is released.

The second method entails some minor acrobatics. The foredeck crew gets into a Lirakis diaper (a three-corner canvas bosun's chair that holds you in even if you're upside down), clips himself to the foreguy so he can't be shaken free, and hand-over-hands himself to the end of the spinnaker pole with the leg of the spinnaker in tow. He then clips the new spinnaker tack into a spare shackle on the afterguy, so the tack of the new spinnaker is at the pole. He waits out there until the new spinnaker is set and flying. Then he trips the tack of the old one out and comes back down to the foredeck.

Of the two methods, the second is far preferable. It's hard to get the new spinnaker to fill properly with a changing strap, but when it's out of the pole, it fills perfectly. There is no loss of speed due to a collapsed spinnaker.

THE DOUSE

The spinnaker takedown on both large and small boats is very similar, the method used being determined more by wind conditions than by the size of the boat.

When lowering the spinnaker to leeward, the only major problem comes from letting it get out from behind the mainsail into strong wind. The crew gathering in the chute gains control of the sail by bringing the sheet forward to a spot just behind the shrouds. The guy is then eased and the halyard lowered, and the sail is pulled in behind the mainsail. However, it is essential that the sheet be in hand and under control before the sail is freed from the guy. Otherwise, the chute will go flying aft and be extremely difficult to capture. On larger sailboats, we first hoist the jib so that the spinnaker is blanketed. Then we lead the lazy sheet to a block well forward near the leeward shrouds and to a winch. We winch the clew of the spinnaker close to the boat before dousing. Then, instead of releasing the guy to run through the pole, the pole is eased to the headstay and lowered to within reach of a crew member who trips the guy. Unlike a jibe when the jaws of the pole are opened to release the guy, here "tripping the guy" means to release the tack of the sail by opening the tack shackle. The sheet is released and the lazy sheet on the leeward side of the boat is winched in so the clew is right near the deck behind the mainsail. With it in that position, the crew gathers in the spinnaker as the halyard is lowered quickly, but not so fast that the spinnaker falls in the water.

There is a tendency at this point for the lazy sheet to be forgotten or even detached from the corner of the sail. This can be a disastrous mistake. Until the spinnaker is completely on board it can fill with wind or water and be ripped out of the hands of the crew pulling it in. With the lazy sheet attached and cleated, the worst that can happen is that the spinnaker trails in the water alongside the boat. But with the lazy sheet taken off, the spinnaker can go out behind the boat held only by the halyard and the sheet (if it, too, hasn't been taken off). This means that the head of the spinnaker will be up in the air filling with wind because the halyard will never be long enough to trail in the water when the spinnaker is out at the end of its sheet. Frankly, the scene produces nightmares, and all because some crew member thought the chute was under control and the lazy sheet could be detached.

There may be times when a windward douse is in order. If you are racing and are about to round a mark leaving it to port, but are on the starboard jibe, consider taking the chute down over the windward side. When you jibe to round the mark, the spinnaker will be coming down to leeward. Or, if you know you must set the spinnaker again and the next set is on the opposite tack, a windward takedown will prepare you properly for the next set. For example, you are sailing an Olympic triangular course. You are on the second reach, heading for the leeward mark on the port jibe. The first reach was very tight and the second reach is broad, which indicates the wind has backed (counterclockwise).

This means that (after beating back to the weather mark) the run will be on the starboard tack. To be ready for a starboard-tack run, the spinnaker on most boats must be set from the port side of the boat. A normal leeward douse on the second reach will leave the spinnaker on the wrong side for the next set. A memory aid: When the second reach is tight, making it difficult to pull the spinnaker around the jibstay to windward, take down to leeward;

when the second reach is more of a run, making it easy to pull the spinnaker to windward, douse to windward.

When dousing to windward, take the pole off and stow it just before you intend to douse. Fly the spinnaker without a pole for a short time. Then, as the halyard is lowered, pull the spinnaker around to windward with the guy. In some larger class boats it's hard to do on a reach, but it can be done quite easily on a run. Many smaller boats set and douse the spinnaker to windward as a matter of course. It avoids having a crew member go to the leeward side of the boat to reach for the sheet. The weight to leeward can promote a broach.

Two other takedowns are fairly similar: the "forward" takedown and the "string" takedown. For the "forward" takedown, the genoa must be up to create the suction of airflow behind it. The pole is let forward to the headstay and lowered; the sheet is trimmed in tight so the foot of the spinnaker is stretched along the leeward side of the boat and, as the boat rounds the leeward racing mark to go upwind, the spinnaker halyard is thrown off completely. I recommend trailing the spinnaker halyard over the side of the boat so it can't kink as it zings out. Crew stands ready along the foot to gather the spinnaker in and stuff it down the forward hatch. When it's under control, the sheet is released, but the guy is not released or unsnapped until the chute is well aboard and mostly belowdecks. The only difference with the "string" takedown is a retrieving line attached to a patch in the center of the spinnaker that leads under the foot of the genoa to a crew member who pulls it in when the halyard is released. Pulling from the middle of the sail effectively halves the time needed to gather the sail in.

COMMON MISTAKES AND ACCIDENTS

There is only one way to avoid all problems with the spinnaker: Don't set one. But if you don't, you will miss much of the pleasure and excitement of sailing a boat on a run.

One common mistake when setting the spinnaker is a fouled halyard. We've mentioned the necessity of checking to be sure it is clear all the way up when ready for the hoist. If you hoist and it's fouled, lower the sail, clear the halyard and start over. On a large boat, send a crew to the top of the mast with a clear halyard, snap it on, take a strain, and release the fouled one.

Occasionally, both the guy and sheet get free during a jibe or a douse when the sail suddenly fills, yanking the lines out of trimmers' hands, the lines run out and the sail streams astern from the halyard. One solution here is to turn the boat dead downwind. In all but the heaviest winds, the sail will come within reach and may be gathered in. Another solution is to pull on just one line if you can reach it—either guy or sheet—and let the other trail. As the captured corner gets close, ease the halyard. If you ease the halyard prematurely, however, you run the risk of having the spinnaker fill way out beyond the boat. When this happens the problem becomes serious. It could endanger the rig, or a small boat may be pulled over so far that she fills with water and the heeling makes it impossible to turn the boat "into" the spinnaker to relieve the pressure; i.e., downwind. It may become necessary to free the halyard completely or cut it.

When a spinnaker is flying off from the masthead of a larger boat in heavy winds, attached only to the halyard, there's a safe, easy solution to a potentially dangerous situation. Send a crew member aloft in a bosun's chair with a long line leading from the deck. He attaches the line to the head of the spinnaker. On deck, the line is led through a block near the bow and aft to a winch. Simply ease the halyard slowly while winching in the downhaul. The boat should be sailed dead downwind so the spinnaker is blanketed by the main as it's lowered. When it's within reach, gather it in.

A spinnaker wrap. Probably the most common spinnaker problem for both large and small boats is a wrap. It happens when the spinnaker collapses for one reason or another and starts to rotate around itself. It can also occur during the hoist if the corners of the spinnaker are not pulled apart quickly enough, or if the bag or sleeve has been inadvertently rotated before the set. When the wrap is very low in the spinnaker, lower the sail and sort things out. Never pull the pole back or head the boat up on the assumption that the wrap will unwind when the spinnaker fills. Instead, get the spinnaker into the dead air behind the main and jib to blanket it. Then shake it out or pull down on the leech to bring it down.

If the wrap is high on the sail, releasing the halyard a few feet should allow the swivel at the head of the sail, which may be jammed in the block, to rotate and unwind the wrap.

A particularly bad wrap is one that is around the jibstay. If it tightens, it can be next to impossible to avoid cutting the spinnaker away. The problem is that in a wire jibstay the strands twist around each other. As the sail is pulled down (assuming that's possible), it is rotated by the twist of the strands and tightens. (On a rod jibstay, the wrapped sail slides down easily.)

Once a jibstay wrap occurs, a couple of things may be tried: one is to send a man up in a bosun's chair to untangle it (in a larger boat); another solution is to jibe the main so the airflow off the mainsail is in the opposite direction and will start the spinnaker rotating in the opposite direction to unwrap itself. It's really quite remarkable how well this works. We worked on a spinnaker wrap for about a half-hour during one race. It was wrapped so tightly I doubted we'd ever get it out. Then, we jibed the mainsail over to the other side and within 15 seconds the spinnaker was free, clear, full, and flying.

Broaching, rolling, and oscillating. No matter what size boat you sail, when carrying the spinnaker you will probably broach, roll, or oscillate at one time or another. It's important to recognize these conditions for what they are, understand their causes, and to know almost instinctively what corrective steps to take when they occur.

A mild broach can result from an overpowering weather helm, which might be caused by a number of factors. When the weather helm becomes so strong that the helmsman is unable to counteract it with the rudder, the boat will broach. Most of the time this means that the boat will just wallow broadside to the wind until steering control is regained and the boat can be headed back downwind.

A major factor contributing to a broach is heeling. When upright in the water, a hull is symmetrical; it splits the water evenly, and is pushed in neither direction more than the other. When a boat is heeled, the bow wave on the lee side becomes quite large and pushes against the curve of the hull as it works aft. The helmsman must steer the boat well to leeward to keep her sailing straight.

Contributing to additional weather helm is the fact that when the boat heels, the force in the sails is out over the water. Fantasize for a moment: Imagine a boat heading toward shore, heeled way over with her spinnaker well off to leeward. We have tied a line to the masthead and have run it all the way to shore where we've tied it to the back of a car as in Figure 44. Now, we drive the car, pulling the mast faster than the hull of the boat can go to keep up. It should now be clear that, first, the boat will rotate until it is parallel to the shore, and then the car will be dragging the whole mess shoreward by the mast as in Figure 45. The hull at this point will be dragging sideways through the water, creating such resistance that the mast will be almost lying in the water from the pull of the line. With the spinnaker out over the water, the total wind force affects the boat in exactly the same way as our imaginary line to shore. The more the boat heels, the more it rotates into the wind; the more the boat rotates into the wind, the more it heels, until we have a full-fledged broach.

Figure 44

In a broach, the rudder becomes almost worthless. The boat is lying on her side, so the rudder is near the surface where it can't get a bite in the water. Because the rudder is more parallel to the surface rather than vertical and perpendicular to the surface, steering to leeward has much the same effect as the elevators on the tail of an airplane. The stern and keel will lift rather than turn. Thus, the more the boat heels, the less effective the rudder becomes in turning it back downwind to reduce the heel. In fact, the rudder will start to increase the heel after a certain amount of heel is reached.

If, in the early stages of a broach, the helmsman is able to turn the boat so that the hull is parallel to the direction of pull (on our imaginary line to the shore), the hull has less resistance and a better chance of keeping up with the sails, and the tendency to broach will be reduced. To facilitate catching the broach before it develops, the skipper and crew can take certain precautions.

Figure 45

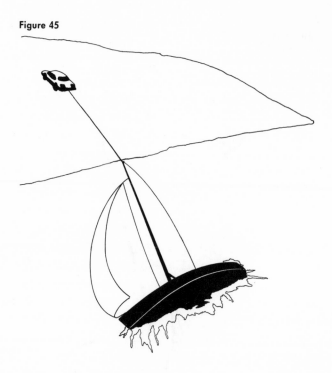

In a small boat, since heeling is the enemy, they must hike out hard during gusts that could precipitate a broach. Another way to reduce heeling is to luff the sails. Since the spinnaker gives the boat a great deal of drive, it is the last sail to luff. First, luff the mainsail. Remember, if your boom vang is tight, the boom is being held down. As the main luffs, the boom end dips into the water and is pushed back toward the center of the boat. Because the main cannot be eased, more heeling will occur and the boom will be pushed even closer to the hull by the water flow. This will cause even more heel and another vicious circle begins, until a broach occurs. So, ease the boom vang. Even maxi-yachts play the boom vang to reduce broaching and to avoid breaking the boom. The boom lifts as the vang is eased and the top part of the sail near the head luffs first. Since this is the part that causes most of the heeling, the heeling is being reduced without much being detracted from the general drive of the sail.

Next, ease the jib (if one is being used under the spinnaker). It is fallacious to think that trimming the jib will reduce weather helm by blowing the bow to leeward, because heeling caused by the tight jib creates more weather helm. When it is obvious that drastic measures are needed to avoid a broach, the spinnaker can be collapsed by easing the sheet a couple of feet. The helmsman must anticipate the need for this and give the command to the trimmer to "break" the spinnaker. When the boat has been steered back downwind and has straightened up, the spinnaker can be trimmed again to fill.

A few other factors can contribute to a broach. If the spinnaker halyard has stretched or is not all the way up, the CE of the spinnaker (its pull) will be farther out over the water and will increase the turning moment. The tack of the spinnaker should be right at the end of the spinnaker pole for the same reason, and the pole should never be solid against the headstay. If the pole is too high, the luff will have a large curve to leeward, causing the drive to be farther out over the water. And if the leech of the spinnaker is cupped rather than flat and free, the trapped air will cause more heeling.

Rolling (oscillating) is another possible problem. The boat in Figure 46 is rolling by the lee and will shortly roll in the opposite direction. In heavy seas this can become wildly exciting. Your boat is almost jibing as the mast rolls to windward and nearly broaching as it heels to leeward. Most of the problem is caused by allowing the spinnaker too much freedom.

In the diagram, the sheet has been eased to near or beyond the jibstay, so the spinnaker is able to get completely around to the starboard side of the boat. It then pulls the mast over in that direction. As the boat heels, a

Figure 46

Downwind rolling:
Spinnaker sheet & halyard are eased too far.

starboard bow wave develops and shoves the bow to port, toward a jibe. The helmsman steers the boat hard in the opposite direction, the spinnaker oscillates over to the port side of the boat, causing heeling and a strong weather helm, which, again, the helmsman counteracts. Thus, the rolling starts. If there is any ease in the halyard, the spinnaker is free to spin in a large arc. Pulling the halyard up tightly reduces the rolling.

There are some extreme wind conditions when no matter what you do you're in trouble. We encountered such conditions during a race in *Sleuth* just before the infamous 1979 Fastnet Race when so many lives were lost. It was a Thursday day-race in the Solent, a downwind start in about 20-knot winds. We had an excellent start and shortly were among the leaders. Looking at the rest of the fleet astern, my wife Doris commented that most of them were broaching out of control as a particularly nasty looking black cloud was catching up with us all. When the wind hit us with 40-knot gusts, we broached. I called for some sheet ease to collapse the spinnaker and had to helm hard over to come off. The chute collapsed and *Sleuth* came off, but she was not totally downwind when the chute filled again, promptly causing another broach. At this point I should have doused the chute because I knew we had to ease the spinnaker sheet a lot to get *Sleuth* dead downwind before the chute filled again. That risked having it fill on the windward side and slew the boat into a leeward broach. Sure enough, that's exactly what happened. The mainsail had a preventer to avoid an accidental jibe, but when we slewed to leeward and the wind got on the wrong side of the mainsail, the preventer stretched, resulting in the mainsail ending up amidships and forcing the boat over flat on the water. I've never been so flattened in a 54-foot boat before or since. Blue water poured down the main companionway in the center of the boat. The spreaders were in the water, the deck was vertical and the keel on the surface. All I could think about was some other out-of-control sailboat holing us below the waterline. A crew member finally managed to ease the preventer and we straightened up. The spinnaker came down in shreds and we continued the race with a winged-out jib. The only solution I have to such wind conditions is to get the spinnaker down in a hurry.

You'll be surprised at how fast you can sail with a jib winged out on a spinnaker pole with the wind over 35 knots. You'll sail almost as fast as with a spinnaker and since you avoid broaches and breakdowns, you'll net out faster.

Off the wind in heavy air the mainsail becomes a large factor in control, particularly in small boats. A powerful boom vang is a must. If the boom is allowed to lift in the air, the top of the leech will fall off so far that it may actually point forward of abeam or at least fold over the spreader and shrouds. Figure 47 shows a cross section of the sail near the foot and near the head. Note that while the foot of the sail is stalled, the top part is getting airflow over the lee side, creating lift in the direction of the arrow. This tends to pull the top of the mast to windward, making the boat roll to windward. Once started, each subsequent roll is a little more severe. The apparent wind goes more forward and flow is picked up lower down in the sail each time the mast rolls to weather, and the faster it rolls, the more forward the apparent wind goes. The more forward the apparent wind goes, the greater the area of mainsail that develops airflow on the lee side, and the greater the lift. The greater the lift, the faster the mast swings to windward, and so on, until the boat is rolling madly. The solution is to vang down strongly and, if the vang can't handle the forces, to trim the mainsheet in a little so the top part of the sail is also stalled.

When rolling conditions exist, consider trimming the jib in flat. That will help to keep the bow downwind, and acts as a baffle to dampen the rolling. Changing course to more of a reach can also help. Further, in such conditions we want to reduce the effectiveness of the spinnaker. By easing the pole forward of square with the apparent wind, and by overtrimming the sheet, we can roll part of the spinnaker in behind the mainsail, thereby partially blanketing it. This also keeps the spinnaker from picking up airflow on the lee side, which, like the main, directs the drive of the spinnaker to windward and places the chute in closer to the sail plan of the

Figure 47

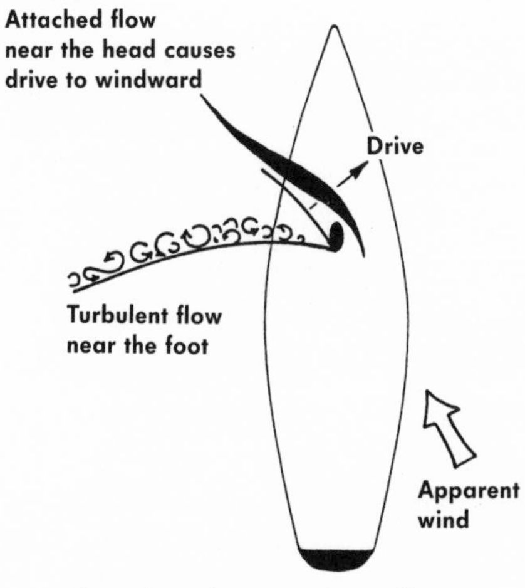

Attached flow
near the head causes
drive to windward

Drive

Turbulent flow
near the foot

Apparent
wind

Excessive twist aggravates rolling.

boat. But don't overdo it. Lowering the pole excessively on a running chute makes the luff fuller in cross section and more likely to collapse. In heavy winds the jolt of the spinnaker filling after having been collapsed can easily break something. Make sure the pole foreguy (downhaul) is tight so the pole can't swing back as the boat heels to windward. Never let the tack of the spinnaker fly out beyond the pole end. Not only is it against the racing rules, it can cause wild rolling.

In small boats, placing your crew weight evenly on opposite sides of the boat will also help maintain stability. Just as children can seesaw faster if they're closer to the middle of the seesaw than when sitting at the very ends, the boat will roll less if the crew weight is spread apart laterally. Finally, change helmsmen if it appears that the present one doesn't quite have the anticipation or timing to counteract the rolling.

Crewing accidents. Because there is so much pressure involved in spinnaker handling and so many variables to consider at once, accidents do happen, even among experienced crew. It's helpful to review them and some of the reasons why they happen.

On most larger boats, one method of dousing the spinnaker is to let the pole forward to the headstay, where the foredeck crew pulls open the snapshackle holding the spinnaker at the pole. Although the downhaul should be tightened as the pole goes forward, it cannot completely control the pole's lateral swing aft as the snapshackle opens and the stretched-out guy recoils when the spinnaker is released.

Not too long ago, during a race, I saw a classic example of this. The foredeck man was reaching over the pole to pull the snapshackle pin and the side of his head was even with the pole on the windward side. I only had time to yell, *"Duck."* (Luckily, he reacted quickly.) As he opened the shackle, the pole swung back viciously, narrowly missing his head.

Another near accident convinced me of the value of carrying a knife. It was in another race, as the spinnaker was being lowered and pulled aboard on the leeward side by two crewmen. Suddenly a wave grabbed it, pulling it through the lifelines and filling it with water. The sheet wrapped around a crewman's leg and a stanchion, pinning the crewman. Imagine the forces involved with a 50,000-lb. sailboat reaching at 9 knots being held back by a spinnaker full of water. Another crew member grabbed his knife and hit the ¾-inch Dacron sheet hard. It parted with one swipe, freeing the leg. I happen to know that it would take about two minutes to cut through a line that thick with a knife that dull under normal circumstances with no strain on the line. For that reason I had discounted the effectiveness of using a knife in an emergency. No longer. I'm a believer.

Many more minor accidents are caused by improper winch use—not putting the halyard on the winch quickly enough during a hoist as discussed previously, not having enough turns on a winch, permitting an override, or from an improperly seated winchhandle flying out of a winch in a runaway situation. Statistically, standing under a spinnaker pole that gets out of hand when it's being lowered has caused more concussions than any other single factor in sailing. The inboard end goes out of control, the topping lift breaks or comes off the winch, or the pole falls out of the mast fitting. The latter happened to me when I was attaching a halyard to the base of a mast. I heard a "swish" and a "klunk" right next to my ear. The pole had come off the mast and landed on the top of a winch on the mast at shoulder height. If my head had been few inches farther over I would have been knocked out cold, or if the winch hadn't been there, I'd have had a broken shoulder. The incident has made me very cautious around spinnaker poles.

Spinnaker horror stories abound, and these few are mentioned here only to encourage caution and awareness when handling a chute. The spinnaker is temperamental and demanding, but well worth the effort considering the increased speed and excitement it produces.

Chapter IV

SEAMANSHIP

Good seamanship is the result of long experience. It's a combination of knowing your boat and equipment thoroughly, of knowing the right things to do and, more important, when to do them. Virtually every boathandling function is an act of good or bad seamanship from the time you step aboard, hoist sail, and drop the mooring until you pick it up again and go ashore.

In this book we give you shortcuts to good seamanship by describing the right things to do. But, when an incident arises, it's experience that will help you instinctively select the proper procedure for the circumstance at hand. That combination of knowing *how* and *when* to apply it is known as good seamanship.

For example, during the 1979 Fastnet Race a devastating storm, which had not been forecast, hit the 303 sailboats racing from Cowes, Isle of Wight, England, around Fastnet Rock lighthouse off the Irish coast and back to Plymouth, England. It was a major disaster. Twenty-four boats were abandoned, five sank and 15 sailors lost their lives. Aboard *Sleuth,* our 54-foot ocean racer—one of the 85 boats that finished the race—we sailed through steep, short seas in 85-mph winds on a beam reach with a triple-reefed main and a #4 genoa. We stayed on a beam reach sailing at a good clip of about 10 knots because that was the most comfortable point of sail under the extreme conditions that prevailed at the time. Though we were 30 to 40 degrees low of course and heading right for the dangerous Scilly Isles, we were depending on the low pressure system to move through and the wind to lift us up to course, which it eventually did.

After the race, a commission studied all the records available and asked each crew to fill out an extensive questionnaire. One of the conclusions of the commission was that the sailboats which maintained the most speed had the least trouble. It confirmed that we had intuitively selected the proper way to handle the situation. We had done so through knowing what to do and when to do it.

Inherent in good seamanship is a thorough knowledge of your boat's equipment, and because line is so essential to every boathandling maneuver, we begin this chapter with a close look at this all-important item of gear.

LINES

There is nothing more essential to proper operation of a sailboat than line. Every maneuver, including anchoring, docking, hoisting and trimming sails, hoisting flags, towing a dinghy, hoisting a bosun's chair, reefing, using a sea anchor, the awning—to mention a few—depends on line. Thus, it's a very important element of seamanship to know how to select, use, and care for line properly.

SELECTION, USES, AND MAINTENANCE

Line is selected on the basis of strength, stretch, and physical properties such as resistance to chafe, ability to float, and color coding. Most lines are made of one of the following materials: manila, nylon, Dacron, Kevlar, Spectra, or a combination of two. These can either be twisted—usually three strands laid together in the traditional method of making rope—or braided. Twisted three-strand rope is less expensive than braid, but it stretches more. Three-strand is also easier to splice into loops or together with another line. Braided line is used where softness and stretch are factors.

Manila is rarely used on modern sailboats. It's rough on the hands, deteriorates faster, is not strong for its weight, and has a hard lay (gets stiff). It's mainly used for commercial purposes because it's cheap, or on yachts that hew to tradition.

Nylon is a synthetic rope with some wonderful properties. It is extremely strong, is reasonably priced, does not rot, and deteriorates very little in sunlight. However, it stretches more than Dacron and chafes very easily. A double-braided nylon line, nylon braided cover, and nylon braided core is a little stronger than three-strand nylon (see Figure 48) but costs so much

Figure 48

Diameter Size	3-Strand Nylon	3-Strand Dacron	3-Strand Polypropylene	Braid: Nylon cover Nylon core	Braid: Dacron cover Dacron core	Braid: Dacron cover Spectra core	Braid: Dacron cover Kevlar core
¼"	2,000	2,000	1,350	2,100	1,800	5,000	5,500
⅜"	4,400	4,400	2,900	4,800	3,750	11,000	11,000
½"	7,500	7,500	4,700	8,300	7,000	19,000	18,800
⅝"	12,200	11,700	7,000	17,000	14,000	27,000	28,000
¾"	16,700	14,700	9,400	21,000	16,000	42,000	
1"	29,400	25,800	15,700	34,000		82,000	

Breaking strength in pounds of various lines

more that many sailors just buy a size larger twisted line than they would buy braided and save the money. They lose space but the weight is about the same. Nylon is used mostly for anchor and dock lines. With a load of 30 percent of tensile strength, twisted nylon stretches 20 percent of its length while braided Kevlar stretches only 1 percent. The strength and stretch are positive factors for those purposes. Instead of jerking the anchor and possibly pulling it free, nylon anchor line stretches in heavy seas and cushions the pull of the boat. Be sure to use chafing gear to protect the line unless it's substantially oversize. Chafing gear often consists of a split rubber or plastic tube that is put around the line at the point of chafe — where it leads through a chock, for instance. Rags, tape, or any material that keeps the line from chafing can also be used.

Because of nylon's stretch (see Figure 48), it is rarely used for sheets. While it's generally assumed that's because the sheet will stretch as a puff hits and cause a properly trimmed sail to sag off, that's not the only reason. Another reason is that instead of providing drive for the boat the puff is absorbed by the line.

Aboard the 58-foot *Dyna* in an Annapolis to Newport Race, we were sailing on an extremely light spinnaker run. The lightest spinnaker sheet we could find was a 1000-lb.-test nylon parachute cord — very light, very strong, and very stretchy. We were not doing well with the competition in the immediate vicinity, so the only thing we could think of changing was the spinnaker sheet. We went to a ⅜-inch Dacron line and, although the spinnaker drooped more from the weight of the new sheet and didn't look half as good as before, we moved right out on the competition.

The speed increase was dramatic and nothing else had changed, includ-

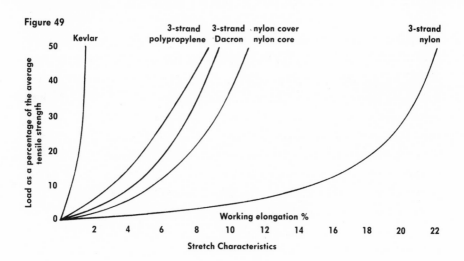

Figure 49

Stretch Characteristics

ing the wind strength. It made such a believer out of me that I don't want to see Dacron or Kevlar sheets trimmed, even on the lightest days, without at least one turn around a winch. When a puff hits, the sheet will pull on the winch rather than on the trimmer's arm (which will naturally extend like stretch in a sheet).

Dacron has less stretch than nylon (see the stretch characteristics in Figure 49) and is better for sheets, halyards, and other running rigging where lack of stretch is desirable. Since braided line stretches less than twisted line, we don't see much twisted Dacron on sailboats because it would lose some of its most desirable property. Granted, twisted Dacron is produced because it's cheaper than braid and can be used where resistance to chafe is needed, but the application on sailboats is limited.

One of the big advantages of both nylon and Dacron is that their strands can be melted and fused with a hot knife to prevent unraveling. When properly done, this eliminates the need for seizing the end of lines with waxed twine. Dacron has the added advantage of being more resistant to chafe than nylon.

Recent additions to rope materials are Kevlar and Spectra. They are extremely light, strong, and virtually don't stretch at all. Thus, one can replace Dacron sheets with Kevlar or Spectra sheets of much smaller diameter and lighter weight. On a large boat, the saving in weight and the ease of handling are considerable and important. On a smaller boat, however, there is a point of diminishing return. The line has to be thick enough to handle without cutting into your hands. If the use calls for ⅜-inch

Dacron, changing to Kevlar may still require ⅜-inch just for ease of handling, so you save a little on stretch and weight, but you sure don't save any money. Kevlar or Spectra braid costs much more than Dacron and that puts them out of reach of all but the most serious racing sailor.

Spectra has some advantages over Kevlar in that it's lighter, stronger, and it floats. It has good UV sunlight, chemical, and abrasion resistance, does not absorb water, and the fibers don't break down and weaken on small sheaves the way Kevlar does. Offsetting these advantages are the facts that it's very slippery, it's more difficult to splice, and it's more expensive than Kevlar. Also, it has a creep problem. It gradually elongates over a long period of time and doesn't return to the original length. I have been assured by manufacturers of Spectra line that the creep is so minimal it's not a factor for sailing applications. It would be more of a factor if you were staying a high TV antenna tower with Spectra instead of wire.

Polypropylene and polyethylene line share a property that makes them appealing for certain uses on sailboats: They float. The most common use is for the dinghy painter. If the painter floats there is no chance for it to get caught around your propeller as you back down after anchoring. There is less need for someone to shorten up and stand by the dinghy painter during the anchoring process. Buoyant line is also useful for securing your boat to shore; because it floats it is very easy to pull behind a dinghy to shore to tie to a tree. In remote anchorages with deep water right up to the shore, this is a good secure way of spending the night. A tree never "drags."

The disadvantage of such line is its slipperiness and hard lay; the line is apt to untie or uncleat itself, even if you use a half-hitch. That's why I recommend splicing it into a snaphook for towing a dinghy. Also, it also stretches about half as much as nylon and is about half as strong. You need a ⅞-inch polypropylene line to equal the strength of a ⅝-inch nylon line. It is also highly susceptible to degradation upon exposure to UV rays and it melts at a lower temperature than nylon.

Once you've selected a type of line for a given purpose, the next step is to choose the diameter and length. The table in Figure 49 gives the strengths of the various diameters. Listed are breaking strengths, and safe working loads are about 15 percent of these. The length obviously depends on the use. For spinnaker guys and sheets, measure 1⅔ to 2 times the length of the boat. A 30-ft. boat would use 50 or 60-ft. spinnaker sheets. Always err on the long side. Sheets are rarely a problem if they're too long, only if they're too short. Because it's advisable not to put a knot in the end of a spinnaker guy or sheet, you want them long enough so that they won't run through the leads during a messy douse.

Genoa and jib sheets should also be longer than you might expect. If you wing your largest genoa out on a spinnaker pole to windward, the leeward sheet still must comfortably reach and wrap around the leeward winch. One-and-one-quarter boat lengths should be adequate for most genoa sheets.

Once you have the right lengths, marking and color-coding your sheets is very important. Many manufacturers of line put colored fleck throughout the line. You might use a blue-flecked line for first reef and a red-flecked line for the second reef. Since red always represents the port side of the boat and green the starboard, use a red-flecked line for a port jib halyard and a green one for the starboard. When it's very important to avoid confusion, use a solid color line. They are available in smaller diameters in a number of solid colors. The only problem with color coding concerns replacement lines. If you have five or six different color-coded lines, you either have to own a coil of each to draw on for replacements or you have to buy cut lengths, which is expensive. In order to be able to buy larger quantities of a given diameter, consider creating color coding by using colored 3M plastic tape on plain white lines. For example, mark all spinnaker-related lines with red tape, all reaching sheets with blue tape, all genoa sheets with yellow tape, etc. The tape adheres well, but can be changed if you change the use of the line. The tape should form a band near the shackle or near the end of the line if the sheet is normally tied to this sail. That way it won't be chafed off through a turning block, and if you hang the line (when you stow it) by the shackle, the tape is easily visible. To refine the method further, add a second band of tape; for instance, to indicate a second reef line. Put corresponding colors next to or on the hooks where the lines are stowed, so the same line is stowed in the same place every time.

Tape is also used to indicate halyards. Put a strip of colored plastic tape for a spinnaker halyard at the point where it exits the mast and another on the top of the winch to which it's supposed to lead. The same can be done with genoa halyards, but add a piece of tape on the approximate turning block the halyard passes through. All this makes it easier for a crew member to grab the proper line and put it around the proper winch quickly and correctly.

For the topping lift, tape different colored bands on the mast. When the inboard end of the spinnaker pole is at the yellow mast band, the yellow band of tape you have put on the topping lift should be at the same spot for the pole to be level. You can use other frames of reference. The yellow tape might be right at the winch, which is easier to see while you're winching, but has the disadvantage that, if you use a different level, the tape may end up on the winch drum and be worn off.

A similar tape guideline is often used for jib halyard tension. Equally spaced marks are put on the mast and plastic tape wrapped around the wire halyard. At the loosest tension the mark on the wire is opposite the topmost mark on the mast, and at its tightest tension the mark is opposite the bottom mark on the mast. It's also important to have a piece of tape come out of the mast on the spinnaker halyard when the spinnaker is within an acceptable distance from the top of the mast, and another when it's hoisted all the way.

When it comes to marking sheets for trim positions, it's best to use indelible marking pens. If the line runs through a block frequently, as when tacking, tape will quickly wear off or — if on wire — may slide. The pen mark isn't as vivid, but at least stays on the line or wire and in one place.

Tape is useful on the leading edge of the spreaders to show where the leech of a non-overlapping jib should trim to in various wind strengths. It should also be used to indicate traveler position.

KNOTS AND WHEN TO USE THEM

Another key to good seamanship is the proper use of knots, cleats, and winches. There are literally thousands of knots, but the few described here will handle 90 percent of the necessary applications.

The bowline. The king of all knots is the bowline, as shown in Figure 50. No matter how tight it becomes, once the strain is released it's easy to untie a bowline. Simply grab the loop that passes around the standing part of the line and push it down along the standing part. This is called "breaking the back of the bowline" and loosens it for untying.

There are also other ways of tying the bowline. In the early 1960s, when I was working in a yacht supply store in lower Manhattan, a garbageman came along to pick up our trash. I had thrown out a two-foot length of line which he dug out of the trash and tied on his truck. I had never seen the bowline tied so fast and asked how he did it. He obliged by demonstrating slowly. First you make a slipknot that slides on the standing part of the line as in Figure 51. Then pass the end of the line around what you're tying and through the loop of the slipknot. Pull evenly on the standing part of the line

The bowline

Tie a slipknot on the standing part, then pull tight for "garbageman's bowline."

and you have a bowline. I dubbed this "the garbageman's bowline" and it's very handy for situations where a knot is needed fast but you have time to prepare for it. For instance, if you want to change from a heavy to a light spinnaker sheet, make the slipknot in the light line first. Then a crew member pulls the spinnaker clew to within reach, you pass the end of the line through it and the slipknot. Voilà! An instant bowline—and the heavier sheet is then unshackled from the clew.

The clove hitch. Another frequently useful knot is the clove hitch, which is used for tying fenders to the lifeline, for tying dock lines to a bollard on a pier, for jib sheets, etc., as in Figure 52. The clove hitch has a few disadvantages. If you tie a clove hitch to something that rotates, the weight of the object being tied can roll the knot right off the end of the line. An example would be a fender being tied to a lifeline that had a plastic tubing around it. It's always best to back up a clove hitch with a couple of half hitches for safety. Another disadvantage is that the clove hitch can tighten up. When using it on a small boat's jib, we use one long jib sheet that's tied in the middle to the clew of the jib with a clove hitch. Since the line goes out in opposite directions, this knot is ideal if you're planning to leave the jib sheets permanently attached to the jib. Once used in this fashion, the knot invariably gets so tight that it takes an awl or screwdriver and pliers to untie it.

For docking purposes, the clove hitch is a great knot. You can pass one loop over a bollard and let it slip to slow the momentum of the boat before you finish off the knot with the second loop. The way to make the clove hitch in this application is to grab the line quite a few feet from the free end. Make a loop, left over right, and drop it over the post. Grab the line again closer to

Figure 52

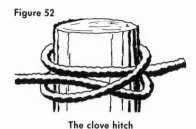

The clove hitch

the free end (between the loop and the free end), make another loop, left over right, and drop it over the post. Pull tight and add a couple of half hitches for safety.

The square knot and reef knot. The square knot gets a lot of press but is rarely used on a sailboat. An adaptation of the square knot, however, is used. It's called the reef knot. After reefing the sail, it's neater and more seamanlike to tie up the excess sail along the foot by lines through the reef points (grommets spaced evenly from luff to leech at the level of the reef). A square knot with a loop pointing downward is formed. Remember that the free ends of the line lay parallel to the standing part in a square knot—otherwise it's called a "granny" knot. Then take the other free end and pass it through the loop and pull the loop snug against it as in Figure 53. This locks the loop in place and the knot cannot become untied accidentally. Yet, when you want to untie it in a hurry, just pull out the locking end, pull on the loop end, and the knot is free.

The figure eight. One of the most common knots used aboard a sailboat is among the first things taught to all new sailors—the figure eight knot shown in Figure 54. This is used in the end of a sheet to prevent it from running out through a block when released and having to be retrieved and re-led through the block. It's also used to prevent the same thing happening to halyards. Unfortunately, this knot unties itself, particularly if the sheet is slightly short and the figure eight is tied too close to the end of the line. I've led a 20-

Figure 53

The reef knot (square knot with a loop)

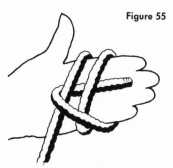

Figure 55

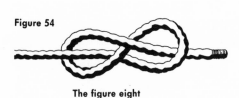

Figure 54

The figure eight

The stop knot: loop twice over your hand,
then pass end out towards your fingers

year campaign through our sailing schools to replace the figure eight knot
with one that doesn't accidentally untie as easily. I call it the "stop knot" and
it's tied as shown in Figure 55. It has the added advantages of being easy to
untie and is a nice handful to grab when it's in the block. Always leave
enough line after the knot, so its easy to grab.

The sheet bend. This is a good knot for tying together two lines of unequal
diameter. Although the true sheet bend is as shown in Figure 56, it's better
to add a second loop of the smaller line for safety, as in Figure 57.

The anchor bend. The anchor bend is shown in Figure 58. It's a secure
way to tie an anchor line to an anchor, but I always feel much safer if there is
a thimble spliced into the end of the anchor line and the end is then shackled
to the chain or anchor. This method avoids the possibility of chafe. Also, a
knot can decrease a line's strength by as much as 60 percent. A splice keeps
100 percent of the line's strength. Make absolutely sure that the shackle pin
is seized either by wire or preferably by plastic electrical ties. The latter are
extremely strong, will not corrode, and will not cause electrolysis. I lost an
anchor one time on a chartered boat by forgetting to check whether the
anchor shackle was seized properly. That's called poor seamanship. We
were lucky not to lose more than the anchor. It's the old story: "For want of a
nail, a shoe was lost. For want of a shoe a horse . . . battle . . . war . . ."

Figure 56

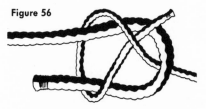

The sheet bend: for tying a small
line to a larger one

Figure 57

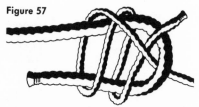

The double sheet bend: an extra loop for
better holding

Figure 58

The anchor bend

The anchor bend may be used, but it doesn't address the problem of chafe. If you do use it on a small anchor for a daytime anchoring, it is a good idea to tape the end to the standing part. I often use duct tape to secure knots. Once taped, there's no way the knot can become untied. I also use tape on halyard snapshackles to prevent them from opening accidentally—especially on a spinnaker halyard. A jib will just fall down on deck if the shackle opens, but a freed spinnaker is a major problem.

The tugboat hitch. The tugboat hitch is great for towing, but it's also useful when there's no available cleat for a winch. It's not really a knot like a half hitch is because the end of the line isn't used. To make a tugboat hitch,

Figure 59

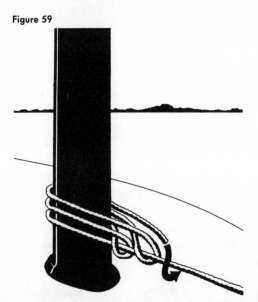

The tugboat hitch: good for towing, can be used around a winch when no cleat is available. Finish off with two half-hitches.

loop a section of the line coming off the winch under the part leading away from the winch and loop this over the top of the winch as in Figure 59. Keep doing this first under one side of the line, then in the opposite direction until there are three or four loops passing under the line leading away from the winch and back over the winch. The joy of this hitch is that it cannot tighten up, yet it will not slip. To release it, just slip the loops off the top of the winch.

The bowline on a bight. There's another knot you should know, but hope you won't have to use. The bowline on a bight is used in lieu of a bosun's chair to hoist a person up the mast. To make one, double a length of line and then start making the bowline in the normal way by forming a loop in the standing part (Figure 60). When you bring the end of the doubled line up through the loop, instead of going around the standing part, pass the doubled line down around the large loops (Figure 61) and pull tight (Figure 62). To use this as a bosun's chair, slip your legs through the large loops. Frankly, it isn't very comfortable, but if you don't have a bosun's chair, it's the only safe substitute I know of.

This knot can also be used for jib sheets on a small boat. Tie it in the middle of the line, passing the doubled line through the clew of the jib. Then pass the free ends through the looped double line, one to one side of the boat and one to the other. It's far easier to untie than a clove hitch.

The rolling hitch. A knot that I consider essential to good seamanship is the rolling hitch. It is used to tie to another line that has pressure on it, such as when freeing an override foul-up on a winch. An override occurs when a crewman on the winch—not watching what he's doing—permits one wrap to pile on top of another as he continues to winch in. The result is a knotted mess on the winch that can't be released because there is no way to take the

Figure 60

The bowline on a bight—step one

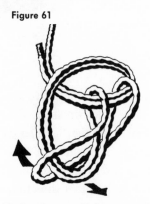

Figure 61

The bowline on a bight—step two

Figure 62

The bowline on a bight — step three

strain off the jib sheet to loosen the coils around the winch. To solve the problem, tie a spare line to the jib sheet with a rolling hitch forward of the winch. Lead this line back to a second winch and take a strain. This frees up the jib sheet aft of the rolling hitch connection and loosens the coils on the winch.

The rolling hitch is a remarkable knot in that it slips along the line it's tied to in only one direction. I have rarely seen it tied correctly even by knowledgeable sailors or in books on the subject. The key to the effectiveness of a rolling hitch is that it pinches the line under it. To tie it: Start the rolling hitch as if you were tying a clove hitch. Cross over as if you were

Figure 63

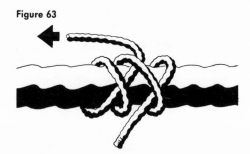

The rolling hitch

going to finish the clove hitch on the other side of the standing part. However, don't finish it. Do a second loop right next to the first loop, between it and the standing part as in Figure 63. Cross over a second time and this time finish it off as if it were a clove hitch. Now, if you pull on the standing part in the direction of the two-hitch side, it won't slip. But you can slide it in the other direction to reposition it on the line if you want to.

LINE HANDLING HOW-TO

Coiling line. All lines, and particularly halyards, should be neatly coiled. If a sudden squall hits, you want to be able to release the halyards quickly and without fear of tangled line. Also, the bitter end (the last end of a rope) of each halyard should be secured so that you can just let the halyard go to get on to the next emergency and know that the halyard won't be lost up the mast.

Always coil a line clockwise. This minimizes kinking. For a proper coil, a righthanded person holds the line in his left hand, letting the line run through the right hand as he stretches out his right arm and then brings the line in to the left hand, forming a coil; the coils will thus all be the same length. If there is a tendency for the line to kink, give the line a quarter twist clockwise with your right hand as you form the coils. With braided line, we don't worry about kinking. It will coil in a figure eight and run free without kinks. However, braided line is "trainable" into the circular coils made with twisted line, and it doesn't seem to hurt its handling characteristics. Always coil starting at the fast end of the line and work toward the free end. (That way, kinks disappear off the free end). If a line is long and is badly kinked, tow it behind the boat and the kinks will disappear. When all but the last arm's length is coiled, finish off by wrapping half the remaining line around the middle of the loops three times, one wrap above the other. Then push the middle of the remaining line through the top loop, pulling the loop back over the coils and sliding it down to the middle. Tighten by pulling on the bitter end of the coiled line.

To hang a coiled halyard, reach through the coil and pull a section of the halyard near the cleat through the coil, twist it and drop this loop over the cleat.

One caveat: Never coil a line by looping it around your elbow; that's a sure sign of an amateur at work.

To prepare a line properly for tossing (to another boat or to the dock, for instance), one end should be cleated to the boat (to prevent the whole line being accidentally thrown to the dock — or overboard). Then the line should be coiled and separated into two coils, one for each hand. One hand throws one coil and the second coil slides off the other hand as it goes out. The best way to prepare this is to coil the line halfway and grasp those coils in your hand. Then continue coiling over your index finger the coils you intend to toss.

Cleating. While using a half hitch to cleat a line was once taboo because natural-fiber lines would shrink, making it impossible to free the line in a hurry, the advent of nonshrinking synthetic lines brought the half hitch back in favor. In fact, there are two good reasons to use a half hitch on a cleat. First, fewer wraps are needed around the cleat to secure the line, so the process of cleating is faster, and second, a half hitch ensures that the line won't slip or become uncleated.

There are one or two arguments against half hitches. They are a little slower to release (although that's debatable) and they can tighten up if there's a great deal of pull on the line. However, if you put an adequate number of wraps around a winch before going to a cleat there should be very little pull between the winch and the cleat. The friction of the line around the winch absorbs most of the pull by the sail. In fact, there is so little pull on the line that if you can tie the half hitch in the first place, there should be no problem freeing it.

The most common cleating system is shown in Figure 64, which consists of a number of turns that end in a half hitch. Note that it starts with one complete turn around the base of the cleat and the free end of the line should lie in the same direction as the previous wraps. Figure 65 shows an alternative system without a half hitch that ends in a wrap around the base of a cleat. This wrap jams against the previous loops and keeps them from coming off.

Overhaul lines (or coil them loosely with coils running off the top so the line can run freely) to avoid having a tangled mess when you need to free a halyard or sheet in a hurry. Always clear decks of line clutter ASAP after action to avoid foul-ups. Also, always be sure halyards in particular and any lines on deck (that might be washed overboard, for instance) are attached to something when not in use. Think it can't happen? Twice we've looked for 150 feet of new line after a race or a sail change and couldn't find it

Figure 64

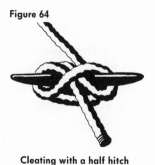

Cleating with a half hitch

Figure 65

Cleating without a half hitch

anywhere. No one saw it go overboard, but that's the only explanation. It's an expensive way to learn a lesson. We're lucky when lessons are cheap, but usually they're costly.

LINES AND WINCHES

Lines always go clockwise around a winch. When putting a sheet on a winch, as soon as there's a little pressure on the sheet, the trimmer adds wraps to avoid losing what has been taken in. There is one fast and safe way to do this. Take the line in one hand and pass it around the winch— clockwise—two or three times, allowing the line to ease through your hand as it goes. Don't ease enough to let the line slip on the drum, just enough to accommodate the extra wraps around the winch. The other hand feeds line to the hand placing the wraps on the winch (Figure 66). Never get the fingers of either hand between that line and the drum.

Also, never pull ahead of a winch or let anyone else pull ahead of a winch unless there are only one or two wraps around the winch. Occasionally an enthusiastic crew will yank the sheet in front of the winch, thinking to bring it in faster, but the only thing he accomplishes is to create an override.

To throw a line off a winch when tacking, uncleat it when the skipper says, "Ready about," and stand ready, sheet in hand. At the call of "Hard alee," grab the sheet about a foot behind the winch and spin the line off the winch counterclockwise very quickly. You should lift the line straight up above the winch as you throw the coils off. This speeds up the process considerably. Again, your hands are not anywhere near the winch.

To "ease" a jib sheet to free the sail slightly, place one hand over the coils on the drum (with your thumb next to your index finger, not sticking out where it can get caught in a loop), and ease the end of the line with the other

Figure 66

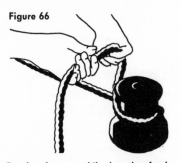

One hand wraps while the other feeds.

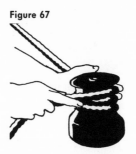

Figure 67

Easing a jibsheet with complete control

(as in Figure 67). The hand on the coils acts like a brake controlling the speed with which the sheet is eased. Without it, the coils may stick on the drum while the sheet is eased, then suddenly jerk out, catching you by surprise and possibly pulling your hand into the coils around the winch. I've heard of people breaking fingers this way.

MAINTENANCE TECHNIQUES

Today's modern synthetic lines are relatively care free. They will collect dirt and will deteriorate slightly from ultraviolet rays in sunlight, so it's best to keep them neatly coiled belowdecks when not in use. Obviously, some have to stay on deck—halyards and mainsheet—but the others should be stowed. When a line gets dirty or picks up tar, wash or soak it in fresh water with a mild dishwashing detergent that cuts grease well. Do not use Clorox bleach, which will weaken the line. A good program of line care is to coil and hang all the various sheets after a cruise or race, rinse them off with fresh water, let them dry naturally and then hang them below in a well-ventilated area. This reduces the chance of mildew and, although synthetics don't rot, it's not good for them to stay wet constantly. If you don't wash the salt out, when you put the lines below to dry the salt will retain moisture in the air and the lines will be forever damp.

The mainsheet should not be left lying on deck where it can collect dirt and moisture, but should be hung up to dry. Dirt and grit can work into the strands of the rope and cut the inside fibers under load, weakening the line. Often the mainsheet is too long and heavy to coil normally. One good method of securing it is to loop it over the boom in long loops that hang on both sides of the boom. Continue looping back and forth over the to of the boom until you get near the end of the line. Then wrap the end around the middle of the line several times and finish with a half hitch.

Chafe or abrasion are constant problems with lines and a good crew is always on guard against it. Chafing gear can take many forms. Most commonly used are split rubber tubes that are tied in position on the line. If it's a line that isn't adjusted much, such as an anchor line, one can even tape rags around the line where it runs through the bow chock. Halyard chafe can be reduced by changing the position of the halyard from time to time. The spinnaker halyard is particularly vulnerable to chafe and if it breaks the results can be disastrous, with the boat running over the spinnaker in the water, catching it on the keel and rudder. On long spinnaker runs at sea, use two halyards with the strain on one at a time. Tape the shackles closed before hoisting, for extra protection. When only one halyard is used, ease it out four inches so it bears on the halyard sheave at a different location. Half an hour later take it up three inches. Change it every half-hour so that a different part of the line bears on the halyard block or sheave. Make sure all sheaves run freely. A synthetic line running over a stuck sheave generates so much heat that it may permanently weaken the line. Also double up other lines that may be susceptible to chafe, such as mooring lines when the boat is being left unattended for long periods, or docking lines when a storm is expected.

Jib sheets run through sheet blocks and often show signs of chafe. Make sure the sheaves are of the recommended diameter for the size of line. A small sheave will bend the line too much and damage the fibers. The chafe usually shows up within a few feet of the end of the sheet where it's tied to the clew of the sail. When the chafe gets too bad, just reverse the jib sheets rather than throw them away. Attach the good end of the sheet to the clew. Many owners buy extra-long jib sheets, so that after both ends have chafed, they can lop off the bad sections and still have sufficiently long sheets. This saves a lot of money spent replacing them.

Lines can also create chafe, as when in contact with sails. The topping lift, which supports the boom while reefing and when the mainsail is down, can severely chafe the leech of the mainsail underway. The constant flopping of the topping lift eventually frays the tabling on the leech. A common solution is to seize a small bullet block to the backstay with shock cord running up along the backstay, through the bullet block and tied to the topping lift. This pulls the latter away from the leech of the sail. Modern boats have a better solution, the total elimination of the main topping lift by the introduction of a hydraulic boom vang. This solid tubular boom vang holds the boom up when the mainsail is lowered for reefing or flaking, so a topping lift is unnecessary.

Running backstays are another source of chafe on the mainsail. If the leeward one is not pulled all the way forward when not in use, but is allowed to rest against the lee side of the mainsail, it will slide back and forth as the boat pitches. It doesn't look like it's doing much harm, but if you inspect the sail closely, you will see that the thread stitching along the seams of the sail is being worn. The answer (for the sake of sail longevity) is to pull the leeward runner forward away from the sail, unless you're in the midst of a series of tacks and can't afford the time.

Another point of chafe is the spinnaker sheet as it leads forward under the boom on the leeward side. One way to handle the problem is to put a snatch block on the spinnaker sheet that is tied with a line through another block on the rail and led to a winch. This keeps the sheet just short of chafing on the boom. When the mainsail is reefed, such a lead is not only reasonable, it's essential. Forget it once and the spinnaker sheet will saw some beautiful holes in the reefed mainsail. That happened to me once, and every time the mainsail was set afterward, a number of repair patches reminded me of my stupidity and marred the beauty of the sail.

Small rips and tears in sails can be caused by burrs on wire halyards— short broken strands of wire that stick out and catch sails, hands, and other line. To get rid of burrs run the sharp edge of the blade of a knife up and down along the wire in the vicinity of the burrs. This bends the burrs back and forth until they break off. Also beware of small tears caused by sharp edges. Tape all cotter pins so the ends don't catch and tear sails or snag lines.

The spreader tips tend to chafe the leech of an overlapping genoa, especially when tacking. Be sure to have your sailmaker add chafe patches where the spreaders touch the sail.

SAFETY TIPS

There are really only two ways one can be hurt by lines. First, by being caught in the line or, second, by a line breaking. I saw a man get caught in the coil of a line that was attached to the tack of a maxi spinnaker when the wire guy broke. He was flung 30 feet in the air and overboard and suffered multiple fractures of his leg and arm. I saw the end of a spinnaker sheet eased to the winch and released in a broach. The tail of the sheet, flopping around the winch on the way out, hit a crew's arm and broke it. I have a friend who lost most of a finger because the bowline he was tying to tow a Star class sailboat wasn't quite finished when the towboat took a strain. And I was nearby but unaware of the unfolding drama when a person was pulled over the side of a cruising sailboat because he stepped in a coil of the anchor line he was easing out in a very strong current. His son handed him a knife in the water to cut the anchor line away below his foot. He made the mistake of cutting the line leading to the sailboat above the water. With the sailboat gone, the current pulled him under and he drowned. The moral is to avoid stepping or standing in a coil of a line at any time and to stay clear of a line that is released from a winch under extreme strain.

The second danger is from lines breaking. In the case of a towline breaking, the line itself can be deadly. However, I find that lines rarely break, because the modern synthetic lines are so incredibly strong. Injury is usually caused by a fitting breaking. For instance, a crew member on one sailboat in the Chesapeake was killed when the turning block for a spinnaker sheet broke and was flung by the sheet at his head. The line was stronger than the block. Never stand in the bight (the angle) of the line leading around a turning block.

While we're on the subject of accidents, avoid placing yourself in line with anything with a large load on it. I know of two deaths caused by the main boom gooseneck separating from the mast and hitting a person to leeward. A near miss occurred on a 12-Meter I was crewing on during America's Cup trials when the spinnaker pole separated from the mast and drove into the deck on the weather side where a number of crew were lying. The force dented the deck, narrowly missing the nearest crewman. Though all the other accidents I mentioned could have been avoided by caution, this one was pure happenstance. Obviously, some accidents just can't be avoided. The reason I'm listing the ones I know about is to give the reader an awareness of danger areas to avoid with respect to the handling of lines and equipment aboard.

LINE COURTESY

It's common courtesy to tie off the halyards in a slip or anchorage at night so the slapping on the mast won't keep nearby crews awake. Using a short line, tie one end around the halyards with a bowline or clove hitch. Pass the other end around a shroud and tie a rolling hitch on itself. Then, just slide the knot along the line to tighten and hold the halyards away from the mast.

Halyards that can be tied away from the mast should be. Snap the shackle to the base of a stanchion, the bow pulpit, or elsewhere forward. Pass the tail portion under the lifeline, grab rail, or other convenient fitting and again tie a rolling hitch on itself. Slide the knot up until snug. Your neighbors will appreciate the small effort it takes to stop the infernal slapping of rope and mast.

Another courtesy detail: When your docking line is underneath a number of others, pass the desired loop up through the other loops, lift it off the bollard and pass it back down through the other loops, which remain secured throughout the maneuver, as in Figure 68.

Returning borrowed line is another expected courtesy of the sea. In any docking situation, you should keep track of which lines are yours and which belong to others and see that they are returned to the proper owners.

Figure 68

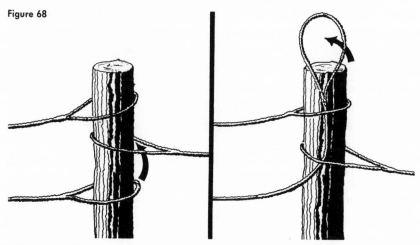

When your docking line is under a number of others, pass it up through the other loops, lift it off the top and pass it back down through the loops.

BOATHANDLING

Vital to your sailing technique is knowledgeable control of your boat's movements through the water when beating (wind on the nose), reaching (wind abeam or slightly forward of or aft of abeam), or running (wind aft) toward your chosen destination. How close to the wind you can sail a steady course when beating, the smoothness of a tack, getting the most out of the boat on a reach and run, and executing a flawless jibe are indications of your ability as a sailor. Essential to efficient operation of the above is good communication with the crew, so standard commands are generally used.

BEATING, RUNNING, REACHING

When beating, i.e., sailing close-hauled into the wind on the starboard tack (wind from the starboard side) or port tack (wind from the port side), you *tack* to change direction. The command of preparation is "Stand by to come about," or the shorter "Ready about," which tells the crew to uncleat the jib sheet and stand ready to release it quickly when the jib begins to luff as the boat turns; then be ready to trim the sheet and secure it on the other side after tacking. The mainsail, which is usually trimmed as flat as desired on a beat, may swing a few inches across the centerline, but usually does not require adjustment during the tack.

The crew acknowledges the skipper's command by replying, "Ready." Then the skipper gives the command, "Hard alee," as he turns the boat into and through the eye of the wind.

When close-hauled, sailing about 45 degrees from the wind, you will tack (your bow will swing) in about 90 degrees. This means that before tacking, you can sight abeam from the windward rail to gauge your heading on the new tack and to assure that the way is clear. To figure how far to turn the boat, note your compass heading, then add or subtract 90 degrees—depending on which way you are turning—and turn until your compass indicates that course.

At times you will note variations in the tacking maneuver: in small boats, for instance, it's a good idea on very windy days to "hand" (hold onto rather than cleat) the mainsheet in case you need to release it quickly in a gust after a tack, or when sailing in crowded waters, to straighten up the boat. Another way to reduce wind force on the sails is to head more into the wind, which is called "feathering" the boat to windward (if the sails luff slightly). In response to a strong gust, a full-fledged luff is necessary.

Should you try to tack without enough speed to carry through the tack, you lose momentum midway because the rigging and flapping sails create resistance to the boat's forward motion, as do the seas hitting the boat head-on. There is no steerageway because there is no water passing the rudder; the boat is said to be "in irons" (or "in stays"). Shortly, however, she will fall off onto one tack or the other. You may continue on that tack or tack again when you have gained enough speed, depending on the situation.

I well remember seeing Danish Olympic sailor Paul Elvstrom tack a Soling a number of times during a race in gusty, 20-knot winds. The smoothness of each turn was exceptional as the mast described a smooth arc from a constant angle on one tack to the identical angle on the other. This is the mark of a good sailor. Through fine adjustments of sail trim and steering angle, the mast stays at a constant angle to the water through gusts and lulls in the wind and crests and troughs in the waves.

When sailing downwind—running before the wind—the change of tacks is called a *jibe*. The skipper's command of preparation is, "Prepare to jibe." Now the crew releases the boom preventer and starts to trim the mainsheet, keeping the boom under control so that it won't swing wildly across the boat. As the boom nears the centerline the skipper says, "Jibe ho," and turns the boat to leeward so that the *stern* passes through the eye of the wind. The crew then quickly eases the mainsheet as the boom swings across, secures the boom preventer on the other side and the boat sails off on the new jibe. With the wind coming from the starboard quarter (about 45 degrees from dead downwind), you are sailing a starboard jibe; from the port quarter, a port jibe. Changing course downwind is "falling off" until the boom crosses the centerline; then you are jibing.

The jib takes very little tending during a jibe. Just uncleat and ease one sheet, keeping the jib under enough control to prevent it from flying out beyond the bow of the boat (where it will start flogging as you pull it in across the headstay), and trim the other sheet as the boat swings.

The novice sometimes gets confused about which way to put the tiller to jibe. He should remember just to turn the bow of the boat toward the mainsail (which is out to leeward) and he can't go wrong. He should also be aware that, as opposed to tacking—which requires a 90-degree course change—only a small course change is needed when jibing.

When running, there is always the possibility of an *accidental jibe,* which can be dangerous. If the wind shifts across the stern, or the helmsman inadvertently permits the boat's course to change so that the wind and the main boom are on the same (leeward) side of the boat, with the wind now flowing from the leech toward the luff of the mainsail, the boat is sailing "by the lee," and there is danger of the wind getting on the "front" side of the mainsail and slamming it across the deck with great force. Unsuspecting crew standing in its way can be badly injured, or the boat's rigging badly damaged by the force of the uncontrolled jibe.

Your first warning that such a jibe is imminent occurs when the jib starts to come out from behind the mainsail and cross to the other side of the boat, or the boom starts to lift. When sailing downwind, particularly in heavy air, the helmsman should always be acutely aware of any change in wind or course direction, and act accordingly.

A second basic problem during a jibe is that in heavier air the boat wants to keep turning and head up into the wind after jibing. While the boom is swinging there's no problem, but when the boom and sail suddenly stop and present a "wall" to the wind rather than flow with it, the forces build up tremendously. Since on a run most of the forces are out over the water (because the sail is eased way out), the tendency is for the boat to round up into the wind. The practiced helmsman soon learns to counteract these forces.

Tacks and jibes should always be well planned beforehand, to ensure that there will be no obstructions on the new course or that the maneuver will not interfere with the right-of-way of other nearby boats when completed. Thus, it's always wise to check the area under the jib when beating, or under the spinnaker or headsail when running, for other boats or obstructions, particularly when changing course.

Reaching is a pleasant and forgiving point of sailing. The boat doesn't heel much and the helmsman may wander off course without fear of an accidental tack or jibe. He may sail a close reach or a broad reach, depending on whether the wind is forward of or aft of abeam and how close to or far off the wind he must sail to reach his objective. In either case, reaching, particularly in a good breeze, is a fast, comfortable, and usually dry point of sailing. However, the alert helmsman will be quick to adjust sail trim for wind shifts, easing when the sails are too hard, making the boat heel more than necessary, and trimming if they start to luff.

SAILING BACKWARD

Oddly enough, it's also useful to know how to sail backward. There are times when the boat starts to move backward and the skipper must instinctively know how to control the direction in which the stern is moving. This occasionally happens when a boat drops a mooring and is dead in the water, i.e., in irons (or in stays). Often the helmsman then calls for someone to "back the jib," only to find that he is at fault and has the helm in the wrong position to make the bow fall off on the desired tack.

Handling the tiller or wheel when backing should be as instinctive as steering when sailing forward. When a boat is moving backward—when leaving a slip, for instance—helm movement is the reverse of what it is when the boat is moving forward. Such maneuvers unfortunately seem to occur most often in crowded areas, when instant instinctive control is important to avoid tangling with or hitting another boat or an obstruction.

Thus, everyone should learn the technique of sailing backward. To practice, do a slow tack into the wind so that you lose almost all headway by the time the bow is slightly past head-to-wind. Then push the mainsail out over the same side it was on originally. The boat will stop dead in the water and start moving backward. Now the helmsman will be able to steer with the rudder and the crew can cease backing the sail, allowing it to luff amidships. The key of the practice is to keep the boat sailing dead downwind backward; if she falls off one way or the other, the sails will fill and the boat will start sailing forward. In a crowded anchorage, this can happen at the wrong moment and can end in collisions with other boats or a pier. Thus, positive helm control when moving backwards is essential.

At this point, I want to comment that it's important to know how to steer a sailboat with a wheel in reverse. I've seen many experienced helmsmen go to the other side of the steering wheel and steer as if the stern were the bow of the boat. Although it works, because they are facing the stern they have to turn to see what's happening to the rest of the boat. It's far better to develop expertise in steering the boat backward while facing forward and glancing aft as you go.

SAILING WITHOUT A RUDDER

On cruising boats, the steering quadrant should be inspected periodically for frayed, burred, or damaged wire and to assure that nothing has been carelessly stowed in the area that could fall into and jam the steering system. However, in spite of all precautions, accidents do occur—the steering system fails irreparably, or the rudder breaks or falls off. If your steering fails in shallow water you should anchor, lower sail, and make repairs. However, if the problem occurs in deep water you may have to steer by the sails for some time.

To do this, you must know how to change the efficiency of the sails fore and aft, depending on your desired heading. By luffing the jib and trimming the main, you create weather helm and the boat turns into the wind. By luffing the main and flattening the jib, you create lee helm—the bow, pushed by the wind, falls off to leeward. To practice, trim the jib flat and ease the main until the boat is balanced and sails straight ahead when the tiller is released. Then change course by trimming the main to head up and pushing the boom out to fall off. When the bow starts swinging in one direction, you must immediately begin the opposite procedures to counteract the swing. To tack, free the jib sheets and trim the main hard and fast. When the boat is past head-to-wind, trim the jib and ease the main to force the bow down. If necessary, back the jib.

Jibing without a rudder is much more difficult than tacking without a rudder because on a run the mainsail causes the boat to turn toward the wind. To try jibing, ease the main completely, making sure the boom vang is also loose, and back the jib to windward. As you fall off to a run, move all the crew to the windward side of the boat and hike out. By heeling the boat to weather, you will create lee helm, and in the same way that a bow wave on the lee bow pushes a heeling boat to weather, a bow wave on the weather bow (caused by heeling the boat to windward) now pushes the bow to leeward.

A number of years ago I raced on the 58-ft. yawl *Dyna,* owned by the late Clayton Ewing, from Newport, Rhode Island, to Cowes, England, finishing at the Eddystone Light. About 1,000 miles from the finish we lost our rudder while carrying a full 2.2-oz. spinnaker in broaching conditions. Clayt immediately broke the crew into two teams, one to work out a sweep steering arrangement of some sort and the other to sail the boat as fast as possible toward Eddystone. With wind building to 50 to 60 knots, the second group, under my charge, didn't have much to do. All we could set was a storm jib that pulled us downwind at a good clip. However, as the wind abated and we needed more sail area, sailing downwind without a rudder became more challenging. We went to a larger jib and winged another out on a spinnaker pole, which worked well, but every time we tried to raise the mainsail, the boat rounded up in a broach. We tried different sized jibs for different balance, but to no avail. Then we decided to try setting a forestaysail. *Dyna* and many other boats have a removable stay that runs from about three-quarters the distance to the top of the mast to the middle of the foredeck. It's a great piece of rigging and I wouldn't want to go to sea without one. It allows you to set a genoa staysail or smaller sail without going all the way forward to the bow. The foot of the sail is over the deck instead of over the water, so you avoid scooping up water in the sail. Also, the sail area is low, so it causes little heeling. We found that by trimming the staysail flat and slightly to windward, we could keep the boat tracking downwind with the mainsail raised. When the main started to cause a broach, we eased the mainsheet and the staysail forced the bow back downwind. If we slewed by the lee, the staysail would then push the bow downwind just before the mainsail jibed.

As the breeze lessened, we raised the mizzen and assigned one crew member to the mizzen sheet and the compass. He eased or trimmed the mizzen sheet and could keep us within 10-degree swings on either side of course in 15 to 20-knot winds. Before we lost our rudder we hadn't steered as straight a course with our spinnaker set.

By the way, the other group solved the sweep problem, but the sweep caused so much drag when it was in the water that we sailed faster without it. We crossed the finish line in fourth place out of the 17 boats participating in the race. That experience confirmed my conviction that there's always something that can be done to continue racing no matter how bad things seem at the time.

If the breeze is light, you can make minor adjustments to the helm by moving crew weight forward and aft. With the boat balanced as described above, move the crew forward. The boat will head into the wind as the curve of the bow bites more deeply into the water. Moving the crew to the stern will cause the bow to fall off to leeward.

STOPPING THE BOAT

While heading into the wind and letting the sails luff will slow a boat eventually to a stop, there may be times when you want to stop more suddenly than that. The distance a boat travels while slowing to a stop is called the distance she "shoots" or "head reaches." This varies greatly with the type of boat and the wind and sea conditions; the stronger the wind, the shorter the shooting distance because of the wind resistance of the rig, flapping sails, and head seas, if any.

To practice stopping, come up to a mark sailing as fast as possible on various points of sail. Then put on the brakes when your bow is abreast of the mark. As a crew member pushes the main out as far as possible, head up into the wind to expose more sail to the wind and to counteract the strong lee helm that will develop. This is a very effective brake. Also effective is moving the helm violently from side-to-side, which throws the bow first one way, then the other in wide swings, slowing the boat. When running, you can slow the boat by trimming the main and jib amidships.

DOCKING UNDER SAIL

One of the obvious measures of seamanship—often observed by a local gallery—is the efficiency and lack of hoopla with which a boat, under either power or sail, is brought alongside a dock, especially if conditions are tricky. Wind, current, speed, and obstructions all play a part in the maneuver.

There are times when you must dock under sail, either because your boat doesn't have an engine or because the engine is temporarily inoperable, so it's important to be able to bring the boat to the dock under sail with confidence.

The boat must be headed into the wind to stop, so each approach depends on the wind direction. If the wind is blowing parallel to the dock, shoot the boat into the wind and come to a stop alongside the dock. If the wind is blowing away from the dock toward open water, there are two options: (1) use the end of the dock and shoot straight into the wind, or (2) shoot at an angle into the wind and luff to slow the boat. Then come parallel to the dock at the last minute.

If the boat is sailing slowly, as soon as you turn broadside to the wind she will start making leeway, so it's imperative to get bow and stern lines to the dock quickly and walk the boat along as she slows.

When the wind is blowing toward the dock from open water, the best approach is with sails lowered (and secured sufficiently so that they will not billow out as the boat turns broadside) if the wind is strong, or with only the jib if it is light. On the approach, round up into the wind, lower and quickly put a few ties around the sails, and drift to the dock. Under such conditions not all landings are perfect and, depending on conditions, your crew may have to toss lines to available dockhands to keep the boat under control until finally secured.

The dock lines needed will be the bow and stern lines, and the "forward spring" line which leads from a cleat on the dock to a fitting forward on the boat to keep the boat from moving forward. The "after spring" leads from the dock to a fitting near the stern to keep the boat from moving aft. Now properly secured, the boat will rest on the fenders provided and will not rub her topsides on dock or pilings.

MOORING UNDER SAIL

When picking up the mooring under sail, in order to bring the boat to a stop with the bow right next to a mooring buoy, you must estimate how far the boat will shoot, then on your approach turn the boat at a spot approximating that distance downwind of the buoy. This is the "turning point." As mentioned previously with regard to stopping the boat, the distance a boat shoots varies greatly with the type of boat and the wind and sea conditions; the stronger the wind, the shorter the shooting distance because of the wind resistance of rig, flapping sails, and head seas. Heavy keelboats tend to carry forward motion longer than light centerboarders, so more distance must be allowed for the former.

The angle of approach to the turning point is very important for two reasons: (1) you want to be able to control your approach speed by luffing or trimming sail as needed, and (2) you want to be able to control your direction by pointing higher or lower as necessary. The approach that best satisfies these requirements is a reach; neither a beat or a run will permit sufficient control or maneuverability.

Therefore, select your course through the other boats in the anchorage on a slow reach toward your selected turning point. At that point, round up into the wind and let the sails luff completely. Any tension at all on the jib sheet can cause the jib to back and force the boat over on the other tack. On a cruising boat, consider dousing or rolling the genoa to get it off the foredeck and out of the way before shooting for the mooring. It's best to stay a few (10 to 20) degrees off the wind; then, if you've misjudged your distance and fall short of the mooring, you can trim sail, fall off, and continue on for another go-around without getting in irons.

A mooring pickup in a light wind with a strong current in the opposite direction has to be executed in a completely different manner. In this case, lower the mainsail and sail under jib alone downwind (into the current). Then pick up the buoy and lower the jib. If you try to pick it up in the normal way, by shooting into the wind with all sail up, as soon as the mooring is secure the current will spin the boat around so that she will be heading downwind. The mainsail will be difficult to lower as the boom jibes back and forth.

When dropping a mooring under sail, again considering neighboring boats, wind direction, current—if any, and your intended exit route from the anchorage. Ask a crew member to stand ready with the mooring line in hand awaiting your instruction. He may even pull the boat one way or another depending on which way you want to leave, or he or another may assist by backing the jib to throw the bow off on the desired side. When the bow is swinging as you wish, and there is enough wind to trim the sails for a clean getaway, he drops the mooring at your nod or command.

Being able to pick up and drop a mooring competently under sail is both a fine point of seamanship and a personal satisfaction.

Rafting. When sailors get together for a party while cruising, they often raft the boats for easy boat-to-boat access. To form the raft, the largest boat in the fleet anchors and others come alongside and tie up. The approach is very much like coming alongside a float, except that the anchored boat is usually headed into the wind, which makes it easier. The main problem is you can't use your lines to check the forward motion of your boat because the anchored boat will just come forward with you. Great care must be exercised to approach very slowly. Have fenders over the side and lines ready. A couple of crew should be ready with roving fenders in hand. Preferably, by prearrangement all the boats involved should put their fenders and lines on the side next to the boat they are rafting alongside. Protection of the other side will be provided by the fenders belonging to the next boat to join the raft. This system works well when tying up and prevents confusion later as to who owns which fender or line when it comes time to disband the raft.

Because the raft swings a little, a perfect approach alongside may ultimately result in a wide space of open water between your boat and the rest of the raft as they swing way from you. For that reason, the safest approach is to poke your bow alongside the stern of the boat you'll eventually be alongside. One of her crew members can grab your bow pulpit or bow line and walk the boat forward toward his bow while another remains by the stern to keep the two boats from touching. They must also check to see that the spreaders of the two boats are staggered so that there's no danger of them hitting in case a sudden wake or swell starts the boats rolling from side to side.

When several boats are involved, more anchors should be set. Just row them out in a dinghy and drop them over the side. Never try to anchor first and then join the raft. However, just because there are a number of anchors out, don't get complacent and remain rafted overnight. More anchors just means more tangled lines and complications if the current or wind shifts in the night or a squall comes through.

Once, when cruising Long Island Sound, we anchored in a small harbor behind a sand spit. The weather was settled and a large group of sailboats rafted near us. As it got dark I was surprised to see they intended to remain rafted rather than split apart. About 0200 all hell broke loose. The rain was pelting down and the wind was gusting to 60 knots. We eased out more scope, but the conditions in the raft were chaotic as the boats tried to break apart and anchor separately. The next morning it appeared all but one had succeeded in coping with the storm, and that one was high and dry in a marsh not far behind us.

In my opinion, the peace of mind derived from riding at your own anchor far outweighs the camaraderie of rafting with friends overnight.

DOCKING UNDER POWER

When docking a boat under power, there are only three factors to be concerned about: wind, current, and boat speed.

If the wind is parallel to the float, it will cause little problem. Given the choice, always approach the float into the wind, because you will be able to control the boat much better with higher engine rpm. To slow down, throttle back and the wind will take care of the rest. On a downwind approach, to slow down you will have to put the engine in reverse. This gives you far less directional control, and reverse on a sailboat is notoriously ineffective anyway.

Wind affects the boat most when broadside to it. If the wind is blowing across the float, approach with your bow heading almost directly into the wind and turn parallel to the float at the last possible minute. With a right-hand prop, the stern will crab to port when you put the engine in reverse to stop the boat. If your port side is to the float, this will pull you closer, so put the prop pull into your consideration.

When the wind is blowing you down onto the float, the procedure is like coming alongside a float that's a few feet upwind of where it actually is. As you approach, land at an imaginary float upwind of the real one. As your forward speed decreases, you will find yourself making leeway. At a dead stop you should find yourself resting gently alongside the real float.

Current is another friend or foe factor. Used properly, current can be a great friend, helping you to get in and out of tight docking situations. Ignored or used improperly, current can create disaster. Usually you want to approach any float in an upcurrent direction. That way you can be powering a knot or two through the water and still remain in the same place over the bottom. If you turn the bow a few degrees across the current, the boat will crab sideways and can be fitted into an extremely tight spot between other boats tied alongside a float. This becomes a problem when there's a strong wind blowing with the current. The wind will tend to blow the bow to one side or the other, and when the boat gets across the current—watch out! A solution in this case is to back against the current and the wind. Thus, the engine in reverse is pulling the stern of the boat into the wind and current, so the rest of the boat lines up downwind like a weather vane. Now put the stern a bit cross-current and the boat will start to crab right into the docking space or slip.

The third factor in docking a boat is speed. Rarely is trouble caused by too little speed. Sure, you need some boat speed to be able to maneuver, but if you can't maneuver, it's not likely you'll hurt much if you're not moving. The big trouble comes from approaching a float or slip too fast. Sailboats build up a lot of momentum that isn't stopped easily and that can damage nearby boats. The slowest possible approach (and departure) is always preferable.

Preparation for the approach should be completed early. Fenders should be placed over the side. Get a bow line, stern line and two spring lines reaved early on the proper side of the boat. One end should be cleated or around a winch, and the line should be led through a chock and back over the lifelines preparatory to tossing the end ashore. It's best to have a loop on the end so you can ask a person on the dock to drop it over a bollard or a cleat. Then you can adjust the line length from the boat and not have to rely on the person ashore who may not understand what you want.

Of the greatest importance is the spring line that leads from a winch through a chock or block amidships and aft along the float. The chock must be at the center of lateral resistance of the hull, keel, and rudder (see Figure 69). To find the correct position for the chock or block, attach a line to the toe rail near the middle of the boat and pull the boat sideways. If the bow comes in more than the stern, move the block aft. If the stern comes in first, move the block forward until pulling on the line brings the boat in sidewise parallel to the float.

Set this up as one of your spring lines. As you approach the float, get that line ashore first and ask the dock hand to drop it over a cleat or bollard aft near the stern of the boat. A crew member should stand ready at the winch to check the forward speed of the boat by easing this line, to avoid crunching the topsides against the float if the boat is moving too fast. As can be seen by

Figure 69

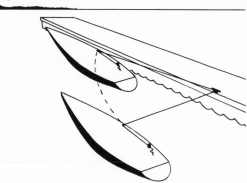

A spring line, properly placed and promptly secured,
can do more for docking a boat than any amount of
jockeying under power.

the diagram, however, once this line is secured, it describes an arc and any
forward motion of the boat brings the whole boat alongside the float parallel
to it because of the location of the lead.

The last line to secure is optional—the breast line. This is usually a single
line from the middle of the boat to an opposite pier or piling to keep the
topsides from rubbing on the float. If you plan to leave the boat unattended
for a while, breast the boat a good distance from the float in case of storm.
Ease all the lines substantially and take up on the breast line. Then pivot the
bow or stern into the float in order to step ashore and tighten all the lines
from the float ends to keep the boat parallel with the float. If you're tying up
to a non-floating dock, remember to allow enough slack to accommodate
the rise and fall of the tide.

The Med-moor. As slip space becomes tighter and tighter, maneuvering
to enter a slip is becoming more and more of a challenge. The Mediterranean style of mooring stern-to a dock, which permits many more yachts to
tie up in an area, was unknown in the U.S. a few years ago, but is now
becoming commonplace.

In Greece, the system is to drop your anchor about five boat lengths from
the dock and back in. First you must select the spot where you want to end
up. If you have come into port early enough in the day, you may find a
sufficiently wide open space between two boats to accommodate the beam
of your boat without touching the others. That's a rare occurrence in
Europe, however, so look for any space you can find between boats. Also,
consider squeezing in between boats smaller than yours, but if you see a
number of smaller boats all together at one end of a quay, the water there

may be too shallow for you, so be careful. In Europe, "Might makes right" more so than in the U.S., and so it's easier for a larger boat to push two smaller boats aside than the other way around.

Having decided where you want to be, maneuver your boat opposite that spot so that your boat is parallel to the others. Drop the anchor about five boat lengths out, or whatever distance seems appropriate for the size of the harbor. We don't go by water depth in this situation. The holding just needs to be good enough to keep your stern from hitting the quay. Your anchor will hold quite well with short scope because it will catch some of the other anchors and ground tackle if it drags. Also, latecomers often lay their chain anchor rodes over yours, thereby increasing your holding power.

Once the anchor is down, the key is coordination between the person on the bow easing out anchor chain and the helmsman who is backing the boat into the space. A couple of other persons with "roving fenders"—not secured in place but rather held in hand to be placed where needed—are very helpful. The bow person eases a lot of scope in the beginning, so the boat can get some sternway and be maneuvered by the helmsman. If the bow starts falling off one direction or the other, he stops easing, so strain on the anchor will straighten the boat out. Ideally, the anchor chain should be secured early enough so that it takes quite a bit of power in reverse to get the stern near the quay. Lines from either side of the stern are then led to rings on the quay and double back to the boat. As the engine is reversed, take in the slack on one side and then the other. This gives you a secure two-for-one purchase. It also makes it easy when you're ready to leave to just throw off one end of the line and pull it through the ring. Finally, put a stern plank to shore for access and egress. Tie it securely to the boat and allow enough overlap ashore so that it doesn't pull over the edge of the quay during the surge experienced in many harbors.

I once saw a beautiful example of "pushy seamanship" in a crowded Greek harbor. There were about 30 yachts tightly packed side by side when a very beamy 60-foot powerboat decided to drop anchor and back in. We couldn't believe he was really going to try to make space between us and the next boat, which was already jammed tightly against us. We waved him away. He ignored our choice phrases attesting to his mental condition and kept backing until his transom was almost touching our respective bows. He then goosed both massive engines in forward gear for an instant. His boat didn't move forward, but the prop wash pushed us and our neighbor aside, creating a hole where there previously hadn't been one. Before the hole closed, he had backed a third of the length of his boat into it. As we were about to touch his topsides he revved the engines in forward again, creating another mammoth prop wash. With the hole again enlarged, he backed the rest of the way in without touching us. It was quite a show and we had to eat our words about there being no space.

BACKING IN FROM A PRESET MOORING

In other parts of the Mediterranean, such as the southern coast of France, rather than dropping an anchor and backing in, you pick up a preset mooring and back in. You approach in the same manner as above, so that you are lined up to back into the desired spot. With a boat hook you either pick up a bow line attached to the mooring or pass your own line through an eye in the mooring buoy and back to the boat so you can ease back, as you wish. At the same time, lift up the messenger line that leads from the mooring to the quay so a crew member on the stern can reach it and can guide the boat backwards. The messenger line can be messy with seaweed and growth, so I prefer to let it run over the boathook out over the side of the boat rather than bring it aboard. Thus the helmsman must rely less on the messenger line and more on skill, so it depends a bit on the experience of the helmsman as to how much you rely on the messenger line to aid in the maneuver. With a poor helmsman get the line to the stern crew right away.

Because each boat has her own mooring and does not need to drop an anchor, this system is obviously less chaotic than the other on both arrival and departure. Although it saves far more space than the U.S. system of docking alongside, it is predicated on the beamiest boat. When a number of narrow boats are using adjacent moorings, there's usually excess space left between them. A common solution to this is a combination of the two systems. Instead of dropping anchors, a mooring system is used, but without messenger lines ashore. The moorings are placed quite close together, so even narrow boats can squeeze next to each other and have their own mooring.

MOORING UNDER POWER

Attention to wind, current, and speed are also important when picking up a mooring under power. Approach the mooring very slowly from a down-wind, downcurrent direction, if possible. The person in the bow with the boathook should aim the boathook at the mooring buoy, so the helmsman can tell about where it is. The crew in the bow should also use the commands "forward," "neutral," and "reverse" to the helmsman as needed, because it's very difficult for the helmsman to know when the bow is directly over the buoy. When the current is very strong, it will be necessary to approach upcurrent regardless of the wind direction. Failure to remember this can cause the person trying to grab and hold onto the mooring line great difficulty. Such a crosswind or downwind approach (upcurrent) should only be attempted after all the sails have been lowered and secured.

Once the mooring line has been brought aboard, led through a bow chock and the loop placed over a cleat, it's a good idea to take the pickup-buoy line (usually spliced into the loop) and cleat it over the loop on the cleat. This prevents the mooring line from slipping off the cleat if slack should develop in the line. Then put chafing gear on the mooring line where it rubs in the chock.

When leaving the mooring, back away from it rather than run forward, to avoid catching the propeller in the pickup line. Remember, too, to shorten up on the dinghy painter as you back down.

THE ANCHOR AND ANCHORING

It's always important for a skipper to know the characteristics and capability of his ground tackle and anchor, especially when in charge of a boat other than his own, as when chartering. For many years we have led our Offshore Sailing Club on cruises to Greece, France, Maine, Tortola, Grenadines, Belize, San Juan Islands, Apostle Islands, Tahiti, and elsewhere. During that time, we have observed how the emphasis of the charter checkout we have been given by each charter agency has changed. Initially, the emphasis was usually on the mechanical systems on the boat and on navigation. Anchoring was covered in passing. As years of charter checkout progressed, anchoring became more and more emphasized, probably because poor anchoring procedures had caused more problems than had anything else. Anchoring problems often occur in the middle of the night when the crew trying to cope with them is half asleep and possibly slightly hung-over.

Among typical anchoring disasters we have witnessed over the years are foul-ups such as one that followed the incredible Statue of Liberty Centennial celebration in New York Harbor in 1986, which we watched from a 40-

ft. sloop accompanied by literally thousands of other boats of all types. After the festivities, we decided to stay at anchor for the night rather than fight a foul current in New York's East River. When you need an "anchor watch" most is when you feel like it least. This was one of those nights. I took the 0100-0300 watch and about 0200 I saw a 60-ft. powerboat dragging past us. I blew our freon horn to try to get someone awake and up on deck aboard that boat, but they were all dead to the world. When she hung up on another yacht, her occupants — at least a dozen of them — swarmed up on deck to fend off and start the engines. Shortly, they were off, anchor up, and powering back to their original spot, where they reanchored. Ten minutes later they were all asleep below, having learned nothing. If each crew member had given up just one hour of sleep to stand an anchor watch, the damage to their boat and others would have been avoided.

Another common anchoring problem is wrapping the dinghy painter around the propeller. Years ago, when crewing on a boat, I was on the bow lowering the anchor as the owner backed down. He hadn't asked anyone in the cockpit to tend the dinghy painter. When the engine stopped, I looked aft and saw only the transom of the dinghy above the surface of the water. The painter had wound around the propeller and pulled the bow under water until the bow reached the prop and the engine stalled.

I saw much the same problem during a cruise in the British Virgin Islands. A charter boat, luckily not one of our group, was anchoring. No one was watching the dinghy painter and it wrapped around the prop. This time they cut the line and the dinghy drifted away. Fortunately, it happened in daylight and the breeze was light, so the dinghy didn't get too far before the crew swam to retrieve it.

One solution to the problem is to use polyethylene line as a dinghy painter, which floats, as mentioned previously. However, it is very difficult to cleat or tie, so it's a good idea to splice and whip a stainless steel snaphook into the end of the painter for securing the dinghy to the boat. The other end of the painter is then spliced and whipped into the dinghy bow eye. This is a foolproof method of securing the dinghy.

When choosing a place to anchor in a crowded anchorage, I drop my anchor almost alongside (slightly aft of) another boat of like characteristics that will be affected by wind and current somewhat comparably to my boat. After I've let out comparable scope, no matter what direction we swing, we will not touch, as in Figure 70. By being slightly aft I can get my anchor up in the morning even if his position has changed to dead ahead of my boat.

If a 360-degree anchor light is required by the rules, be sure to put one on

Figure 70

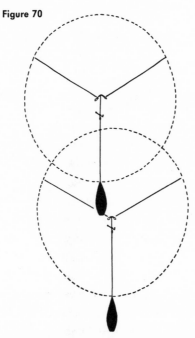

Drop you anchor near the stern of an anchored boat. As both boats swing they can't collide.

your bow about six feet above the stemhead fitting. It's required unless you are anchoring in a "special anchorage" area designated by the Coast Guard and shown on the nautical chart.

In very protected waters with only a light breeze on a hot summer's night, consider taking the anchor line to the stern from the bow, so the stern will head into the wind. This allows the light breeze to come down the companionway and any aft-opening hatches to cool off the sleeping area.

As for an anchor's holding power, the major variables are the type of anchor and its weight, the angle the anchor line makes with the bottom, and the type of bottom. Figure 71 illustrates the most common types of anchors. For instance, a Danforth© anchor holds well in a muddy, rocky bottom, but poorly when the bottom is grassy (covered with seaweed). A plow anchor is better at grabbing on a grassy bottom. The best bottom for anchoring is hard sand. A yachtsman's anchor has to be heavy to be effective and is awkward to handle. The Bruce anchor has yet to become popular in the U.S. It is probably the most effective all-around anchor of all. The heavier the anchor of any type, the better the holding power.

The table in Figure 72 is taken from manufacturers' suggested anchor weights, but is strictly a guideline. A 50-ft. boat could weigh over 50,000

Figure 71

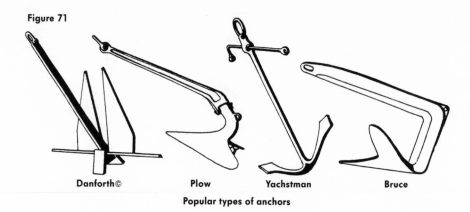

| Danforth© | Plow | Yachstman | Bruce |

Popular types of anchors

pounds or less than 20,000 pounds. It could have multiple masts, high topsides and large superstructure or could have a streamlined aerodynamic profile. The former would have tremendous wind drag and need much heavier anchors than the other, yet they are both listed at 50 feet. Moreover, the wind itself can have more or less power depending on its density. Dense air will cause more wind drag on an anchored boat than less dense air. The density changes with barometric pressure, temperature, and humidity. High temperature and high humidity with low pressure creates a low density of air whereas low temperature and low humidity with high barometric pressure creates high density. In other words, cold, dry air is denser than warm, moist air and will have much more force on each square foot of surface.

The smaller the angle the line makes with the bottom, the better the

Figure 72

Boat Length in feet	Drop-Forged "CQR" Plow	Cast Plow	Bruce		Danforth© Hi-Tensile fluke	Danforth© "Deep-set" Hi-Tensile fluke
			Working to 30K	Storm to 50K		
25'	15	20	4.4	11	12	3
30'	20	25	11	16.5	12	3
35'	25	35	11	22	21	7
40'	35	45	16.5	33	21	7
50'	45		22	44	36	9
60'	60		33	66	63	16
70'	75		44	110	150	16
85'	105					60

holding. If the line is almost vertical, the anchor will lift rather than dig in. However, if the line is almost horizontal, the anchor will dig in hard. The most common method to reduce this angle is to let out more line or "scope." A four-to-one scope is enough for temporary anchoring such as a lunch stop, but a seven-to-one scope is recommended if you want to sleep well at night and not worry about dragging. This means to let out anchor line equal to seven times the depth of the water you are anchoring in, and be sure to consider the tide factor as well. In Long Island Sound, for instance, if you anchor in eight feet of water at low tide and let out 60 feet of anchor line (7:1), you are only going to have about 4:1 when a six-foot tide brings the depth up to 14 feet. Also, you may have anchored at slack tide with little current. When the current starts to flow fast, you may start to drag.

Use your depth sounder to determine water depth where you're anchoring—15 feet, for example. Add the expected rise of tide—say, 5 feet—for a 20-ft. total. Multiply the result by six and let out 120 feet of scope. Until you are well aware of how much line this represents, it might be useful to place colored plastic markers along the line at 20-ft. intervals.

Another way to increase holding power by reducing the angle the anchor line makes with the bottom is to drop a weight along the line on a messenger called a "sentinel." Snap a snatch block on the line with the weight attached and lower it 20 feet or so. This has an added advantage of making the line from the bow to the weight more vertical than before and reduces the risk of the anchor line wrapping around the keel if the current shifts during the night. Setting out two anchors will also keep the line from wrapping around the keel.

Some cruising skippers set out two anchors at 45-degree angles off the bow. This helps reduce swinging when there is limited room in an anchorage, but does not add much to holding power. The holding power is the square of the weight of the anchor or of the two anchors combined. Square a 12-lb. anchor and you have 144. Square an 8-lb. anchor and you have 64. Two 8-lb. anchors give you a holding power of 128, still not up to that of the single 12-lb. anchor. However, the foregoing doesn't take into account that if one anchor drags, there's still another to save the boat.

Furthermore, if the current changes and you're using a single Danforth anchor, it's possible for it to flip over and not dig in the other way either because of weed. With two anchors out at approximately 45 degrees either side of the bow, the greatest angle either can rotate on the bottom is 90 degrees. Each anchor, once set, will just rotate rather than pull out, and will be reset as the boat passes over it with the current.

The best way to set two anchors across the wind is relatively simple. Choose your anchoring spot, drop one anchor and pay out anchor line over the windward side of the boat while powering directly across the wind. It's better to power than to sail. Head the bow 10 to 15 degrees into the wind to offset leeway. Predetermine the amount of line that will be used and cleat it at that point before you make your run. For instance, if the depth is 20 feet and you decided on 140 feet of line, get both anchors ready, each with 140 feet of line flaked on deck and cleated. When the end of the first anchor line is reached, drop the second anchor and pay out its line. You will end up solidly anchored by the two anchors and able to absorb all sorts of wind and current changes without excessive swinging.

Adding a length of chain between the anchor and line will also increase holding power; the chain then must be lifted before the anchor is affected. Many sailors advocate an anchor rode made completely of chain. Chain has more catenary—the parabolic curve between the anchor and the point of attachment on the boat—than line. The result is a very low angle to the bottom near the anchor and a more vertical direction near the bow of the boat. This makes the holding power excellent, and the boat swings much less.

With a nylon rode, the boat often "sails" around its anchorage, while with a chain rode the boat acts more as if it were tied up to a mooring. Nylon stretches and absorbs some of the shock of the boat pitching in heavy seas, but it can chafe and break where it leads through the chocks or if it wraps around a coral head. Chain won't. However, in extreme conditions chain can break. It's only as strong as it's weakest link, and doesn't compare in strength with nylon.

The other disadvantage of chain is weight and handling. When it's all aboard and stowed it is far heavier than rope. Since it is invariably stowed in the forepeak, the bow of the boat will always be excessively heavy, particularly since one needs a heavy anchor windlass to overhaul chain. This must be located up on the foredeck where it can be most beneficial. The result is that when underway the boat will pitch much more in seas because of the weight forward, making for an uncomfortable motion and greatly reducing sailing performance. Also, chain is hard to handle and can be very dangerous if it "gets away" (releases out of control).

When anchoring in areas where the water is very deep, such as the Society Islands in the South Pacific, a combination works quite well. An anchor rode made up of 60 feet of chain and 300 feet of nylon seems to be a good answer for anchoring in 70 to 90 feet of water every night. The chain increases holding power and resists the abrasion of coral heads, and the rope reduces the weight of the whole arrangement. One drawback is that when weighing anchor, the transition of the rope to chain on the windlass can be difficult because you have to switch from the chain drum on the windlass to the rope drum. If I were asked to vote on the chain/line controversy, I would have to cast my vote for a combination such as the above. In shallow water the rode would be all chain. As the wind increased and you added scope, you'd gain the advantages of line. I would also have aboard a smaller anchor with an all-line rode for lunch stops and for protected-water anchorages with a mud or sand bottom which wouldn't snare and chafe the line.

One other way of increasing holding power that appears to be quite effective is "backing an anchor" — having two anchors in a series, with one attached to the other in line by a short piece of chain. Thus, even if one pulls out, the other is set.

When approaching your selected anchorage, have your anchor ready on deck. If the anchor line is stowed in the forepeak, make sure plenty of it has been pulled out on deck so that the anchor will reach the bottom without pulling more line out of the hawsehole (the hole in the deck leading into the forepeak anchor line storage area). The line, of course, should have been carefully stowed in the first place. If a tangle develops under the deck, it's a nasty mess to handle in an area that's hard to reach. Make sure, however, that the bitter end of the anchor line is secured, either in the forepeak or on deck, before the anchor is put over. Then lower the anchor into the water gently until some of the weight is reduced by water pressure and then let go.

After the anchor is down, back the boat or let the wind blow her downwind. Ease out scope as she goes, and when you have let out all your intended line, snub the line around a cleat so that the momentum of the boat will set the anchor. On a sailboat with a fine bow and high topsides, the bow blows way off to leeward. It may blow so far that the stern ends up upwind of the bow. In that case, take the engine out of reverse and, rather than wait until the boat finally lines up with the wind again, power in forward gear downwind. Watch that you don't run over the anchor line and wrap it in your prop. When enough scope has been let out, snub the anchor, put the engine in neutral and let the boat's momentum set the anchor. Then, secure the line, reverse the engine, and test the set of the anchor. You can tell whether or not it's dragging by grasping the line; the vibration will be transmitted through the line to your hand. If it becomes obvious that you are ending up too close to another boat that was there first, raise your anchor and try again. The courtesy is, "He who anchors last, moves first."

Next, take compass bearings on nearby landmarks or lights so you can check later on to determine whether or not you've dragged the anchor. There are three caveats to this advice. If the landmark is nearby, the normal swinging on the anchor will radically change the bearing and you may think you are dragging when you aren't. If the landmark is far away, you will have to drag a long distance before there is a bearing change. If the visibility deteriorates you can't see the landmark, so bearings have limited value.

On one cruise, our flotilla of chartered sailboats anchored close together near some reefs. In the middle of the night, I woke up to find us bumping against the bow of a companion boat. Rain was driving down and visibility was only a few feet. Our impulse was to get the anchor up immediately and move to another spot. We took up enough scope to stop bumping and started the engine, but I told the crew not to get underway until I plotted a safe course. The wind direction had completely reversed and had we headed in the direction we had previously been oriented, we would have ended up on a reef. When you are disoriented, sleepy, and have a problem to face, try not to do anything rash. Take the time to plot a safe course, decide on how many minutes to run that course, turn on your running lights, and trust your compass. It's the best friend you have.

On another cruise in Tortola, we tried to anchor in a harbor on Jost Van Dyke. It was late in the afternoon and the anchorage was crowded. The wind was blowing on shore, so we rounded the sterns of the anchored boats and headed out between them to drop our hook. It was clear that we would be unable to drop the anchor and drift backwards without fouling one of the boats on either side, because we couldn't track in a straight line until there was enough scope out to take a bite with the anchor without dragging. So we chose to go upwind of the fleet, power straight downwind through the fleet, drop the anchor over our bow between two of the anchored boats, and when there was enough scope out so that we were behind the other anchored boats (but not too close to shore), we snubbed the anchor line. The anchor grabbed and spun us around 180 degrees, right in the spot we wanted to be for the night.

The crucial part of this maneuver is to put the engine in neutral as you drop the anchor and pay out the line lest it get caught around the prop. Also, the anchor line should be flaked on deck so it can pay out quickly without snagging, and the bitter end must be cleated. You must be powering at a good clip when you drop the anchor, so you'll continue in a straight line. It's a system that's rarely called for, but under special circumstances, it's one that really works.

If you are concerned about dropping the anchor from the bow because of the chance of fouling your prop, take your anchor and line to the stern. Power slowly downwind and drop the anchor where you want to place it. You have complete control and can power between other closely anchored boats. Also, since you don't have to put your engine in neutral, you can power more slowly, which makes it easier and safer to pay out scope. When you reach your desired location, snub and cleat as before and, when securely anchored, take the end of the anchor line up to the bow (outside all stanchions and shrouds) and cleat it. Then release the line at the stern. This method, though taking more effort and preparation, is a surer and safer method of anchoring in a crowded anchorage.

Occasionally, before putting the anchor over you may wish to attach a tripline, a light line attached near one of the anchor's flukes that will pull it out backward, in case it is snagged. A small buoy attached to the tripline will float directly above the submerged anchor. This also gives the skipper a mark to head for in order to get the boat right over the anchor before raising it.

To raise the anchor, start the engine and motor toward it. A crew member on the bow should be pointing toward the anchor position as he gathers in the line because the helmsman will not be able to see the direction of the line. Hand signals work best here as voice communication may be lost in the noise of the engine. When the anchor line is vertical, the crew snubs it around a cleat and uses the forward momentum of the boat to break the anchor out. The engine should be in neutral and the boat at a complete stop as the anchor is raised. Forward motion bangs the anchor against the bow.

If the anchor doesn't break out as the boat rides over it, the crew should cleat the line and the helmsman puts the engine in forward gear and hits the throttle in an attempt to break the anchor out. If at first unsuccessful, he can then try different angles. In heavy seas, try an alternative method: When the bow goes down, take up slack in the anchor line and snub it. As the bow rises on the next wave, the boat's buoyancy may break the anchor free. The slack may have to be taken in on a series of waves before the line is vertical enough for the maneuver to work. If this system doesn't work, lead the anchor line back to a jib sheet winch and try to winch it up. Failing this, don your mask and flippers to look the situation over for a solution.

If, after looking the situation over, you decide the anchor line is wrapped around a coral head, ease out 60 feet or so of anchor line and power with the helm hard over heading the bow to the outside of the circle. This allows the boat to circle around the snag with a constant outward pull on the line, but

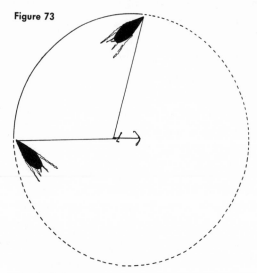

Figure 73

Put the helm to port to generate outward pull while circling clockwise.

keeps the line from wrapping around the keel. To reverse the direction of rotation, reverse the engine until the boat and anchor are in line, turn the wheel so reversing puts the bow to the other side of the anchor, then power forward with the wheel hard over. Thus, for counterclockwise circling, the helm is hard to starboard in forward gear and vice versa for clockwise circling, as in Figure 73. This should unwrap the line if you can see which way it's wrapped. If you can't see, circle in both directions. If there's no "give" or loosening in one direction after two or three circles, go four to six circles in the opposite direction. The nice thing about this method is that you are putting great outward pressure on the line. The boat will be almost parallel to the line and will be pulling every degree of a circle rather than just a few angles—as is the case when the bow is vertically over the fouled anchor and you power forward in a few directions.

When the anchor eventually breaks the surface, clean the mud off before bringing it aboard and then make sure it is well lashed down on deck before setting sail.

THE DINGHY

Everyone has a "funny dinghy story" to tell: how it overturned, was swamped by a passing powerboat, or lost at sea—not funny at the time, however, and in some cases expensive. Dinghy handling is a sometimes neglected detail of seamanship.

While the stable inflatable and Whaler-type dinghies abound to give us a false sense of security, traditional, less stable dinghies are here to stay and do require careful handling. Although they are easier and more fun to row than inflatables, they do tip easily if passengers are careless in stepping aboard or too rambunctious en route. Many a loaded-with-supplies-cameras-and-duffel dinghy has overturned at the dock or boat because of a passenger's ungraceful step off-center or on the gunwale. Boarding passengers should be instructed by the rower where to step and sit for best trim in prevailing conditions, and should do so quietly. If the rower is practiced, he will have the routine down pat and all will be well.

Watching someone row a dinghy who knows how is one of the rewards of the view from the cockpit when you're enjoying an anchorage. It's like watching the Harlem Globetrotters in a full court press—dexterous and flawless. The novice faced with rowing a dinghy should take the dinghy into a cove when no one is around, throw a wood chip overboard and practice coming up to it from all angles to develop good oar-handling technique. Add a sailbag or two to equate a load.

Overloaded dinghies are a frequent sight at group rendezvous, but nine times out of 10 the seasoned sailor doing the rowing has the weather, waves, current, and load factor figured and his crowded dinghy with five inches of freeboard makes it to the dock. The 10th-time disaster does occur occasionally, however, usually when an outboard-powered dinghy rushes by thoughtlessly creating a wake. Keep that in mind when loading your dinghy and be prepared.

More dinghies are lost at cocktail parties than at any other time. You row over to the host boat to find several other dinghies hanging off the stern. I recommend tying your dinghy to a stanchion with a bowline rather than cleating it with all the others. Often there are two or three dinghy painters on the same cleat and the first person to leave the party uncleats the others to free his painter and then recleats them with one hand while holding his own painter in the other. After a few drinks he occasionally misses a painter or two, possibly yours. When you come to get your dinghy darkness has fallen and—surprise—the dinghy is nowhere to be seen. If you're cruising in the Caribbean, it's somewhere between your harbor and Central America. Lots of luck in finding it.

Avoid the problem: Tie it with a bowline; tie it separately; tie it yourself.

The need for having someone tend the dinghy when backing the boat down and methods of securing the dinghy painter have been described previously, but the proper way to tow and stow a dinghy at sea to prevent its loss are as follows.

When you tow your dinghy in any seas, it's a good idea to double up on the towlines. Use one as a primary painter and another as a safety line tied to another fitting on the dinghy and led to a different cleat on the boat. Either take the rowlocks, oars, and/or outboard off the dinghy or make sure they are well secured. The former is the best policy. Tow the dinghy well aft of the sailboat on the back of about the third wave astern so the dinghy rides bow up rather than scoots down the face of the wave.

In bad sea conditions or on a very long passage, particularly at night, don't tow the dinghy at all lest it swamp and break the towlines. Rather, hoist it aboard with the main halyard and a three-part bridle attached to the bow and two corners of the dinghy transom. Then lash it upside down on the cabin top or foredeck. That should be a one- or two-person job, and you will rest a lot easier knowing your dinghy will be secure.

HEAVY WEATHER

Heavy weather is a subjective concept. Every sailor has his or her own perception of what it is. A crew accustomed to daysailing translates a simple broach into a death-defying knockdown. For me, a knockdown occurs when the spreaders are in the water and the boat is slow to recover. To round-the-world cruiser/racers, what I call a knockdown may be only a broach. They no doubt encounter these conditions many times in the Roaring Forties.

But what isn't different in each case is a crew's reaction to heavy weather. First, it's a foregone conclusion that a certain number of crew will be seasick, and since the extent to which mal de mer incapacitates an individual is personal, some crew will become useless, others will be walking invalids, and the lucky ones will try to ignore the illness and continue to do the job at hand. In any case, in very heavy weather your boat will not be sailing at full crew strength. So, you say, just pick experienced crew who won't get seasick. That's more easily said than done.

In 1979 we sailed in a transatlantic race from Marblehead, Massachusetts, to Cork, Ireland. Most of the crew continued on to sail with me aboard my 54-ft. sloop *Sleuth* in the disastrous 1979 Fastnet Race. Four of the crew who had shown no signs of seasickness across the ocean soon looked like death warmed over during the Fastnet. Four out a crew of 12 is a 33% loss of manpower. That meant the others had to take up the slack under very trying conditions. In such situations, the good helmsmen must steer longer and the crew on watch must awaken healthy off-watch crew to help shorten or change sail. Even mundane chores like cooking and sail trimming must be handled by the reduced crew, increasing the work load on each of them. There's little time for rest.

This brings us to the next enemy: fatigue. Unless the crew can get some rest, their reactions will slow and they may make poor decisions. For instance, the jib rips and a crew member rushes forward to gather it in, forgetting to snap his safety harness into the jackline running fore and aft. It's a small oversight caused by fatigue and may not matter; on the other hand, the oversight could result in the loss of that crew member over the side.

Many years of ocean sailing have taught me that in storm conditions as the weather builds healthy crew reacts in various psychological stages.

Stage one is exhilaration. This is a wonderful time. The crew is innervated by releases of adrenalin as the boat charges through the seas or scoots down waves. Advice to the watch captain is prolific. "Don't you think it's time to reef? What about changing to a number three jib?" Everyone has something to add. Normal shipboard humor revolving around non-sailing topics such as sex is also profuse, and the ship's motion under radically shortened sail is still relatively comfortable.

Stage two is concern. Conditions have begun to exceed the comfort level of the majority of crew. Humor becomes more focused on sailing. "Sailing is like hitting your head against a brick wall . . . it's so nice when you stop." Suggestions and advice are less frequent except from the more experienced crew. Part of the problem is that if a suggestion is accepted and involves work, the suggester will probably have to carry it out. Since just moving around the boat is hard work, anything else is work on top of work.

Yet, at this stage a lot can still be done, such as tying down loose items belowdecks, moving storm sails to accessible areas, doubling up a jib sheet, adding safety lines through the leech reef cringle around the boom, and charging batteries against later need for power for a spotlight or radio transmission. Rest and food for the off-watch must continue. The watch chief can and should delegate authority in specific areas to the most competent crew to keep them busy and keep their thoughts constructive.

Stage three is fear. Either some accident or breakdown occurs that indicates the boat's or crew's vulnerability to the storm, or the wind and seas now exceed everyone's experience and expectations. Humor may still be there. On one boat I sailed on, there was a standing joke about the optimist and pessimist brothers. At Christmas, their parents, who wanted to cure the kids of these traits, filled the room of the pessimist with presents only to find him standing in the middle of them crying his heart out because, he said, "There are so many presents, I don't know where to start." They filled the room of the optimist with horse manure and found him standing on top of the pile, happily digging away. Asked what he was doing, he answered, "Wherever there's this much shit there's gotta be a pony!" Whenever we were in a storm—knee deep in it, so to speak—someone would call out, "There's gotta be a pony out here somewhere."

At this stage the crew becomes introspective and quiet. Advice, so freely given earlier, is rare. The captain is on his own. The buck has stopped and if you're the person it stopped with, you feel very strongly your responsibilities to the others and their dependency on you.

Stage four is panic. I have never seen this stage because I've never been on a boat where faith in the boat and/or the captain has eroded to the point where panic has set in. It may have been aboard in an unrecognizable form—such as a person taking to his bunk with "seasickness." Panic is an overpowering terror that can affect the whole crew at once. It paralyzes logic and reason and often results in a rather hasty decision to abandon ship.

Aboard *Sleuth* in the 1979 Fastnet Race, we reached stage three. After the race was over I learned of an interview with Henry Kissinger, who had had remarkable successes in seemingly impossible negotiations in the Far East. He was asked if he ever had doubts before or during the negotiations. He said that he was riddled with them, but was determined not to show any doubt to either his side or the other. That was the secret of his success.

I had come to the same conclusion aboard *Sleuth* during the Fastnet. Our most experienced crew member, an around-the-world racing veteran from France, interrupted my efforts at navigation (our navigator was seasick) at about 0400 in the worst part of the storm saying, "Steve, we 'ave zees probleem." The last thing I wanted was for the rest of the watch to hear of a problem, but I knew that in the darkness all ears were tuned in. Nobody could be sleeping under those conditions. The problem, as he described too loudly, was that we were heading directly for the dangerous Scilly Isles. I explained that although we were on starboard tack and 50 degrees below course to Bishop Rock (which had to be left to port), when the low pressure area passed through we would be lifted as the wind veered and would easily get around it. He voiced the fear that since we had been reaching along for five hours and the wind had shifted only 10 degrees, we were traveling as fast as the storm and would end up on the rocks. I had the same doubts, but said, "We're going fast. We're reasonably comfortable. Do we have a problem now?" "No," he answered. "Then," I said, "when we have a problem, we'll do whatever is necessary to solve it."

Not another word was uttered by anyone about problems. The low passed through and we were lifted around Bishop Rock.

The introspective aspect of a stage-three reaction manifested itself in my standing orders for the crew not to listen to the radio. I didn't want anything to distract us from coping properly with the storm. I reasoned that we had no accurate position. All our electronic instruments including our speedometer and log were out of commission and we were on dead reckoning. We would be lucky to know our position within five miles and I doubted that other boats in the race could boast any better accuracy. Moreover, at night in the mountainous seas we couldn't find a boat unless she were within 100 yards of us. So, if we heard a distress signal, all it could produce was anxiety enhanced by the knowledge we could do nothing about it. Nevertheless, we turned on the radio the next day when we passed a boat lying a-hull in case she was trying to contact us. That short time was enough to pick up a transmission about a sinking boat. The depressing effect on the crew made me thankful we had not listened to the radio during the night and heard other distress calls about which we could do nothing.

Once you are aware of the four crew reaction stages — exhilaration, concern, fear, and panic — the longer you can keep your crew at the exhilaration stage, the better off you'll be. Not only do these stages impact on the crew as a whole, but they also affect each individual. Experience is the strongest factor in helping crew to remain in stage one. As noted previously, the broach of the daysailer that causes a stage-four panic in one crew member exhilarates another only because the latter has experienced the condition before and has faith in the boat and his or her ability.

Even if you don't have the experience necessary, you can try rationalizing to keep yourself from panicking. Think of the worst storm you've been in and then pretend that what you are experiencing is no worse than that. Then remember the lovely day that followed that storm and think how beautiful it's going to be when this storm passes through. Remind yourself that no matter how bad it gets, it always improves.

Remember, too, there's always got to be a pony out there.

Nevertheless, no amount of mental preparedness or rationalization can replace experience in handling heavy weather. Let's look at some of the weather situations you might encounter. The first and most common is a squall.

Squalls are small, local, often unpredicted, storms. They form on hot summer days as a result of nearby land heating up. This causes the air to rise and large cumulus clouds to form. These thunderheads are often anvil-shaped and quite dark down low. There may be almost no wind as a squall approaches, and then suddenly you're met by a strong blast coming out of it. Then, as the squall passes, the wind shifts—often as much as 180 degrees. Other types of squalls are associated with frontal passages and can be fairly accurately forecast. For warm-front passages, the wind will never clock more than 180 degrees. If the weather forecast has predicted a front to pass through, you may expect some prefrontal squalls in the neighborhood.

The problem for sailors is to determine beforehand just how intense the squall will be. Quite often the experience you have had from past squalls in a given location will suggest what to expect for future ones. For instance, when a nasty-looking squall hit us once or twice a winter in the Bahamas it was as bad as it looked, blowing 60 with a driving rain. In the Virgin Islands, a squall that looked exactly the same as it approached rarely had over 35-knot winds. The result is that one views a squall with a great deal more caution in the Bahamas than in the Virgins. Yet nothing is absolute and many squalls have the potential of causing great damage. Near Captiva Island, Florida, a squall's intensity can be deceiving. A few winters ago, we were hit by a squall that developed into a twister five miles after it passed us, knocking over house trailers on nearby Pine Island.

It's best to treat any approaching squall with respect. Try to look for signs that might measure its force and don't be fooled too much by darkness. On a bright, sunny day a low bank of clouds in the distance casts a shadow underneath that looks very ominous. Yet, when the bank arrives, there's nothing there except a solid blanket of low-lying clouds instead of the sun you had previously. Had you shortened sail because of it, you'd have felt very foolish. Without any vertical development of the clouds, there's not apt to be much increase in wind velocity.

The squalls I get concerned about are those that stand out as very dark on an already overcast day, which means the cloud layer is very thick right down close to the water surface. Often there's a pink tinge underneath which I can't account for, but when you see the pink tinge—watch out! It's apt to be a dilly. Obvious whitecaps in the distance also warn you of a high-intensity squall. If you're lucky enough to have other boats between you and the squall, watch how the winds affect them. If you see them suddenly knocked flat as the squall hits them, quickly shorten or douse sail yourself. If they just disappear into the darkness of the squall without appearing to be affected by it, don't be lulled into believing the squall has no power. After the boats disappear from your sight it's possible they might be hit by a blast. However, if there's no strong wind visible on initial entry into the squall there's not apt to be much wind farther into it.

If you're not racing, squalls are handled differently depending upon the type and size of sailboat and the sailing area. A small keelboat daysailing in relatively tight waters may have to anchor after dousing sails.

The proper way to prepare for a squall in a small sailboat is first to make sure that any flotation compartments or hatches that keep water out of the boat are secured. All crew should put on flotation vests. Next, get the anchor out and coil the line properly so it can run freely. Run the bitter end of the line through the bow eye and aft to the mast. Wrap the line twice around the mast and tie a bowline. Now overhaul the line through the bow eye and coil it neatly in the cockpit. Do this before the squall hits, because getting up on the foredeck in the middle of the squall can be very dangerous. If you slip overboard there's no way the crew can come back to pick you up if the squall is extremely violent. Anchoring from the cockpit in the middle of a squall, without leading the line to the bow, can cause complications. The boat will be broadside to the seas, which will put a great strain on the anchor, the line, and the point of attachment to the boat. Something will have to give. If it holds for a while, the waves will smash against the side of the boat and fill up the cockpit.

If you are certain you can sail back into the harbor before the squall hits, that's the best solution to the squall management problem. Don't attempt it if you are not certain. Nothing's worse than being hit by a squall in an area of restricted mobility surrounded by shoals. It's far better to get away from shallow water, even if it means heading away from the harbor, if you can't get safely inside before it hits.

If you expect to be hit by the squall and can't make it to port, the first sail to lower on most small boats is the mainsail. When the first blast hits, the mainsail will lay you over (if it hasn't been doused) and easing the mainsheet doesn't help much. The boom hits the water and the heeling of the boat pushes the boom in just when you want to ease it more. Because you are unable to ease the mainsail, the heeling increases and eventually the boat will swamp—the cockpit will fill with water.

So, get the mainsail down. Assign the crew emergency positions so each person knows his specific task: releasing the mainsheet, boom vang, and cunningham, or unhooking the halyard while holding the boom up to free the leech. Remember that all tasks are much more difficult to perform when it's very windy, so allow a little extra time. Be sure to take the halyard off the mainsail so it can't accidentally fly out like a spinnaker attached only by the head and foot. Then flake the mainsail on the boom as neatly as possible, wrap the head around all the flakes once or twice and tie the whole sail snugly with the mainsheet.

With only the jib up in heavy winds you will be able to sail as high as a beam reach, but it is doubtful that you will be able to make any headway to windward. The stronger the wind becomes, the more you will have to run before it. If running before it at high speed is not getting you anywhere advantageous, you will probably want to reduce speed by dousing the jib and running "under bare poles." Lower the jib and keep both jib sheets tight as the sail comes down so the clew is centered right in front of the mast and the foot is stretched taut. In a small boat, reach forward from the cockpit and tuck the body of the sail under the foot to avoid having much of the sail go over the side. If possible, try to wrap the spinnaker pole foreguy or the ends of the jib sheets around the sail to furl it. Don't go up on the foredeck. Stay in the cockpit and if you can't get the jib neatly rolled up and secured, don't worry about it. As long as the foot is tight and the sail is well lowered, you won't have too much trouble.

All this is fine where there's plenty of sea room, but in the presence of land or shoals, movement over the bottom must be reduced or stopped. This is where our anchoring preparations come in. Double check that the anchor line won't wrap around anything—such as someone's leg—as it runs out. With a good head of speed, round up into the wind and lower the anchor over the side. Since you have overhauled the line aft of the bow eye, you can wrap it around the jib sheet winch and pay it out. This should be done relatively smartly. Using the jib winch allows you to increase the scope more slowly after the anchor has a good bite. It avoids the possibility of breaking the line, which could happen if you tossed all the line overboard and waited for the anchor to bite and the boat to reach the end of the line with one gigantic jerk. Remember there are presumably heavy seas running and the boat could be surging down one of these seas when the end of the line is reached. Moreover, paying the line out under control keeps the bow headed into the seas, thereby offering less resistance to the waves. And last, the chance of someone or something getting caught in the line zinging out is diminished.

Now that you are anchored and the anchor line is running over the foredeck, tuck the jib under it to prevent the jib flapping in the wind. Both now and when underway, keep the boat as dry as possible. Water in the boat makes it sluggish to handle and lowers the freeboard. Waves are able to come over the side more easily the lower she gets and soon you won't be able to keep up with the waves.

On large boats at sea when a squall approaches, you reef or change headsails or roll up the jib. Unlike aboard small boats, the first sail to douse is the jib. It's usually larger than the mainsail and more fragile, unless you have changed down to a storm jib. By sailing with a reefed mainsail augmented with a little engine power, a sound cruising boat can handle almost any squall.

When it comes to more extreme storms, there are a number of methods of handling them in comfort. Unfortunately, I have no firsthand experience with these methods because I've sailed through every storm I've encountered, including the Fastnet storm. In a way, that could be called another method of handling a storm: Reduce sail to a minimum and sail fast on a close reach to broad reach, depending on the seas: more *into* breaking seas, more *off* rollers. In extreme conditions running off downwind with just a little spitfire jib works well.

One of the standard methods of coping with a storm is heaving to. This is a handy technique to know and to practice, whether you want to just stop sailing for a while and relax for lunch, or are caught in a violent storm and want to ride it out this way. To heave to, trim in the mainsail tight and cleat it. Back the jib to the windward side and cleat it. Since the mainsail will be forcing the boat forward and up into the wind and the jib will be forcing the boat backwards and the bow down away from the wind, an equilibrium can be maintained. The tiller or wheel can be tied in the position that best augments the equilibrium—usually to leeward. The boat will move very slowly through the water making quite a bit of leeway depending on wind strength.

A friend of mine has sailed thousands of miles with just his wife as crew on a keel/centerboard cruising boat. When a storm hits, he reefs the main, heaves to, and raises the centerboard. The boat makes such rapid leeway that it leaves a flat "wake" to windward that seems to level oncoming breaking waves. He and his wife then go below and play cards for a day or two until the storm passes, enjoying relative comfort without being tossed around by the seas.

Another method of coping with a storm is called lying a-hull. This means dousing all sail and letting the wind and seas take you where they will. I feel this method is dangerous unless a helmsman stays on deck to steer. The boat will still be drifting at three to five knots and needs to be positioned to avoid being smashed broadside by breaking waves. Dragging warps (long lines) or a sea anchor over the stern can take the place of a helmsman in keeping the bow downwind. This also slows the progress of the boat downwind in case you're running out of sea room. But remember, the closer the boat is to equalling the speed of the wave, the less force the wave will exert on the boat as it hits. One of the problems with running under bare poles or sailing downwind in a storm is that it may keep you in the storm longer. The most powerful sector of a storm is the leading righthand quadrant. If you're in that quadrant, the necessity for good storm-handling tactics will be greatest. If you run off, you will be sailing in the direction of travel of the storm and stay with it longer as in Figure 74. Proper tactics are to try to get to the weaker side of the low where running off takes you away from the storm. On one Bermuda Race in *Dyna,* our navigator said an unpredicted low was approaching as we were sailing close-hauled on starboard tack toward Bermuda. We tacked to port and sailed a few hours in lousy conditions that night, but by dawn we were surfing down waves on course. Figure 75 shows why. We were second boat across the finish line and easily won our class on handicap since we were the bottom-rated boat in Class A.

Another method of handling storms is to pay out a sea anchor from the bow. A sea anchor resembles the wind sock you see at airports, but is made of heavy material to withstand water pressure. It does an excellent job of slowing the boat down, but I have problems with having a boat surge backwards down waves as the sea anchor takes hold. The more natural movement is forward.

In another chapter we discuss man-overboard recovery procedures. I've sailed in conditions when, if anyone had gone overboard, it would have been virtually impossible to retrieve him or her with any procedure. I love the saying, "The difficult we do immediately; the impossible takes a little longer." I really should not use the word. However, the main concern is keeping everyone on board at all times and never having to find out if the "impossible" is possible.

With that in mind, the more difficult the task, the easier it is to lose someone overboard. With modern reefing techniques and the strength of the new synthetic sails, storm trysails have become dinosaurs.

The storm trysail is a sail that feeds into an auxiliary track leading into the mainsail track above a furled mainsail. It is loose-footed, has no battens, and sheets to the rail. The sailcloth is many times heavier than the regular

Figure 74

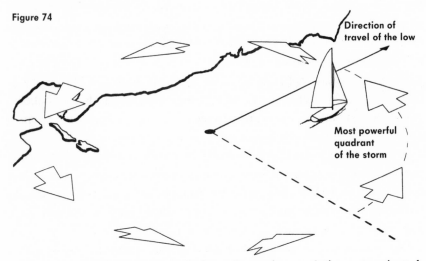

Direction of
travel of the low

Most powerful
quadrant
of the storm

Running off on starboard tack, even under bare poles, can keep you in the worst quadrant of the storm for a longer period. At the very least, jibe to port.

Figure 75

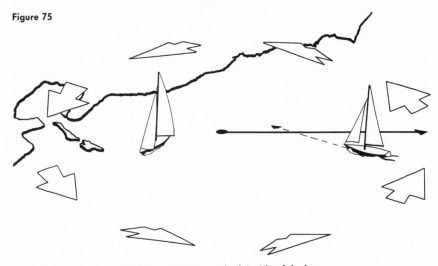

Tack to port to get to the fair side of the low.

mainsail cloth. To set a storm trysail, the crew has to douse and furl the main, lug the storm trysail up on deck, and feed it into the groove, attach a halyard, reeve port and starboard sheets and hoist. This is a lot of unnecessary work in heavy seas and 50–70-knot winds if the regular mainsail can be reefed down to the size of a storm trysail or smaller.

With jiffy-reefing techniques, it is easier and safer to reef a main than to take it down completely and furl it. Assuming the mainsail is not a lightweight racing main, but rather an all-purpose passagemaking sail, it should hold up well in heavy winds. By reefing instead of changing sail, fewer crew need to leave the security of the cockpit, so there's less chance of losing someone overboard.

However, I would not eliminate a storm trysail from a sail inventory. If the mainsail blows out, it's a decent backstop. It's strength, lack of battens, and loose foot make it useable in extreme conditions or in case the boom is broken.

Another sail that works well in heavy weather is the storm staysail. It is hanked on a stay—the inner forestay—that runs from the mast to the middle of the foredeck parallel to the headstay. To set it the crew doesn't have to go forward all the way to the bow where the motion is violent. Set at a fairly wide position of the boat, the staysail is not likely to catch a wave and be pulled over the side. Also, it doesn't affect steering as much because it's not near the bow of the boat. It's an excellent reaching sail because when set it doesn't have the tendency to scoop the bow wave as much as a jib on the headstay does on a heavy-weather reach.

Chapter V

THE WIND

═══════════════════════════════════

One day, when one of our Offshore Sailing School instructors asked a student where the wind was coming from, he got a surprising reply. It's an often-asked question intended to develop a novice's awareness of wind direction, but this student thought the instructor was asking for the wind's source, not direction. Her answer was that the trees shake their leaves, which creates wind, and that's where wind comes from. At least she wasn't afraid to give an answer, but let's try to get a better handle on the wind than that.

READING THE WIND

Wind is a movement of air from areas of higher pressure to areas of lower pressure. At the equator there is a band of low pressure where heated air expands and rises. This band is called the "doldrums." It is characterized by calms, cloudiness and frequent squalls. At about 30° north and 30° south, latitude, there are bands of high pressure called the "horse latitudes," which is also calm, but clear. At 60° north and 60° south, there's another band of low pressure, and at the north and south polar caps there are high pressure areas. Note in Figure 76 how the air sinks from aloft over the bands of high pressure and then moves north and south toward the low pressure bands and rises again. This creates a large circulation pattern. The middle of the diagram shows what would be the direction of air flow if the earth didn't rotate. Since it does, the direction is deflected as indicated.

If you look at a weather map, you will see lines called isobars. These are

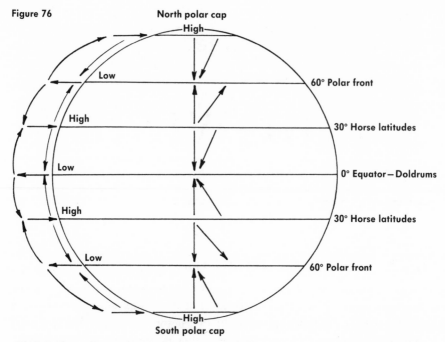

Figure 76

North polar cap

High

Low

60° Polar front

High

30° Horse latitudes

Low

0° Equator – Doldrums

High

30° Horse latitudes

Low

60° Polar front

High

South polar cap

Wind circulation blowing from high pressure areas to low pressure areas, rising and returning

lines connecting points of equal pressure at various locations on the map. These lines are much like the lines on a topographical map. A mountain, for instance, will show up on a topographical map as many lines close together, each line indicating a set amount of altitude above sea level, such as 20 feet. This incline of the slope of the mountain is called its gradient. A steep slope is a steep gradient. It's the same with the pressure gradient in meteorology. When the lines are close together, we have a steep gradient—a larger change in pressure over a short distance. This difference in pressure creates wind and the steeper the pressure gradient, the stronger the winds. When sailing on the east coast of the U.S. you can call weather sources (such as airports in cities to the west of you) to get the barometric pressure difference between their location and yours. Then, based on a table of the difference in pressure and the distance in miles between locations, you can determine the increase or decrease in wind strength that will prevail when the system reaches you. In preparation for a race or a sailing passage, you can also use other sources of weather information available to you—the weather channel on cable TV, the National Oceanic and Atmospheric Administration (NOAA) weather radio station (NWR for short), newspaper weather maps, or facsimile charts if your boat has a receiver and printer.

Since a fast-moving weather system will cause major wind shifts, it's important to remember how the wind rotates. Wind blows *clockwise* and angles slightly outward around a high pressure area. Around a low pressure area, it blows *counterclockwise* and angles slightly inward toward the center of the low. If you face the wind and extend your right arm at a right angle to the direction you're facing, your arm is pointing to the center of the low. This is called Buys Ballot's Law and it can be very helpful to you in determining the location of a low and its effect on the wind.

When looking at a weather map to try to decide which way the wind is going to shift, I find it easier to move my position through the system in the

Figure 77

Move your position through the low parallel to the direction of its course to visualize what wind direction changes you'll encounter.

direction opposite to which the system is moving, rather than trying to imagine the system as it moves past my position. Look at Figure 77, showing the winds around a low-pressure area. We expect the low to move to the northeast—in the direction of the arrow—and in 12 hours to be at the point of the arrow. We draw an arrow from our position (at the X) in the opposite direction, and the winds we see along the length of the arrow are those we might expect during the next 12 hours. For us, the wind will "back" (move counterclockwise) from the south and southeast and even the north as the low passes to the south.

While the gradient or weather system wind is relatively predictable when you're at sea, near land it's a different story. Other things affect wind direction and speed, particularly geographical influences. Generally, it tends to be beneficial to sail near a shore. Usually there's some sort of windshift that can be useful to the sailor.

The vagaries of the wind are many, however, and the racing sailor who hugs the shore could be dismayed to find that boats farther out are moving while he's becalmed. This is often caused by "lift-off" of the wind as it approaches a high shore, as shown in Figure 78. Though the "blanket"

Figure 78

The wind starts lifting far offshore when an onshore breeze approaches a high bluff.

Figure 79

Wind blowing offshore over a high bluff creates a lee, a calm area, near shore.

Figure 80

Wind blowing obliquely towards land tends to bend in the direction of the shore.

effect of such a high shore is obvious when the wind is blowing away from the land (Figure 79), many sailors don't realize how far away from shore the wind can lift off the surface to rise over cliffs when the wind is blowing toward the shore.

Near the shore, wind often has a different direction and velocity because of topographical influences. Wind blowing obliquely towards the shore often tends to parallel the shoreline (Figure 80), while wind blowing obliquely away from the shore tends to bend out at right angles to the shoreline before bending back to its original direction (Figure 81). This change in direction can be very helpful to a racing sailor. He sails on port tack toward the shore until he is headed as he gets near it; he then flips to a starboard tack and sails in a nice lift along the shore (Figure 81).

Figure 81

Wind blowing obliquely offshore tends to bend perpendicular to the shoreline as it departs shore.

Other geographical influences are those that channel the wind, such as valleys, points of land, or even city streets. Chicago, for instance, is a good example of the latter. An offshore wind will funnel right down the larger streets toward the water and you can pick up quite a blast by being right there to receive it. Before a race, study a topographical map of the area and note any steep hills, river valleys, or bays accentuated by high land.

Of utmost importance to your performance in onshore races is local knowledge of how the sea breeze works. On many days in spring and summer, the land heats up rapidly while the water remains a constant temperature. The air over the land heats, expands and rises. The cooler air over the water moves in to replace it causing a wind near the shore called a sea breeze. This breeze is strongest when the temperature differential is greatest. In the early spring, the seawater is still cold so on a bright, sunny, warm day there will be a stronger sea breeze than there will be later in the summer when the water has warmed up.

Now, look at a topographic map and try to determine the direction the sea breeze will take when it comes. If there is a large town with many streets and parking lots nearby, these will heat up faster and more air will be rising at that area, creating the possibility of a stronger breeze and a slight deflection in direction toward that area. On the water, observe the sky. As a cloudless, sunny day progresses, you will see cumulus clouds build up over the land when the air rises. With experience you'll learn when the buildup will translate into a sea breeze, usually late morning or early afternoon. It's at this point the study of the weather map comes into play. If the land is to the east you would expect a westerly breeze to develop. However, if the gradient wind—the weather system wind—is an easterly, the two winds might cancel each other out, with only a calm remaining, unless the warm gradient wind lifts above the cooler sea breeze.

If the day is a little cloudy and the easterly gradient wind is strong, you might expect the westerly sea breeze to just reduce the strength of the easterly wind. If the gradient wind is a westerly early in the morning, you would expect the westerly sea breeze to reinforce that wind and create a fairly strong breeze in the afternoon. Of course, there are many variables. Every different angle and strength the two breezes make relative to each other creates a different direction and velocity for the resultant wind just like any vector. Rather than just relying on a weather map, try to obtain from an airport the direction of the wind at 1,000 to 2,000 feet above the surface. If these winds are within 50 to 100 degrees from the direction of the sea breeze, the surface wind will be strongest. At night, when the land cools off, a reverse breeze — called a land breeze — blows offshore from the land. Also, during daylight hours in the fall, when land is cold and the water is warm, a land breeze can form. To determine what's going to happen, input as much information as possible and make an educated guess.

It is very important to be able to recognize wind. Wind is invisible, but its effect on our surroundings is not. There are many signs that tell us where, in what direction, and how strong the wind is, or how it might change. Look at the land. Usually there's smoke from a stack that will show the wind direction and a possible change in direction. Compare the direction the clouds are moving with the surface wind. Given the right conditions, this higher level wind may come down to the surface and change the surface wind direction, as happens in gusts. Because wind aloft more often than not is veered (clockwise) in relation to the surface wind, such gusts may also be veering when they hit.

Look at the water surface. On light-air days you can see ripples that indicate the presence of wind. Be careful not to confuse ripples caused by current with those caused by wind. Even on windy days such ripples are noticeable on bigger waves and indicate even stronger gusts approaching. Experienced racing sailors can see these dark patches — "cat's paws" — approaching and can determine whether the gust is going to have an advantageous angle when it arrives. They are called cat's paws because they fan out as they approach. On the near side, a close-hauled boat will be headed, and on the far side, lifted. Seeing this takes a keen eye and years of practice; not every sailor is good at it.

While observing these wind patches on the water, also note other sailboats in the distance. Their direction and angle of keel can give you information about the wind they have, and what it will probably be when it reaches you.

When you're sailing in enclosed waters, your wind may be affected by local tidal current direction. In many bays and sounds, an incoming current can bring in cool water that will set up an even greater temperature differential between the water and land. This, in turn, can set in motion a slight onshore breeze that you might be able to anticipate.

If you are sailing anywhere along the east and west coasts of the United States in light winds coming from any direction except northwest, north, or northeast, you may expect that as the day goes by there will be a continual wind shift. More than 50 percent of the time, the wind veers — shifts to the right (clockwise) as you face the wind. Since you always want to sail toward the next shift when beating, you should be on the right side of the course when the wind shifts so you'll be headed on port tack and have a starboard-tack lift to the weather mark. By "right side of the course," we mean to the right of a line drawn from the start to the weather mark. The boat farthest to the right makes out best when the shift comes (unless the shift is so large she overstands the mark on a starboard tack). However, if the shift goes the other way, she also has the most to lose—she's out on a limb, so to speak. When you have no idea what will happen to the wind, it's better to sail near the middle of the course, but remember that the right side will pay off more times than the left.

At this point, let's make sure we are speaking the same language in regard to wind. The actual wind that blows across the water is the "true" wind. A true wind is "backing" if it's changing counterclockwise—from north to northwest. It is "veering" if the direction changes clockwise—from east to southeast. The wind that results from a combination of forward boatspeed and the true wind hitting the boat is the *apparent* wind.

It's not enough to just know the direction of the apparent wind. We need to adjust the sails to use the power of the wind most efficiently. Telltales help us do this. We usually place wool telltales at three levels up the jib and at the ends of the battens of the mainsail. If we were to put them at other locations along the leech of the main, flutter would disrupt their flow.

The wool telltales on the jib indicate when the airflow is smooth and attached. Their most important function is to show a stall, which is impossible to see without them. The sail is an airfoil and if it is trimmed in too tight the wind will not be able to flow over the lee side of the sail very far before it separates from the surface and becomes turbulent. Then, just as an airplane stalls when it tries to climb too abruptly, the sail loses its lift or effectiveness. When the air becomes turbulent on the lee side of the sail, the leeward telltale will flutter, indicating a stall. There's very little heading difference between a stall and a luff. A boat that is indicating a stalled jib may need to head up only 5 to 10 degrees before the windward telltales starts to flutter, indicating a luff.

Although you never want to sail with the leeward telltales fluttering, there are times when the boat sails best with the windward one fluttering. For instance, in a strong wind and a smooth sea, you may be able to "pinch" a little—carry a slight luff in the jib—and sail faster with the windward telltales jumping. Falling off to the point of smooth flow on the windward side of the sail can cause the boat to heel excessively and slow down.

The general idea is illustrated in Figure 82. Diagram A shows even flow on both sides of the jib and good jib trim for the given course. Just before the

Figure 82

A. Proper flow. Both telltales stream aft.

B. Just before the jib luffs, the windward telltale flutters.
   1. If close-hauled, fall off.
   2. If reaching, trim sheet.

C. When leeward telltale flutters, jib is stalled.
   1. If close-hauled, head up.
   2. If reaching, ease sheet.

sails luff, the windward telltale will jump around, as in Diagram B. The leeward telltale will still flow well, but the curve of the sail is obstructing the wind (which is more toward the bow of the boat) from attaching to the windward side. Thus, the windward telltale flutters. The solution when closehauled is to fall off, and when reaching to trim the sail. Diagram C shows a stalled jib. The wind is hitting the sail more from the windward side and is unable to make the sharp curve around its lee side without breaking away. Here, the solution when close-hauled is to head up and when reaching to ease the sheet.

Wool telltales on jibs are very useful when reaching. A racing crew has to "play" the jib constantly on a reach—trim when it luffs and ease when it stalls. Without the telltales, it is extremely difficult to know when the sail is stalled.

The reason for three levels of telltales on the jib is to avoid excessive twist. Wind velocities are faster higher off the water and a certain amount of twist is desirable to keep the same angle of incidence of the jib to the apparent wind at the head as at the foot. Surface friction slows the wind nearest the water substantially compared to wind just 30 feet or so above the water. This means the wind at the top of the mast is farther aft than at the bottom. Think of it as if the top of the sail was sailing in a continual gust compared to the bottom. In a gust, with a constant boat speed, the apparent wind goes aft. To make the same angle of attack to the wind, the top of the sail must be more twisted than the bottom. Too much twist will indicate a luff on the uppermost telltale of the jib. To correct this we move the jib lead forward and create more downward pull on the leech. Another solution would be to trim the jib tight, but that would tend to stall the bottom of the jib. The bottom telltale on the lee side would flutter, indicating a stall, in that case.

APPARENT WIND

The wind shifts we discussed that refer to the compass—veering and backing winds—are based on the actual wind blowing across the water. This is the *true* wind. The shifts that relate to the boat—headers and lifts— are affected by the speed the boat is traveling through the water. The result of these factors—the true wind and the boat speed wind—is the *apparent* wind. Everything on the boat that indicates wind direction is indicating the apparent-wind direction—the masthead fly, telltales on the shrouds, ciga- rette smoke, and electronic wind indicators all show the apparent wind.

Novices become aware of the phenomenon when they sail close-hauled for the first time. They've read that a boat can sail roughly 45 degrees to the wind direction, yet the telltales on the shrouds indicate that the wind is much farther forward, perhaps 25 degrees from the bow, but when they tack, they discover it still takes 90 degrees to complete the tack.

To understand apparent wind, imagine you are in a motorboat. It's dead calm. As the boat moves forward and reaches a speed of 10 knots you feel a 10-knot breeze from dead ahead. This is a boat-speed-created wind since there is no true wind. If, however, the motorboat were heading due east at 10 knots and there were a 10-knot true wind blowing from the north, you would not feel two different winds (i.e., boat speed from the east and true wind from the north), but rather a resultant wind from the northeast that is a combination of the two winds—the apparent wind.

The apparent wind direction and velocity are easy to determine if you

Figure 83

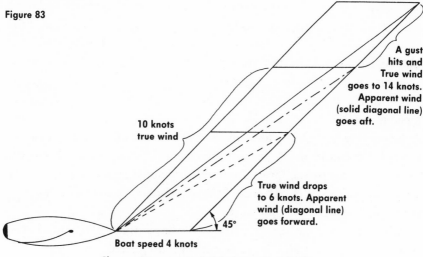

10 knots
true wind

A gust
hits and
True wind
goes to 14 knots.
Apparent wind
(solid diagonal line)
goes aft.

True wind drops
to 6 knots. Apparent
wind (diagonal line)
goes forward.

45°

Boat speed 4 knots

Changes in apparent wind during gusts and lulls

know the true wind velocity and your boat speed. If your boat tacks in 90 degrees, you know that the true wind is 45 degrees from your bow. Say the boat is sailing at four knots as in the parallelogram in Figure 83. With a true wind of 10 knots, the dot/dash diagonal line of the parallelogram is the apparent wind direction. By drawing similar parallelograms for a boat sailing at four knots on various sailing angles—beam reaching, broad reaching and running (with the same constant true wind of 10 knots), you can diagram the apparent-wind direction and velocity for those sailing angles. If you diagram each sailing angle as the wind clocks, you will end up with parallelograms for a boat on a run that resemble Figures 85 and 86. (Incidentally, this is a hypothetical case because a boat that reaches or runs at four knots couldn't maintain that speed close-hauled. Let's assume that the boat in the close-hauled diagram is larger and therefore faster.

The above diagrams assumed a constant true-wind speed of 10 knots. Now let's see what happens when the wind increases. In Figure 83, the extension of the true-wind line to 14 knots indicates a four-knot increase in wind velocity and the solid diagonal line indicates that the apparent wind has come aft. Working this out graphically illustrates basic wind axiom #1: *When the wind increases, the apparent wind comes aft.*

Thus, as a gust hits it causes greater heeling and less drive because of a changing angle of incidence (the angle the apparent wind makes with the sails). The net result is that the sails are now improperly trimmed and you must either head up or ease the sheet or traveler to fill them.

This particular change in apparent-wind direction is very important, especially on light days. If you have a three-knot breeze, the wind velocity in a puff is apt to more than double it to six or more knots. However, if the wind is blowing 15 knots, a gust may get to only 20 or 22 knots—only one-third higher. Therefore, the movement aft in apparent-wind direction is often greater on light days than it is on heavy ones.

Conversely, the dotted lines in Figure 83 show the resulting change in apparent wind if the wind suddenly dies. With boat-speed remaining constant and the wind velocity lowering to six knots, the apparent wind will go forward. Obviously, in the absence of any wind, the only breeze felt would be that produced by the forward motion of the boat, and that would come from dead ahead. Wind axiom #2: *Any reduction in true wind velocity brings the apparent wind forward.*

This happens on light days, particularly to large cruising boats that have a great deal of momentum. The sails will start luffing and you think you are sailing too high. Actually, the boat may only be going through a light spot or "hole" in the wind. You must make an immediate decision: Is it a valid wind shift—a header—or is it just a hole? If it's the former, you must head off to fill the sails; if it's the latter, you could kill what little speed you have by heading off instead of shooting through the light spot with momentum and picking up the breeze on the other side of it. Usually the wisest course is to head off very slowly and evenly. If you're still luffing after turning 20 degrees away from the wind, it's probably a flat spot.

Note "slowly and evenly" above. The skipper who turns downwind too quickly aggravates the situation if it's just a hole in the wind. The turn itself forces air against the lee side of the jib, causing it to luff or back. He will soon find himself 30 degrees below his previous course with the jib still luffing because of the turning motion of the boat.

If the skipper decides the luffing is due to a header—i.e., the wind has shifted toward the bow—he will tack. But he should be wary. As he turns the bow into the wind, the jib will fill as the apparent wind comes aft due to the turning of the boat. Because the jib has stopped luffing, it can appear that the wind has shifted back to its original direction and the skipper may think he has been lifted (the wind direction has changed more toward the stern), when actually it is only the pivoting of the boat that has caused the change.

An inexperienced skipper will then stop his tack and return to his original course. At first it will appear that he has made the correct decision because, by making the incomplete tack, he has slowed the boat, which puts the apparent wind fairly well aft. However, as the boat picks up speed, the

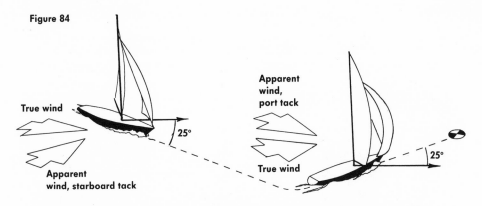

Figure 84

apparent wind will again come forward and he will find himself sailing in the same header as before.

Referring to the parallelograms, note the relevance of the following:

Wind axiom #3: *Apparent wind direction is always forward of the true wind, unless the latter is coming from dead ahead or dead astern.* This fact becomes important in determining when to jibe. To reduce the chance of an accidental jibe, most skippers will sail with the wind coming over the quarter rather than from dead astern. This brings the apparent wind quite far forward. Note in Figure 84 that the boat is sailing at a 25-degree angle from dead downwind and the apparent wind is forward of that. In order for the boat to sail at the same angle to the destination after the jibe, the jibe must be made when a 50-degree turn will head the boat toward the destination. To make such a determination, the skipper must judge fairly accurately the direction of the true wind. Ripples, foam, and streaks on the water give an indication of the true wind direction, but a more accurate indicator is to sail dead downwind momentarily and see how much the boat has to be turned to attain that point of sail. In our example, the turn will be 25 degrees, so he wants to jibe when another 25 degrees will point to his destination.

Wind axiom #4: *As the true wind comes aft, the apparent wind speed lessens.* The diagrams illustrate this very well, but the importance of reduced apparent wind speed is most noticeable when a run is compared with a beat. If a boat is running downwind at nine knots in a 16-knot true wind, the apparent wind will be only seven knots (16 knots minus nine). The breeze you feel is very light. On a beat, the boat speed may decrease to about six knots, but the apparent wind will increase to almost 21 knots, or three times greater than when running. Even if there were a direct relationship between wind strength and wind force, this would be a substantial increase. However, wind force varies with the square of the velocity. A five-

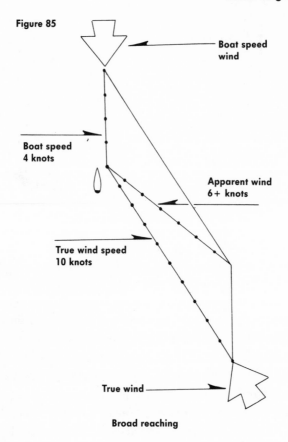

Figure 85

Boat speed wind

Boat speed
4 knots

Apparent wind
6+ knots

True wind speed
10 knots

True wind

Broad reaching

knot wind squared is 25. A 10-knot wind squared is 100. So, as the wind speed doubles, the wind force quadruples. In the above example, the wind force is nine times greater when beating than when running.

The effect is that the amount of sail area that could be carried easily on a run may very well overpower the boat on a beat, and you may have to consider shortening sail. Keep this in mind whenever you set sail on a broad reach or a run. You may have a hard time getting back home when you decide to turn around.

Wind axiom #5: *When the true wind is near astern, a small change in true wind direction will make a large change in apparent wind direction.* Compare Fig. 85 with Fig. 86. Note how small a change there is in the true wind direction, and how far aft it caused the apparent wind to swing. Such a large change in apparent wind direction when running makes steering very difficult for the inexperienced helmsman. If he steers slightly by the lee, the apparent wind will swing well by the lee. Threatened with a possible jibe, the helmsman turns the boat the other way, causing a large swing in the

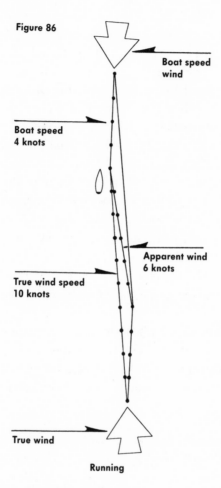

Figure 86

Boat speed wind

Boat speed
4 knots

Apparent wind
6 knots

True wind speed
10 knots

True wind

Running

apparent wind to the windward side of the boat. To avoid broaching, he steers downwind again and the cycle repeats itself. A flying jibe can result.

Wind axiom #6: *When the boat is on a beam reach to close-hauled, the apparent wind speed is greater than the true wind.* The faster a boat sails, the greater the apparent wind speed. The greater the wind speed, the faster the boat can go, limited only by the resistance of the water being pushed aside by the hull. Light sailboats of certain hull configurations skim the surface of the water— "plane" —at relatively high speeds because of lack of hull resistance on the water. Iceboats, for example, attain tremendous speeds (over 100 knots) because they encounter minimal resistance to forward motion. They are basically creating their own wind.

Now let's consider instances where wind speed remains constant but boat speed varies. For instance, if the boat starts surfing down the face of a wave (much as a surfboarder uses a wave), the apparent wind goes forward. Sometimes it goes forward to the point where it will flatten the spinnaker back against the mast and rigging; at other times the boat may slow down. Then the apparent wind comes aft and its velocity will increase. As noted previously, when wind velocity doubles, the pressure on the sails and rigging quadruples. When a boat runs hard aground at high speed, she is often dismasted because the rig and sails tend to keep on going even though the hull has stopped; also, the apparent-wind pressure on the sails has suddenly increased tremendously.

This occurred to *Mare Nostrum,* a 72-ft. yawl, on the 1955 transatlantic race from Cuba to Spain. We were carrying a spinnaker, mainsail, mizzen and a mizzen staysail (sort of a jib for the mizzen) in fairly fresh winds of about 20 to 23 knots. The swivel on the spinnaker halyard broke and the chute streamed out ahead of the boat. Before we could get it aboard, it filled with water, went under the bow and hooked on the keel. This slowed the boat so suddenly that the top half of the mizzenmast toppled forward under the increased load on the mizzen staysail.

So, always remember that whenever there is a change in either boat speed or boat direction, or wind velocity or wind direction, there must also be a change in the apparent wind. A helmsman must be alert to it and he must either change his course accordingly or the crew must trim or ease the sails.

Chapter VI

NAVIGATION: PILOTING

Navigation is broken down into two categories: celestial navigation and piloting. The former is a system of navigation based on the positions of celestial bodies, which is used by navigators when out of sight of land. In this book we are concerned with piloting, which is coastwise navigation based on landmarks, buoys, soundings, bearings, and other points of reference.

Piloting consists of transferring your position to a chart. It requires that you determine your position ("fix"), locate the fix on the chart, and use the rest of the chart to answer certain questions. The fix has answered the question, "Where am I?" But you also want the answers to other questions: Is the water deep enough for the boat's draft? Where are the nearest dangers—rocks, reefs, shoals, riptides? Referring to the chart, you want to be able to determine a course or courses to steer that will allow safe passage to deep water or to some other destination.

THE CHART

The chart is an expertly researched road map of the sea. It is printed under the auspices of the Department of Commerce and is available at many nautical supply stores. The area a chart covers and its identifying number are listed in the *Nautical Chart Catalog,* which is an easy way to find any one particular chart.

You will notice in the catalog that charts come in different scales. They are all roughly the same physical size, but cover different size areas. Every chart has a scale with which to measure distance. A mile on the scale of a "large scale" chart is longer than a mile on the scale of a "small scale" chart. Therefore, a chart that enlarges a small area, is a large scale chart. Such charts are used for entering harbors, where precision and accuracy are necessary. When planning a passage, however, a small scale chart covers more distance and is easier to refer to.

Although charts are printed in different scales, the most common are 1:80,000, 1:40,000, and 1:20,000. On a 1:80,000 chart, one foot is equivalent to 80,000 feet on land, or roughly 13 nautical miles (NM). On a 1:20,000 chart, one foot equals 20,000 feet or about 3.3 NM. Obviously, there will be less detail when you crowd 13 miles into a foot of chart space than 3.3 miles, so the latter is a large scale chart, which shows more detail.

The traditional equipment used to plot courses are the parallel rulers for moving a course or bearing from the compass rose to your position on the chart—or to that of a landmark you have sighted—and dividers to measure the distance. Although these instruments and a pencil are all one really needs for plotting a course, a protractor is also very useful.

The protractor is laid on the chart so that one edge is parallel to the line of longitude. This gives a reference to true north. The center of the plastic square is a compass rose, and when you rotate the plastic arm to the desired course, it gives you a *True* course line. Some protractors feature a double compass rose; the second one can be rotated to adjust for variation, so the arm will show a *Magnetic* course. The advantage of such a protractor is that you don't have to correct the magnetic course continually when you are doing multiple plots in the same area of variation. It's like having a movable true and magnetic compass rose when there isn't one printed on the chart. See the discussion on the "The Compass: Variation and Deviation" later for more on magnetic courses.

Distances

For the purpose of navigation, the earth is considered to be a perfect sphere which is 21,600 nautical miles in circumference. The north pole is at the top of the globe and the south pole is at the bottom. Lines running north and south around the earth passing through these two imaginary poles are called meridians of longitude. The horizontal lines are parallels of latitude. Since a circle is 360 degrees, the parallel lines of latitude divide the earth into 360

Figure 87

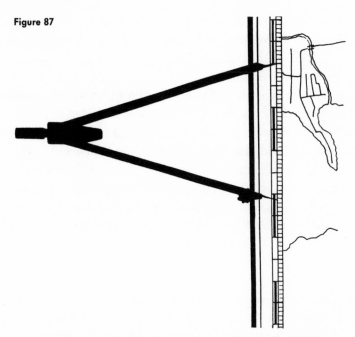

Measure distance by latitude: one minute equals one nautical mile

equal parts of 60 nautical miles each. There are 60 minutes to a degree, so one minute of latitude is equivalent to one nautical mile, which is somewhat longer than the statute mile we use ashore. A statute mile is 5,280 feet; a nautical mile is 6,076 feet.

To convert statute to nautical miles, multiply by 0.87; to convert nautical to statute miles, multiply by 1.2. It is the same when converting knots to miles per hour and vice versa.

To measure the distance between two points, we use a pair of dividers. Spread the dividers so a tip falls on each point. Now, place the dividers along the edge of the chart, as in Figure 87, and count the number of minutes of latitude (shown on many charts as alternate dark and light increments, each divided into tenths) that fall between the two tips. In this case it's 3.15 minutes, which converts to 3.15 nautical miles. If we sail that distance in one-half hour, we are sailing at 6.3 knots. A knot is one nautical mile sailed in one hour. Since most nautical charts are Mercator projections, a minute of latitude is a different distance at different latitudes. For this reason, measure the distance at the same latitude as your position.

If the distance you want to measure is greater than the spread attainable by the dividers, spread them along the edge of the chart a workable number of miles (minutes of latitude), say five miles from tip to tip. Then lay one tip on your starting point. The other will rest on a spot five miles down the course. Walk the dividers so that the first tip lays five miles farther down the course, and so on, until your destination is reached. It would be would be unusual for the last measurement to be exactly five miles, so the dividers will probably have to be pressed together so the tip rests on the destination, and this reduced distance can be measured on the edge of the chart.

To measure long distances where only a rough estimation of distance is needed, I use my hand. The spread between my thumb and little finger is almost exactly 10 miles on a 1:80,000 scale chart at the latitude of New York, so I can measure 70- or 80-mile distances quickly and within a few miles of accuracy this way. Check your own hand spread on different scale charts and different latitudes. This may work for you too.

Reading a Chart

On the chart, buoys are shown as small diamonds with a dot or circle underneath to indicate their exact location. A purple color around the circle means it's a lighted buoy. The color of the diamond, usually purple, black, green, black and white, or all white, corresponds to the color of the buoy. Next to the diamond is a number in quotes, such as "23." Anything in quotes on the chart is written on the buoy. Red buoys all have even numbers; black or green buoys, odd numbers. The chart will further describe the buoy as a bell, a gong, or a whistle.

For example, the information about Execution Rocks lighthouse in Long Island Sound reads: "R Bn Fl 10sec 62ft 16M HORN," which tells us that it is a radio beacon flashing every 10 seconds and is 62 feet above mean high sea level, it has 16-mile visibility, and sounds a horn during foggy weather.

To the left of Execution Rocks on the chart is a diamond that is half purple and half green. It has "RG" written near it followed by an "N." This means it's a red and green junction buoy with horizontal bands and the uppermost band is red, indicating the preferred side of the channel. Also, the "N" means that the preferred channel is as if the buoy were a nun (all red). The rule is that we leave red buoys to starboard as we enter a harbor or sail from a larger body of water into a smaller one. A simple phrase to help remember this fact is "Red Right Returning." Leave red buoys to starboard as you enter a harbor. If you sail in international waters, however, it's the reverse. Only the U.S. has this system of red to starboard.

There are also many other items of useful information on the chart. Note the colors: white areas are deep, navigable water; light blue areas are usually less than 20 feet deep and green areas are out of the water at low tide. The depths of the water are usually marked in feet at mean low water. Extreme low water could mean depths four or five feet less than shown on the chart, so take that into account.

Along the East Coast of the U.S. the tides are semi-diurnal: two high tides and two low tides in a 24-hour period. The tide height changes about 25 percent the first and last two hours of a tide, and about 50 percent during the middle two hours. Thus, if you're in an area with a six-foot tide, during the first two hours the depth will drop 1.5 feet; during the next two, three feet, and the last two, 1.5 feet. This is a factor to take into consideration if it's necessary to cross a bar or a shoal that you know is too shallow for your boat at dead low tide, yet has deep enough water at certain times during the tidal fall. The U.S. government prints the *Tide Tables* book listing the predicted times of high and low water and heights of tides. On some charts the depths (soundings) may be in meters or fathoms (six feet equals one fathom), so check the explanation on the chart itself.

Also shown on charts are depth contours. These contour lines connect all the areas of equal depth and are very useful in navigation when using a depth finder. On the beige (dry land) area of a chart, any object that could be helpful in obtaining a navigational fix is located and marked. Tanks, towers, conspicuous buildings, spires, and others are all pinpointed.

THE COMPASS: VARIATION AND DEVIATION

Variation is the angle between the geographic meridian (a line passing through both geographic poles, north and south) and the local magnetic meridian (a line passing through both magnetic poles). For instance, your compass will point to the magnetic north pole and at any given point this will be so many degrees to the west or east of true north, which points to the geographic north pole. In a few spots on earth there is no variation and your magnetic compass will point to true north. Your chart will have the number of degrees of variation written on it for the given area.

Figure 88 shows the number of degrees of variation in the northeast. Up in Greenland, for instance, the magnetic north pole is 35 to 40 degrees west of the true north pole as a compass direction. The angular difference is called variation. Printed on most charts is a compass rose. It's a circle drawn on the chart which is graduated in 360 degrees. The outer circle gives you the true north direction. The inner circle on the compass rose is called the

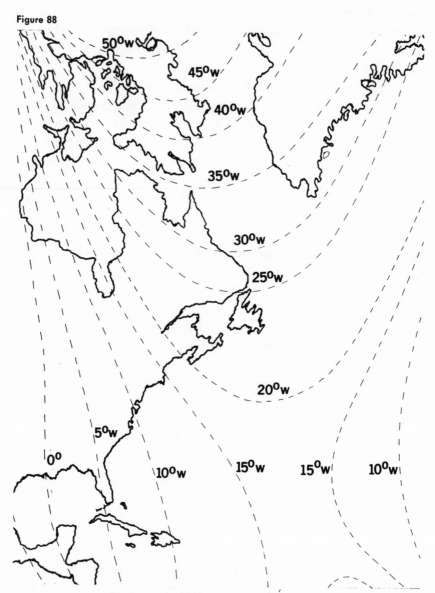

Figure 88

Variation charts show the amount at any location.

magnetic rose. The variation of the locality is easy to see by the angular difference of these two circles. The variation is also written at the center of the compass rose along with the annual rate of change. For example, "VAR 12° 45′W (1983) ANNUAL INCREASE 5′," reads, "the variation is twelve degrees and 45 minutes west as of the year 1983 with an annual increase of five minutes per year observed." You would have to apply the annual rate according to the date and age of the chart. This usually doesn't amount to much, but the careful navigator will at least be aware of this fact.

Deviation is the compass error caused by the metal on the boat that attracts the compass needle. On sailboats it rarely amounts to much, but it should be taken into account for accuracy even if it's only a degree. This error is measured when a compass adjuster "swings" your compass and, by the use of magnets, reduces the error caused by the magnetic pull of local metal on the boat. Deviation is the difference between the direction the compass needle should point—taking variation into account—and the direction is does point. The adjuster may not be able to correct all the deviation, so will make a deviation table. This will show you the deviation for various boat headings. If deviation is small enough to be of little concern—say, one or two degrees—then your compass error will be equal to variation alone. Then you can take all your bearings and courses in magnetic readings and, being careful to use only the inner circle of the compass rose (the magnetic rose), plot directly.

You can also determine your deviation in a less formal way and correct it yourself. To do this, place your boat next to a navigational aid with a known position, such as a buoy. Draw a line on your chart north from the buoy (allowing for variation) and note which landmark in the distance the line passes through. Point your boat at the same landmark and see what your compass reads. The difference is deviation. By adjusting the magnets on the side of the compass, reduce the deviation by one-half. Then head east and determine the deviation in that direction. Reduce it by one-half by adjusting the magnets on the front and back of the compass. Continue with south, then west, and then repeat the process until most of the deviation is gone.

Both variation and deviation errors are expressed as either easterly errors (the compass needle points to the east of north) or westerly errors (the compass needle points to the west of north). They can be combined. For instance, if the variation is 10 degrees E and the deviation is 2 degrees W, the net compass error is 8 degrees E.

By combining the errors we can use a very simple acronym to determine direction. CADET, which stands for Compass, Add East for True, simply means that if you have your compass heading, just add any easterly combined compass errors to obtain the true heading. By just remembering CADET, you'll find that all the rest falls into place logically. If you add easterly errors, you subtract westerly errors. If you have your true course from the chart and you want to know what compass course to steer, you reverse the procedure and subtract easterly errors and add westerly errors.

Let's say you have taken a bearing on a lighthouse to obtain your line of position. It bears 276 degrees. Your deviation is 1 degree E and your variation is 7 degrees E. Your chart does not have a magnetic compass rose, only a true one. You add 8 degrees to 276 degrees to get a true bearing of 284 degrees, which you plot on the chart.

Once you have determined your position, you set a new course for your boat. Walk the parallel rulers over to the true compass rose and determine that your true course is 093 degrees. What course will the helmsman steer using the compass aboard? With a compass error of 8 degrees E, we subtract that from 093 because we are going from true to compass, not compass to true as in the acronym CADET. The answer is 085 degrees.

DEAD RECKONING

Your "dead reckoning position" (DR) is the position determined by applying your course and distance from a previously determined position. There are a number of theories how it came to be called "dead" reckoning. One is that it's short for "deduced" reckoning because your position is being deducted from the input of your speed and distance. That "dead" was "ded" in middle English lends some credence to this theory. Another theory is that dead means exact as in "dead ahead." Dead reckoning, therefore, is as exact a reckoning of position as can be obtained with the existing variables.

A third and more intriguing possible derivation was that it came from the log used on early sailing ships called a chip log, which was made from a flat, triangular chip of wood with lines led from each corner that met a few feet away where they were attached to a single towline. The result was like a sea anchor that remained stationary when in the water. Along the towline were equally spaced knots and the line was coiled on a spindle much like that used to fly a kite. To measure the speed of the sailing ship, the chip log was put over the side and the line ran out. A 128-second sand glass was turned upside down and the number of knots that passed through the crewman's fingers by the time the sand ran out was equal to the number of nautical miles the ship was traveling per hour. So, though the knots originally were units of distance, they soon became known as units of speed with a built-in sense of "per hour," which is why we never say "knots per hour." If five knots passed through the crewman's fingers, to say "five knots per hour" would have been inaccurate because it was five knots in 128 seconds, the equivalent of five nautical miles in one hour. "Dead reckoning" most likely came from reckoning your position from the point where your chip log was dead in the water since you didn't measure your speed all the time, only when you wanted to update your position (or if there was a significant change in wind strength).

BEARINGS

Now you are ready to determine your position with a series of bearings transferred to your chart. In taking bearings in order to obtain a fix, the primary concern is to correctly identify a shore-based object or aid to navigation and locate this on the chart. A bearing taken on a building is useless to you unless the building is indicated on the chart. Study the chart, looking for prominent objects in your vicinity that are indicated on it, such as lighthouses, buoys, buildings, or tangents of a prominent landmark or hill. Try to find these by looking carefully at the shoreline or known objects (recently passed navigational aids are a good place to start, such as channel buoys). Pick at least two objects that have a good angular separation. Two objects 90 degrees apart would be perfect, but you rarely find this. When doing this, you have actually fixed the boat's position by "eyeball" navigation and you are just trying to verify your position by more positive means.

Quickly sight across your steering compass or use a hand-bearing compass to take your bearings. Observe the bearing closest to your bow or stern and the most distant landmarks first: they will change the slowest. Then take the bearing closest to your beam and the nearest buoy or landmark and note the time to the nearest minute. Write these down and plot these lines on the chart. Using parallel rulers or triangles, transfer the angles from the compass rose over to the object observed. Where these lines cross should be your position at the time of the fix, not at the present moment. You were there five minutes or so ago when you took the bearings. Make sure your write the time of the fix on the chart.

POSITIONING

Given a known latitude and longitude—such as from loran—you then pinpoint your position on the chart using parallel rulers and one-handed dividers. The latter are dividers with curved tops which, when squeezed, spread the tips of the dividers. Squeezing the legs farther down brings the tips closer together. Lay the edge of the parallel rulers along the line of a parallel of latitude and then walk them to the proper latitude along the side of the chart. Then measure with the dividers the longitude from a meridian line along the top or bottom of the chart and duplicate it along the parallel rulers. Press the point of the dividers into the chart at the proper spot hard enough to make a little indentation, which your pencil can find and mark.

PLOTTING

Since sailboats are subject to the vagaries of the wind, it's difficult to set a particular course and speed in order to end up at a desired destination on a given schedule. Of course, you can set an initial course and determine your estimated time of arrival (ETA) based on the speed you are making through the water adjusted for current, which gives your speed and course over the bottom. But if the wind dies you won't make the speed on which you based your calculations, and you'll spend longer in the current, which will require a course adjustment.

If the wind shifts, your speed may change because you're on a different point of sailing, either faster or slower, even if the wind velocity doesn't change. The wind may shift further so you no longer lay the course you originally desired and have to beat for your destination. In short, you are constantly updating your position as you sail along and are forever changing the course to your destination. The navigator who doesn't keep careful track of his DR plot will get lost.

First, we must start from a known position. We plot our course to the destination and after we have traveled a while we plot the distance we have covered on the course we've been steering and mark it as our dead reckoning position, noting also the time.

We use the 24-hour clock in navigation, so 1515 in the diagram is 3:15 p.m. Just add 12 hours to any p.m. time to get the 24-hour clock time. Always use four digits—9:18 a.m. is marked as 0918. Courses are always written with three digits—093 in the diagram. (If it was written simply "93," a person reading another's handwriting might mistake a line or a smudge and read "193" or "293.") We add "M" to the course to show it's magnetic or "T" for true. If you're using a chart with a magnetic compass rose and courses drawn on it are always magnetic, you may start deleting the M.

We usually know two or three variables when we try to determine our position. Since we started at a known location and kept track of our speed and time run in a particular direction, we can figure out the distance. We measure the distance from the first location in the direction we have been sailing and determine the second location. These are simple Speed-Time-Distance problems. Many people have difficulty remembering the equation, so we teach our students to jot down just one formula on a piece of paper or edge of the chart so it's handy for use. Commonly called the "D Street" method, the formula looks like this:

$$\frac{D}{ST}$$ where D is distance,
S is speeed and T is time

Now, put your thumb over the item you want to find and what remains is the formula to get there. For instance, you want to find speed. Cover S with your thumb and D/T remains. Divide distance by time to arrive at the result: speed.

In noting the time of your fixes or taking bearings, use minutes evenly divided by six. For example, use 06, 12, 24, 30, etc. for your time, because 06 minutes equals 0.1 hours, 12 minutes equals 0.2 hours, 18 minutes equals 0.3 hours, and so on. This makes your time even tenths of an hour and your speed, time, and distance formula becomes easier to work.

An hour or so after your first DR you update your position and discover three good landmarks or navigational aids on which to take bearings. In Figure 89, a radio tower marked on the chart bears 020 degrees, a buoy bears 170 degrees, and a point of land has just obscured another point of land behind it. I recommend you use the third example all the time, because you don't have to take a bearing and be subject to the possible errors caused by the compass swinging or by your parallel rulers slipping, etc. Just watch for two islands or points of land to come into line. Note the time. Then, on your chart, locate these objects and align them with a straightedge, draw a line, and there is your bearing; no compass required. It's a simple procedure, but very accurate and fast. Each of these bearings is a line of position (LOP) to the object. Where two or more LOP cross, you have a fix. Just mark a dot representing your position in the middle of the triangle, note the

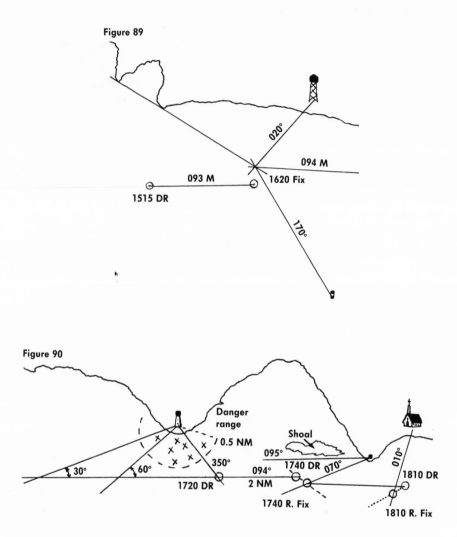

Figure 89

Figure 90

time, and plot a new course to your destination, in this case 094 degrees M. If you have a log that reads the number of miles you have been sailing, it's always good to note the log reading on the chart at the time of the fix. Also, if you have a depth sounder, check the depth of the water at the time of the fix and compare it to the depth shown on the chart for that location. This can confirm the accuracy of the fix. Use the depth sounder for all DR plots also.

As you continue along the coast, there's a point of land ahead with rocks off it. You want to be sure to be far enough off the point to avoid them. There are various ways to do this. One is to use a sextant on the object and consult tables that tell you your distance off. Another is to use a range finder.

However, you must know the height of the object, which isn't a problem with a navigational light because its height is usually written on the chart, or is at least listed in the government light list. Then describe an arc with a compass (as in Figure 90) that encompasses all the rocks and hazards.

Let's say it's half a mile in this case. Mark it down as a danger range of .5 NM (nautical miles) and make sure that your range-finder readings keep you outside this distance off the object.

If you do not have a range finding device aboard, there are other ways to stay clear of the rocks. Keep careful track of your course and speed. Plot a bearing on a landmark such as the lighthouse in Figure 90. If you know you're sailing six knots and it's been five minutes between two bearings, you will have sailed half a mile. After five minutes of sailing, take and plot a second bearing. Place your dividers so the points are half a mile apart. Set your parallel rulers on the compass course of your boat's heading and run them across the two bearings until the dividers show the bearings to be half a mile apart. Then draw your course line and see if you clear the rocks. Remember that an adverse current means you won't have sailed half a mile in five minutes and you could very well be closer to shore than you estimate. In a fair current the opposite is true.

Figure 90 shows a method sometimes used to determine distance off an object. A bearing (called a "relative bearing") is taken relative to the bow of the boat. Let's say it's 30 degrees. When that bearing becomes double—60 degrees—the distance you have sailed between the two sightings equals the distance to the object from your boat when you took the second bearing. It's called "doubling the angle." Another is called "bow and beam" bearings. Take a bearing when the object is 45 degrees off the bow of the boat. When the object is abeam, 90 degrees from the bow, the distance run from the time of taking the first bearing equals the distance to the object when abeam.

Continuing along the shore in Figure 90, you have taken a DR position at 1720 after sailing an hour from the previous fix. You have combined it with a bearing on the lighthouse of 350 degrees M, but it's not a fix because it's only one LOP—not two or more—and you know there's a shoal that you must stay to seaward of, so you draw a line on the chart from the light on the next point that just clears the shoal. This line turns out to be 095 degrees M and is called the "danger bearing." Any bearing we subsequently take of the light that is 094 degrees M or lower keeps you clear of the shoal. If you take a bearing and it's 096 degrees M or higher, you are inshore of the 095 degrees danger bearing and could possibly hit the shoal.

You are still sailing six knots. Twenty minutes later at 1740 you take a bearing on the light and find it bears 070 degrees M. You know you have sailed a course of 094 degrees M and have sailed 2 nautical miles in 20 minutes. Your DR doesn't cross with the new bearing. Advance your first bearing 2 miles so it runs through the 1740 DR and is parallel (350 degrees) to the first bearing (the dotted line). The point where it intersects your bearing on the second object is called "a running fix." Mark it "1740 R Fix" and continue your 094 degrees heading from that new fix. Half an hour (three nautical miles) later at 1810, you take a bearing on a church ashore and find it to be 010 degrees M. Your 1810 DR doesn't coincide with the bearing. Advance your second bearing (070 degrees M) three miles to the 1810 DR (the dotted lines) and the point it crosses the bearing on the church is your 1810 running fix.

OTHER FIXES

Keep in mind some of the various types of fixes available to you:

1. *Radio direction finder and depth sounder.* Along some coasts the depth contours are fairly steep and roughly parallel to the coast. By combining an RDF bearing (described later) that's relatively perpendicular to the shore with a depth sounding that's roughly parallel to the shore, we get an approximate fix.
2. *Bearing and distance.* Take a bearing on a landmark on the chart and measure the distance from it by Telefix or other device. The bearing is a line of position; the distance crosses it, giving a fix.
3. *A visual bearing and distance off determined by contour heights.* All charts show the topography of the land masses. The height and steepness of the hills is shown by numbers and topographical contours.

Until I started to look closely at these contours on the chart, many sections of the shoreline looked like many others. When the contour lines are close together, indicating a steep slope, it's quite often easy to spot the hill it represents. The heights of the peaks are usually marked on the chart. Of two nearby summits, one may be 400 feet high and the other 600 feet high. When you look at the shore, the perspective of the two summits to one another can give you a good idea of your geographical relationship to them.

Use the known height of the peak with a distance measuring device to get the distance off. Then cross the bearing line of position at that distance to get a fix.

HELPFUL NAVIGATION TIPS

Since the lubber line of the compass is in line with your boat's bow, a simple and accurate bearing can be taken just by pointing the boat at the landmark or buoy whose bearing is desired. This works well even if you have to alter your course slightly to place the object dead ahead.

Another secret to safe navigation is to be very skeptical of your work. Once a fix is plotted, check it by looking around to see if it makes sense. According to your position, do nearby objects appear in the proper perspective? Is that island really on your starboard bow as your fix shows? This is the type of reasoning you follow to check yourself.

Nothing beats reading the number right off a buoy if it's close enough in order to verify that it's the right one. Once you've navigated a while in fog, low visibility, and current, buoys that seem to confirm your position often turn out to be wrong ones on closer inspection. If you don't check the number or otherwise confirm your position, you might make a course alteration on the assumption that your navigation is correct and really end up in trouble. If you aren't sure, quickly plot a second fix to check the first, and so on. With practice you will gain confidence in your work and will more easily be able to catch mistakes before they can place you in danger.

It's a good idea to circle danger areas on the chart near your expected course, particularly ones in unusual spots such as a shoal surrounded by miles of deep navigable water. Also, circle the range of lights ahead of time so when you see a light you'll be able to eliminate immediately the ones that are out of range: for a 10-mile light, describe an arc with a compass/pencil with a 10-mile radius from the light. When you see a light and you aren't sure if it's a near or distant one (and in fog sometimes it's difficult to tell), squat down to look at it. You will still see the near one, but the distant one will disappear because of waves and the earth's curvature.

Another tip: Sometimes the characteristics of a light—or other information on a chart—is in very small print and hard to read. If there's no magnifying glass handy, use one side of the binoculars held upside down. Make sure the eyepiece is very close to the print and your eye is right next to the large lens. The binoculars act as a magnifying glass when used in this way. Try it, it really works.

CURRENT

Current comes with tidal depth changes, and is an important factor in navigation when the current velocity becomes a large percentage of the boat's speed. Therefore, it's particularly a factor in sailing. A sailboat averaging five knots may be sailing in a current 20 to 40 percent (one to two knots) of its speed. The speed of the current is called its "drift" and the direction to which it flows is its "set." For instance, sailing in a two-knot westerly current, you have a two-knot drift and westerly set.

The *Tidal Current Tables* printed by the U.S. government give the maximum flood and ebb current and the time when the current changes direction. Tidal current charts are printed for 12 bodies of water on the east and west coasts, and are very handy in navigating and planning a cruise.

Let's say we locate our present position on the chart and find that the current is 1.0 knots in a direction of about 251 degrees. We transfer this information to a chart as in Figure 91. We are sailing from A to B. The course is 353 degrees M. First we draw line AC one mile long, indicating the effect of the current on the boat in one hour. Next we take the boat speed (five knots in this case) and describe arc D to intersect course line AB at point E. Line CE will be the course to steer (006 degrees M), and A to E will be our progress toward our destination in one hour, our speed made good in knots. If the current velocity or direction changes over the period of time it takes us to reach our destination, we can use an average current for our calculations.

Rather than transfer all these courses over to our position on the chart, the same course to steer can be determined by drawing the current diagram right on the compass rose in the same manner. Figure 92 shows how it's done.

When your DR includes allowances for current and leeway, most navigators call it an "estimated position" and mark it "EP" on the chart with the time. Some navigators even draw two separate plots — one DR and one EP — until a fix can be obtained.

Figure 91

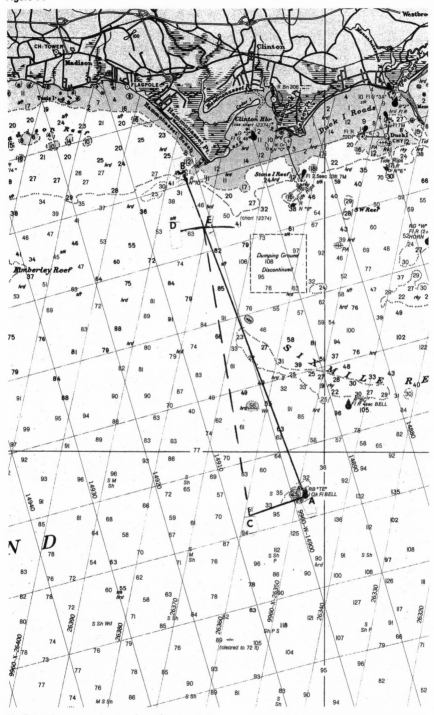

To determine course to steer in a given current:
1. Draw course AB.
2. Draw current direction and velocity AC.
3. Describe arc equal to boat speed CD.

4. CD is the course to steer and AD is the speed made good over the bottom.

Figure 92

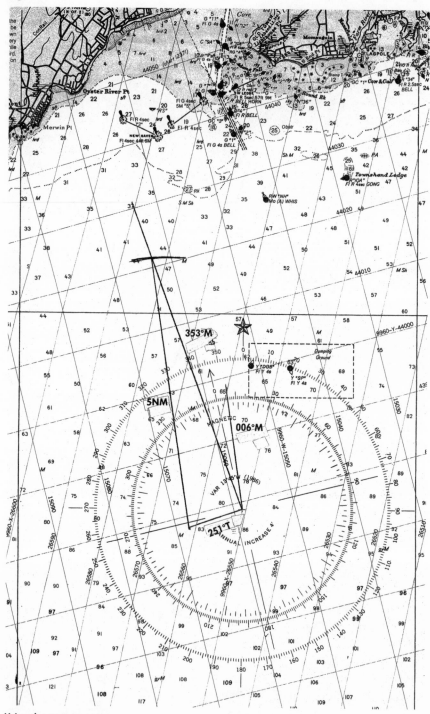

Using the compass rose:
1. Draw course: 353°M.
2. Draw current (251°T, 1.0 NM).
3. Describe arc representing speed (5 NM).
4. Draw line parallel to it from center of rose.
5. Read course to steer (006°M).

RADIO DIRECTION FINDER

In restricted visibility, such as rain or fog, or when distances are too great to take visual bearings, a radio direction finder (RDF) may be of use. An RDF is a radio receiver with a directional antenna using low frequencies of 190 to 500 kilohertz (kHz). The location and the characteristics of such beacons are usually found right on the nautical chart. Marker radio beacons mark the location of such things as harbors and breakwaters for homing purposes. Major radio beacons are used for fixing your position. You use the antenna to locate where the transmitting station bears from you (its bearing). One radio bearing will give you an LOP, and two more will give you a fix.

However, there are some errors to watch for. One is called "night effect." An RDF is apt to be unreliable at night. Also, there is RDF deviation, which is caused by the metal on the boat. Unlike compass deviation, RDF deviation cannot be corrected, but it is possible to determine how much there is by checking RDF bearings from a known position.

LORAN, SATNAV, GPS

These offspring of modern technology are marvelous gadgets. They permit you to pinpoint your position, which is usually read in longitude and latitude directly off the instrument. You can program numerous waypoints—buoys or geographical spots—along the way to your final destination. You can ask for the bearing and distance to the next waypoint and the instrument will also tell you your speed over the bottom, your cross track error (how much off course you are), what effect seas and current are having on your course and speed, and your ETA (estimated time of arrival). These are constantly updated.

In short, instruments are wonderful, so who needs to navigate? I once sailed a 30-mile, around-the-buoys race on our 54-foot ocean racer without a navigator, and I steered the whole race. I just programmed the race marks in the loran before the start and had continual readings on their range and bearing all the way around the course.

But the problem is, these instruments make navigators lazy. If you suddenly lose battery power or your electronic instruments malfunction, you could be in trouble if you're entirely dependent on them and have not been recording and advancing your position on the chart. You will have no record of the boat's course and speed from the last known position. You will be lost. Also, for lack of practice, you will probably have lost the ability to navigate by other means to find out just where you are.

Problems can also arise when the careless navigator gets a bearing (course) for a destination from the loran but neglects to plot it on the chart to make sure the course doesn't pass across a shoal, ignore buoys, or even pass over land. Obviously, the loran doesn't know whether or not there's land between you and your next waypoint; it only knows the direction and distance of the waypoint. You must check with the chart. While most navigators carefully check the course on the chart initially, some fail to recheck it against the chart later, when, due to leeway, current, wind, or helmsmanship, the instrument indicates a different course to the destination. This new course may, in fact, lead right over a shoal, which you won't know unless you check the chart again. Such sloppiness has put more than one boat on the rocks.

The point is that such instruments should really be used to check your piloting and they should be relied upon only as backup, not as your only source of navigational expertise or information.

The problem of over-reliance on navigational instruments came home to me on the 1987 Fastnet Race on the 81-ft. maxi *Nirvana*. We were on the relatively long open-water stretch from Lands End, England, to the Fastnet Rock lighthouse off the coast of Ireland. I came on watch and asked the course as I took over the helm. "Two-eight-six," answered the helmsman whom I relieved. I had been steering 286 degrees for an hour and a half when the navigator told me the course was 299 degrees. Evidently the other watch had not wanted to waken the navigator to check the course, so a crew member took a look at the SatNav, which gives the course to the waypoint in true compass headings rather than magnetic. That 13-degree change of course was the difference between setting a spinnaker or sailing with the jib. When we settled down on the correct course, we immediately set a spinnaker and picked up 1.5 knots of boat speed. This could have been done a couple of hours earlier if someone hadn't thought navigation had become so simple that all you did was read the numbers off a black box.

Loran (Long Range Navigation) has been with us longer than SatNav (Satellite Navigation) or—the newest—GPS (Global Positioning System). Loran was developed during World War II, but by today's standards is hardly "long range." While GPS is becoming available worldwide, loran has numerous areas where the signal is weak or unreliable, such as the Caribbean and Bermuda. Only in the past few years has loran become cheap enough, compact enough, and versatile enough to be found on most small cruising sailboats.

Loran works on a system of signals transmitted from a master station and secondary stations. The instrument measures the time delay of receipt from each station. It's really just a sophisticated clock. The time delay (TD) between stations is shown on charts as a "loran overlay," and you plot the lat/lon positions indicated on your loran on the overlay grid. Where they cross is your position.

One drawback to loran is the unreliability and weakness of many of the signals. Signal weakness can result from your distance from the transmitting stations, alternators on your boat's engines, fluorescent lights, precipitation static from weather fronts, and sky wave interference near sunrise and sunset. Fortunately, we can check the signal strength with the signal-to-noise ratio (SNR), and most instruments will blink when the SNR is too low. So, although we won't be misled and put ourselves in the wrong location, neither can we put ourselves in the correct location when such conditions exist.

Along comes SatNav to help with the problem. Satellite navigation instruments pick up the signals from satellites that are on a polar orbit. As they pass overhead, the instrument receives the signal and translates it into a position based upon the course and speed of the vessel programmed into the instrument. It takes about 20 minutes per pass, so an error of up to two miles or so can be made if the course and speed are input incorrectly.

Also, SatNav is sensitive to "height of eye" (the height of the antenna), so if the installation is faulty, other errors will occur. Moreover, you have to wait for a satellite to pass overhead to obtain a single fix. Since the satellites are in polar orbits, the closer you are to the poles, the more often you can get fixes in a given period. In mid-latitudes it can be 40 to 80 minutes between fixes; near the equator, up to eight to 10 hours. So, although SatNav can provide a fix all over the world compared to loran's limited areas, you have to wait for it.

The next generation of electronic navigation, GPS, is impressive. It gives continuous fixes anywhere in the world within a 30-ft. accuracy. In fact, some models give an accuracy of 10 feet, and you get an updated fix every second instead of waiting 40 minutes, as with SatNav. There is even a hand-held model. The prices of SatNav and GPS are about the same. Loran is cheaper, but has been around much longer. I expect GPS—which runs $3,000 to $8,000—will come down in price over the next few years.

Just remember that all these devices are dependent upon battery power and if that gives out they're unusable, so in case of a power failure, you had better know backup methods of navigation for your area.

THE LOG

The ship's logbook is the key source of plotting information for the navigator. Rather than plot all the time, the crew records the course and speed of the boat in the log, so the navigator can update the information every few hours. Close to land and on short trips, course and speed are recorded every half hour, while on longer trips and at sea, every hour is sufficient. You might ask how you can give a navigator a course and speed for a half-hour period when you have been swinging 20 degrees in following seas and surging from five to 10 knots. The answer is to give your best judgment of the average for the period. You will be amazed at how accurate the results are when you finally get a fix, even after 10 or 12 hours of averaging. A modern electronic log records the nautical miles covered. Record the miles run in the logbook every half hour or hour. This backs up your estimate of speed.

When the navigator decides to update the boat's position, he or she can either plot each log entry or average them together. Averaging will give a fairly accurate course, but not distance. The plot is recorded on the chart with the time.

Chapter VII

RACING TACTICS

Sailboat racing is challenging. To race well takes a combination of intelligence, canniness, strength, stamina, concentration, and persistence. These translate into the two essential components of winning: boat speed and tactics.

WHAT ARE TACTICS?

If we accept the broad dictionary definition of tactics, "the means to an end" (which is to win), we can include boat speed in this definition. This makes tactics the most important single factor in successful sailboat racing.

Let's take a narrower view of tactics that eliminates some of the elements of boat speed—sail trim, sail shape, spinnaker work, tuning, crew positions, reefing, helmsmanship, and others. If races were held against the clock instead of against other boats, these factors would contribute to a winning effort. We'll consider tactics as "the means to win in proximity with other sailboats," as opposed to winning against the clock. By this definition certain types of boats are sailed less "tactically" than others.

In many ways sailboat racing tactics are constantly changing and evolving just as society changes and evolves. In fact, many recent changes in racing reflect the change in society's attitudes. There was a time when sailboat racing was a casual Saturday afternoon contest between gentlemen. If a sailboat hit a racing mark, the skipper retired from the race, period. As the attitude toward racing became more competitive and winning more important, some skippers decided to take the chance of disqualification rather than retire after hitting a mark.

The injustice of this came to a head during the 1968 Olympics in Mexico when Carl van Duyne, U.S. Finn class representative, hit a mark during a race. No one saw the accident, but Carl did the honorable thing—he retired. A few races later, a competitor from another country brushed a mark with his sail. Other Finn sailors, and even the international judge stationed at the mark, saw it. The sailor did not retire, was protested, and was not disqualified because he vehemently denied hitting the mark. Since the rule depended on the honor system, the competitor's word outweighed observations by others.

This incident, more than any other, led to the change in the penalty for hitting a racing mark. No longer must a boat retire or be disqualified. Instead, she may do penalty circles and continue the race.

The incident is, however, symptomatic of both a gradual deterioration of the moral fiber of society and a changing attitude toward the importance of winning. Many of today's sailors seem to believe that winning is more important than abiding by the rules. One youngster at an Optimist Pram championship was asked why he had brought two rudders. His unabashed reply was that the second one was designed for sculling when the wind is light. Sculling—the rapid back-and-forth movement of the rudder to propel the boat forward—is strictly illegal, but it is in widespread use in dinghy-type sailboats.

Also illegal are rocking (rolling the boat from side to side), pumping (trimming the sails rapidly and easing them slowly) and ooching (moving crew weight forward and aft). Some of the foregoing are legal within certain limiting parameters when used briefly to promote surfing or when, under a rules option, the race committee raises a prescribed signal. But their use to propel the boat around the race course in light air is in flagrant violation of the rules.

Another maneuver in this category is "roll-tacking," which was originally developed to improve the speed a small boat could carry through a tack. In theory it is similar to trying to fly a kite on a windless day. As long as you are running with the kite string pulling the kite, it will rise in the air. The forward movement creates a breeze and, in turn, this creates lift. When you stop running, the kite falls. Similarly, if we can create wind by swinging the mast and the sails, the sails will stay full and create lift even if there is little or no actual wind. To do this, as the boat turns the crew hikes out hard, swinging the mast and sails up and over. The sails stay full even though the bow has passed through the eye of the wind. The crew then leaps across the boat and hikes out hard on the new windward side, swinging the mast back up toward the wind as the boat settles down on the new tack. Thus, the sails luff only for an instant instead of throughout the tack. New rules limit the amount of swinging allowed.

Once the technique of roll-tacking was perfected, however, it was soon discovered that doing it with precision and intensity numerous times in succession could propel a dinghy upwind in light air much faster than normal sailing, and its use for this purpose was also declared illegal.

Repeated jibing is another illegal maneuver. It is common knowledge that a good pull on the mainsheet in light air during a jibe will scoot a light boat forward faster than just letting the boom come across on its own. Some years ago, I was crewing a Thistle in the midwinters at St. Petersburg Yacht Club. We were sailing downwind toward the finish line in first place, with the second-place boat's bow even with our transom. Suddenly he executed two fast, violent jibes, which propelled him to a first-place tie with us. Although we felt this was morally wrong, his argument was that he decided to go for the other end of the finish line and then changed his mind. It's easy to find some justification for a series of jibes or tacks. This situation, though, has become exaggerated, with some competitors in dinghies doing 15 to 20 roll-tacks from the starting line to get ahead of the others.

Although these maneuvers are all essentially illegal, they are still widely used, and the result is that dinghies should now be taken off the list of "tactical" sailboats. If one tacks to cover another, the latter can, by rocking, pumping, sculling, unweighting (bouncing up and down), or torquing (bearing off, heeling, and hiking out hard as he comes back up to course), nullify the effectiveness of the (legal) cover.

How far will some sailors go to win? At a recent regatta it was discovered that a number of boats had been sabotaged. Spreader bolts had been sawed halfway through so that in a heavy wind masts would be lost. The hope was that vandals had done the damage because no one could believe that another competitor could or would stoop so low. The truth has not yet been uncovered.

A few years ago two teenagers were racing a small centerboard boat. After numerous capsizes in heavy winds one of them could no longer get back into the boat after righting it. He slipped away and drowned. It was discovered later that the teenagers had been carrying lead weights in their pockets to make them heavier for hiking out, in total contravention of the rule against movable ballast.

Just before the start of an ocean race in England in 1971, an Italian yacht, late for the start, was powering at full speed toward the starting line with only a minute to go before the gun. We raised a protest flag since the crew should have turned off her engine—or at least gone into neutral gear—five minutes before the start. More surprising than the rule infringement was their reaction to our protest. They couldn't believe it, as if they considered the rule a minor one made to be broken. One wonders if they also use their engine on the race course when it's calm and there's no other yacht around to spot them.

These are examples of incidents that are clearly illegal. The problem is that propulsion such as "pumping" is now considered immoral rather than illegal, and that justifies its use in many racer's eyes these days, when winning is often considered more important than mere morality.

In this chapter we are dealing only with legal racing tactics, on and off the racecourse. These include not only boathandling tactics but psychological tactics as well, which are a part of every sport.

For instance, say you are being closely covered by another boat, and you want to split tacks with her. Yet every tack you make is matched by the other boat either on your wind or close to it. Just keep tacking. Never give up after two tacks just because you think she's going to match every tack you make. Usually you'll break away after the third tack, when she decides that a tacking duel with you is not worth the distance lost to other boats.

Psychological tactics are used off the racecourse, too. Before a big series, when most everyone is somewhat nervous, competitors often bait one another. One might comment how tired another looks; one crew member might try to get a rival skipper drunk the night before; a competitor rubs a funny-looking potion from an unmarked bottle on the bottom of his boat before launching and claims it reduces skin friction 30 percent, and so on.

Bantering designed to put a competitor on guard or to break his concentration while racing is a reasonable psychological tactic. For example, the legendary Arthur Knapp was being beaten to the finish line by a particularly nervous skipper in first place who kept looking back to see if Arthur was gaining. Every time he looked back Arthur slapped the side of the boat or spun a winch, which so rattled the skipper ahead that Arthur managed to squeak by him and cross the finish line in first place.

Another tactic along the line of Arthur Knapp's was that of a very good downwind skipper who would engage nearby skippers in conversation to distract them from steering well. He had no trouble talking and steering so he invariably gained.

During an SORC race, *Heritage,* a much larger boat, was to leeward of *Sleuth* without luffing rights on a reach. She came up, was blanketed, fell off, and tried unsuccessfully to break through farther to leeward. She came up again, and the crew tried to distract me with shouting and close-quarters maneuvering off our lee rail. They yelled that I was illegally coming down on them even though I was steering a steady compass course. I called back that if they luffed me once more they were ending up in a protest meeting and I then ignored them to concentrate on steering. Shortly, they dropped back and went past our stern to windward of us.

After finishing races, some skippers sail very hard back to port to demoralize others. If a skipper and crew appear to be so fresh after a long race, what fantastic physical shape they must be in, and how can they be beaten in the next race? During the 1976 Olympic trials I saw Dennis Conner and Con Findlay planing back to the harbor in a fresh breeze with spinnaker *after* a race. Con was flat out on the Tempest's trapeze, pumping the spinnaker sheet, and Dennis was aggressively playing every wave and hiking out hard in every gust. Their competitors must have been impressed at the strength, agility, and intensity of the two. It certainly could mean a threat in a head-to-head confrontation in the next race.

Among other tactics are practical jokes, and if you let yourself be taken in by them, you deserve the consequences. Once, during a Mallory Cup eliminations we switched boats with another crew for a second race, as is common practice in this type of round-robin series. The spinnaker appeared to be prepared, neatly packed in a container as if the previous crew had forgotten they were to switch boats. Our skipper was a little smug that a competitor was so "out to lunch" as to do our work for us. Since the foredeck was my responsibility, I wasn't about to set a spinnaker I hadn't packed, so I dumped it out of the container. Underneath the neatly folded covers of the sail on top, the spinnaker was tied in knots. Although I can't imagine doing that to another competitor, I'd only have had myself to blame if taken in by such shenanigans.

Now let's turn to some of the more usual tactics sailors use. But first, to understand tactics as they are discussed, it's necessary to thoroughly understand the terms used. The following list will be an easy reference when needed.

GLOSSARY

Backwind: An area of turbulent airflow astern of a sailboat

Barging: A windward boat illegally taking room to start to leeward of a starting mark

Break a cover: Get free from a covering boat

Blanket zone: An area of badly disturbed airflow directly downwind of a windward boat

Covering: Staying between the competition and the destination

Covering from behind: Staying in the same wind and sea conditions as the boat ahead so he does not get away

Current stick: A stick, weighted to float vertically, with which to estimate the current direction and strength

False tack: Start to tack, then abort it when head-to-wind

Favored end: The upwind end of the starting line

General recall: When all the starters are recalled for a new start either because of a timing error or too many boats are over too early to be identified

Header: Wind moves towards the bow

Layline: The imaginary line that takes a close-hauled boat directly to the windward mark without either overstanding or having to tack again

Lift: Wind moves towards the stern

Lines of equal position: An imaginary line perpendicular to the wind direction. Any boat on it is as upwind as another on the same line and is even with the other

Luffing: Altering course toward the wind

Ooching: Sudden movement of crew weight forward or aft to propel a small boat

Overstanding: Sailing past the layline and having to reach off for the mark after tacking

Pumping: Persistent or rapidly repeated trimming and releasing of any sail

Rocking: Movement of crew weight or adjustment of the sails or centerboard to create persistent rolling of the boat

Roll-tacking: Using crew movement to improve the speed a sailboat carries through a tack and reducing the period of luffing to a minimum

Safe leeward: Lead boat has a "safe leeward" on boat on her weather quarter because the wind bent aft by the lead boat's sails creates a header for the windward boat, who cannot bear away because of proximity of lead boat

Sculling: Repeated forceful movement of the helm back and forth to propel the boat

Shooting the wind: Heading the sailboat directly into the wind and drifting to a stop

Splitting tacks: Sailing close-hauled on one tack while the competition is on the other tack

Torquing: Rolling the boat to windward, thereby increasing the apparent wind in the sails

Unweighting: Bouncing crew weight up and down to gain advantage in waves

Windward (weather) mark: The mark that ends the beat.

It is also essential that the reader study and eventually acquire a thorough knowledge of the racing rules. Send for your own copy of them and always carry it with you when racing. For your copy of *The Yacht Racing Rules,* write to the United States Yacht Racing Union, Inc., P.O. Box 209, Goat Island Marina, Newport, RI 02840.

THE START

The best incentive there is to win a sailboat race is to get a good start, and to do that you must follow three rules: (1) be on the line at the instant of the starting signal; (2) be at the best location on the line; and (3) have clear air.

The first rule requires a good sense of timing. There are usually 10 minutes in a starting sequence. Under one frequently used system the committee boat hoists a white "warning" shape (often a canvas cylinder) 10 minutes before the start; it is lowered six minutes before. At five minutes, the blue "preparatory" shape goes up; at one minute before the start it comes down. At the start a red shape is displayed. Be sure to begin your timing when the shape goes up, rather than at the gun. However, if the line is long and crowded and you cannot see the shape, watch for the smoke from the gun and start your timing then; the sound takes too long to reach you to be a reliable starting signal. If you miss a time signal, be sure to restart your timer when the next shape comes down. Most crews use a stopwatch to keep track of the time elapsed, but some also use a tape-recorded countdown. Of the two types of stopwatches, sweep second hand or digital, the latter is adequate if a crew is calling out the time remaining, but in my opinion, a sweep second hand gives a better feeling of the passage of time. It's usually best to have two stopwatches going in case one fails or is damaged.

It is very important to keep track of the color of the signals (shapes) and the order of start of the various classes; otherwise you may miss your start. Dick Deaver of North Sails once used a competitor's confusion over the starting sequence to his advantage. He was in a match race series—pairs of boats racing against each other—starting at 10-minute intervals. Dick was paired against Australian Jim Hardy of 12-Meter fame. For some reason, Jim thought the starting interval was a five-minute sequence and maneuvered himself into a very fine position relative to Dick just before the five-minute gun. Realizing that Jim was planning to start five minutes early, Dick played along. He started along with Jim, but in a very poor position. Dick then initiated a tacking duel to make Jim think that the race was on. By tacking well, Jim was lengthening his lead on every tack. Eventually, at 2½-minutes to go to the correct gun, with Jim Hardy well ahead, Dick broke off the tacking duel, turned back to the line and started all alone at the correct signal. By the time Jim figured it out and sailed back to start correctly, he was a long way behind.

Dick emphasizes that Jim took it as a good sport, but this incident shows that even the finest sailors in the world can make mistakes.

Knowing the time remaining before the gun does not necessarily get you to the line on time. I find that skippers often sail too far away from the line, misjudging the time it will take to get back. On *Sleuth* I use a three-minute pattern: I am near the line with three minutes to go to the start. After sailing away from the line for half that time, I will still have over a minute to go on final approach. This is enough time for even a 54-footer to pick up speed. Most other boats use a longer pattern—four to six minutes. Often, they are coming back on starboard to start while I'm still going away. If it looks to me as though the first boats are very early, I let them go by and find a hole to leeward and ahead of the later boats that appear to have timed it correctly. If we all appear to be early as we approach the line, I have the option of luffing them to slow the boat down. If, however, we're late, I have room to fall off to drive the boat faster.

With a close-hauled start, it's important to know just what heading you can make on each tack. Let's say you want to start on starboard tack at point A, as in Figure 93. You have determined previously that you can sail 330 degrees close-hauled on starboard. As you sail away from the line, you take compass headings on the committee boat. If you find that the bearing has changed from 020 degrees to 350 degrees too quickly, it means you will pass the 330-degree course well before you need to jibe or to tack back for the line. This will possibly place you in a dangerous barging position (for an explanation of barging, see page 00). Fall off to run more parallel to the 330-degree course, to converge with it more slowly. You are now sailing farther away from the line, so you will have to turn back earlier than before to compensate for the slower speed when close-hauled rather than reaching. In addition, you will have to adjust your course for other boats to avoid having

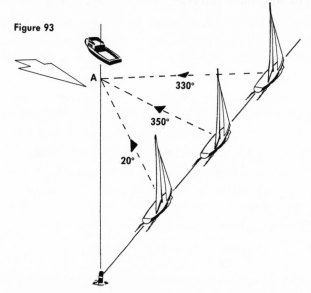

Figure 93

330°

350°

20°

Take bearings to the committee boat so you don't get too far past the close-hauled course to the line.

Figure 94

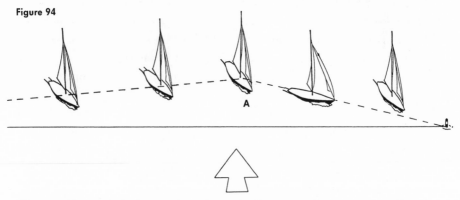

The crew of boat A thinks they're right on the starting line. Starting line "sag" is a problem of perspective.

them either directly to windward of you when you return or on your leeward quarter, where they can force you over the line early. All these course adjustments mean changes in your timing. For me, it is easier to judge the time it will take to cover a short distance than a long one, which is an additional reason for a three-minute pattern. In smaller boats, which accelerate more rapidly, the pattern may be even shorter. (In dinghies and catamarans there is hardly a discernible time pattern. You just choose your spot on the starting line, sit there with sails luffing until seconds before the gun sounds, trim in, and go.)

This pattern, correctly undertaken, will get you near the line at the gun. The next problem is to know how close to the line you are. There is often a large sag in a line of boats starting, because skippers often judge the location of the starting line by their relation to other boats. Consider the skipper of boat A in Figure 94. He looks toward the race committee boat and thinks that two competitors are right on the line to windward of him. A glance toward the buoy makes him feel that the nearest boat to leeward may be over the line early and is reaching off. The other boats appear to be right on the line. The truth is that all the boats are well behind the starting line. The skipper of boat A is the victim of a mistaken perspective, since he cannot look at both ends of the line at the same time.

The solution is to find a way to look in only one direction to know how close you are to the line. This is done by taking a range. The most common way to do that is to line up the starting line with a point on shore. Whenever I crew, I urge the skipper to get a range before the start.

Figure 95

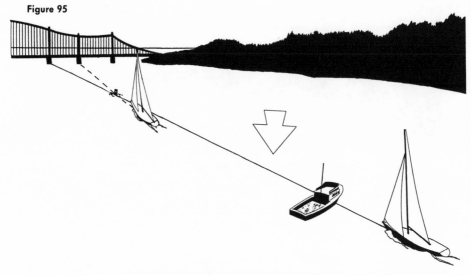

Get a range of the starting line with a landmark.

One time, when sailing a series with an internationally known skipper, I was having trouble getting the point across. He said, "Okay, Steve, we're on the line now, and the buoy is lined up with that outer bridge span." My response was that even with the skipper's long and varied experience, he was only guessing that we were on the line when he said so. We sailed around behind the committee boat, and while reaching toward it, we lined up the starting line flag with the buoy. The true range was the buoy in line with the inner span (see Figure 95). My skipper was flabbergasted to discover that he was so far off in his judgment. The bridge was an ideal range, but you can use anything along the shore, such as a roof or a tree. You must remember as you approach the line that your range was taken from the cockpit. Allow for the fact that your bow will reach the line before you are on the range. On large boats such as maxis, a spotter on the bow will call the time to the tactician or helmsman. The range can be taken reaching down the line when the boat is positioned so the centerline and backstay line up with the committee boat flag while the bow is lined up with the buoy. When the boat is at this position, take a range on the shore behind the buoy.

The timing and distance from the line can be guessed by how quickly the bearing changes along the shore. The farther you are from the buoy, the slower the bearing changes, as shown in Figure 96. If the bearing is changing fast, be careful not to poke your bow over the line. If it's changing slowly, you can get quite close to the cockpit range you took and still be safe.

Figure 96

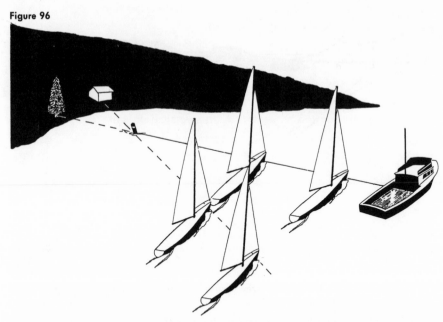

The closer you are to your range marker, the buoy in this case, the faster the range changes.

Figure 97

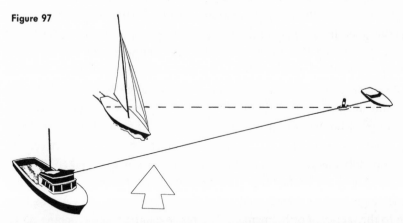

A race committee stake boat can also be used as a range if anchored on the extension of the starting line.

Always remember that the race committee may move the buoy between starts of various classes, or change the position of the committee boat. Since it's difficult to get a range in the last five minutes before the start, watch to see if the line is being changed. An outboard motorboat puttering around near the buoy, a person on the bow of the committee boat near its anchorline, general recalls in previous starts, or a bunching of the fleet at one end of the line in earlier starts are all indicative that the line may be adjusted, negating the range you took.

Often the race committee places a stake boat at the far end of a long starting line to aid in calling the boats that are over early and are blocked from the view of the committee boat. If done properly, the stake boat will anchor right on the extension of the line, and one crew member will sight the line toward the committee boat through a vertical pole or mast as in Figure 97. You can use the buoy and the vertical pole as a ready-made range.

At the committee-boat end of the line there also is a ready-made range. One person sights the line from behind the vertical mast or pole that constitutes the committee-boat end of the line (see Figure 98). If you are near that end, it's very easy to tell if you are on his line of sight. At the start of the 1979 transatlantic race from Marblehead to Ireland, I reached up on starboard tack to leeward of the fleet. *Alliance,* to windward, possibly could have blanketed us, but she was killing speed because the helmsman thought he was early. I could see that the man "calling" the line was sighting far ahead of our bow, and I pushed on ahead. This allowed me to hit the line right at the gun, get the best start in the class, work out in front of *Alliance,* and give the crew a good boost for the start of a long race.

I feel a good start is very important psychologically. It does the crew a world of good to feel they have won the start, and they will work twice as hard to maintain their advantage. It's always "cotton mouth" time for me, because we are maneuvering with other large yachts in close quarters. The damage that could be done in a collision of boats from 50 to 80 feet long is fearsome. Their power and momentum is tremendous.

At the start in the next to last race of the 1979 Antigua Race Week, I was sure *Sleuth's* number was up. The starboard end of the line was favored. As

Figure 98

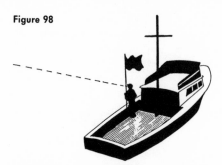

If you are blocked from seeing the buoy end of the line, note the direction the spotter is looking.

we approached the line, the 79-foot *Kialoa,* along with two other maxis, *Mistress Quickly* and *Condor of Bermuda,* was overtaking us at twice our speed. *Kialoa* came within two feet of hitting our starboard quarter. As she headed up to avoid us, she collided with *Mistress Quickly,* and went over the line early. *Sleuth* was being held up by a boat to leeward, and there was no place we could have gone to avoid the mess. Because so many boats were

Figure 99

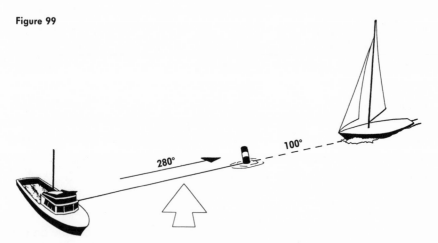

By sailing on an extension of the starting line towards the committee boat, you determine the starboard tack bearing of the line.

Figure 100

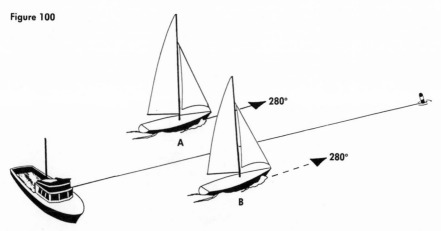

Then as you reach back on that course you can tell by buoy position if you're above or below the line. This is helpful for a middle-of-the-line start on a long starting line.

over the line early, there was a general recall, and we had to go through the whole procedure again in the 20 to 25 knots of wind prevailing at the time. My first reaction was to thank God we hadn't been hit and no one had been injured. My initial plan for the restart was to be cautious and conservative. It then occurred to me that every other skipper must be feeling the same way, and so I resolved to "go for it" on the restart. The starboard end was still the place to be, and we were there right at the gun. As I suspected, we were all alone and had the best start.

If you're on a starting line where there is no land or stake boat for a range and you're starting near the middle of the line, there's another way you can judge your distance from it. Before the start, get the compass bearing of the line. Sail out beyond the line. Then sail toward the buoy, lining it up with the flag on the committee boat. On port tack, as in Figure 99, the bearing is 100 degrees. It follows that the bearing on the starboard tack is 280 degrees. There are times when we are reaching along the line on starboard tack to avoid going over early. If we sail a course of 280 degrees, and the buoy is off our starboard bow (as in Figure 100, position A), we're still short of the line, and can afford to get closer. If the buoy is to port (as in Figure 100, position B), we're already over, and had better get down to the proper side before the gun goes.

The best starting skippers are those who have complete control over their boats. They know her turning radius so that they can swing around the stern of another boat. They know how fast they can stop the boat by backing the mainsail, and how much lee helm this will give them. They know how fast they can accelerate to prevent a windward boat from driving over them. I once watched Arthur Knapp at the start of a "frostbite" race in dinghies. He placed his boat right at the committee-boat end of the line in about 12 or 15 knots of wind. By trimming, luffing, moving his weight, raising and lowering his centerboard, and judicious helmsmanship, Arthur was able to keep his dinghy within three feet of the same location. Boat after boat tried to hang in there with him, but drifted off to leeward. At the gun he took off with the best start.

There still comes a time when, no matter how good your timing or ability to maneuver your sailboat, you get caught in a bind and can't avoid going across the line early. For example, you may want to luff up to kill your speed, but the committee boat or a number of individual boats are in the way and thwart your intentions. You may then decide to run down along the line, but some leeward boats are there holding you up. There is no way to avoid being early. This generally happens when the starboard end of the line is

Figure 101

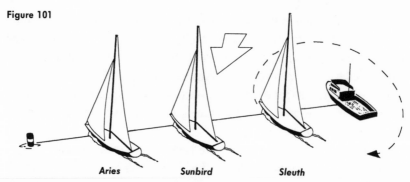

Aries   *Sunbird*   *Sleuth*

If you know you're going to be over early near an end of the starting line, bite the bullet and go around without waiting for the starting signal.

Figure 102

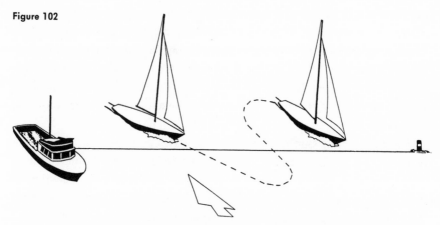

If you're over early with the port end favored, run in that direction to restart.

well favored, and boats are approaching almost at right angles to the line. Instead of the port-end buoy being well forward of abeam and only a small dip needed to keep from going over early, the buoy is actually almost abeam, and a major alteration of course is necessary.

Once, in 1980, when we were racing *Sleuth* in Antigua Race Week, these same circumstances prevailed at a start. We were early, with *Sunbird* holding us up and nowhere to go. We could have dipped a little or killed our speed a bit, but I knew that it wouldn't be sufficient to avoid being early since the buoy end was so far back. So I plowed ahead, knowing we were over early, but determined to round the committee boat as fast as possible. We were closest to the committee boat, with *Aries* and *Sunbird* to leeward, all three of us going for the line. They, too, were over early, and, possibly because they felt we were blocking the committee boat's line of vision, neither returned to start and both were disqualified (Figure 101). Since our rerounding took only 35 seconds, it was not much more of a disadvantage than a very poorly timed start. The key is to bite the bullet and reround fast. If you kill your speed, even though you know the start can't be saved, two things can happen. First, those who have timed it properly can drive over you to windward and keep you from tacking for a while, and, second, you will have so little forward speed that the tack and jibe needed for rerounding will be terribly slow.

Once having gone over the line early, too many skippers sail on, trying to decide how to get back to start. They may have boats both to windward and leeward of them, and can neither tack nor jibe. The solution is to slow the boat energetically by luffing (both heading into the wind and luffing your sails). This will allow other boats to sail by and make room to leeward. You have all your rights until you're actually returning to start. Every boat length you sail away from the line is another boat length you must sail back. After turning back, head straight across the line at right angles to it. Remember that you must "keep clear of all yachts which are starting or have started correctly," until you're wholly on the pre-start side of the line or its extensions. If you have the choice, it is better to bear off to a run when the port end is favored because you don't have to change tacks (see Figure 102). You will be heading toward the upwind end, and you can just dip the line to start on starboard tack. When the starboard end is upwind, the reverse is true (see Figure 103). Tack, if possible. You're going to have to go back to

Figure 103

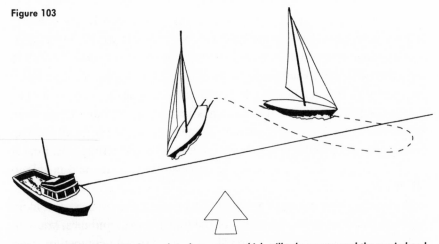

When the starboard end is favored, tack to return, which will take you toward the upwind end.

the line on port tack anyway, and a tack takes you much closer to the favored end.

There are a few other factors that can change your timing and mess up a perfect start. One is current, the other is a change in wind strength. A combination of the two can transform a small mistake into a disaster. When the breeze is very light, the percentage of wind-strength change can be great. A two-knot breeze is doubled with a four-knot puff, a 100-percent velocity change; a 15-knot wind only increases 33.3 percent in a 20-knot puff. Since wind force on the sails quadruples as the wind velocity doubles, you can see how important the puffs and lulls can be at the lower speed ranges. The problem in timing the line often comes from a light wind that is dying. A boat that strays too far away from the starting line in a light breeze may end up in a hole, and take an hour to get back; I've seen it happen. While all the other starters hugged the line, one boat sailed to a point three minutes away from the starting line in a light breeze. As luck would have it, the breeze died where she was, but held near the line. By the time she finally started, the fleet was rounding the weather mark a mile away. The absolute rule for light air is *stay near the line!*

Since your competitors' sails disturb and block the wind more in light air than in heavy, you should avoid getting into a large pack if possible. In some cases this is done by initiating a "dip start." Sail around to windward of the line, particularly if there's a current carrying you downwind. Just before the start, dip across to the correct side of the line, harden up, and start.

There are a few caveats when making a dip start. The person spotting the line for the race committee will see you on the wrong side of the line before the start, may not have seen you completely clear the line if his attention was momentarily directed elsewhere, and may call you over early when he sees you in a good position right after the gun. Moreover, if you are reaching or running down on starboard tack, all the boats to leeward of you have right of way because as windward boat you must keep clear. Unless you can find a hole, all the boats already on the line can hold you up on the wrong side of it. For that reason, an approach on port tack is often better than starboard. In Figure 104, boat A on starboard tack is unable to find a hole, and ends up running parallel to the line with boats holding her to the wrong side. Boat B on port tack sails against the flow of starboard-tack boats, and is able to select a hole to jibe into.

With current setting you downwind, this type of start makes even more sense. If you sail around upcurrent of the line and the wind dies, you will drift across to the proper side, and still be upwind of your competitors who

Figure 104

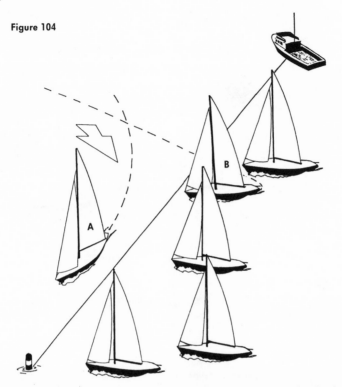

Starboard tack boat A can't find a hole because she's sailing more parallel with other starboard tackers. Port tack boat B, sailing against the grain, finds a hole easily and jibes into it.

have drifted even farther downwind of the line. You are in the same relationship to the other boats as before, but it's as if the line moved upcurrent as the fleet was pushed downcurrent (see Figure 105).

If you want to start at the starboard end of the line with the current carrying you downwind, a "barging start" can be relatively safe. By "barging" we mean placing yourself in a position where a leeward boat can luff you into a starting mark. In this example (see Figure 106), the committee boat is at the starboard end, because with windward starts and marks left to port, that's the way the line is usually set up.

The "anti-barging rule" states: "When approaching the starting line to start . . . a leeward yacht shall be under no obligation to give any windward yacht room to pass to leeward of a starting mark surrounded by navigable water . . ." In Figure 106, boat A is on a close-hauled course to the committee boat end of the line. Although it is commonly accepted that boat C is barging because she is reaching in from an area above the close-hauled course (indicated by the dotted line), boat A is also barging because boat B, with luffing rights, can deprive her of room at the committee boat until the

Figure 105

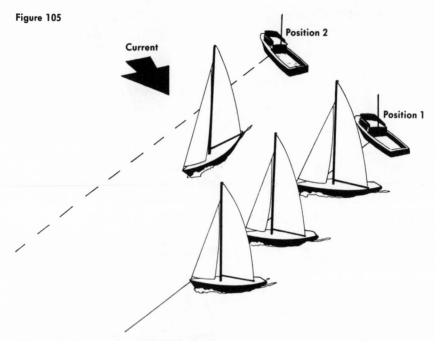

If the wind dies completely, it's as if the starting line moves upcurrent. A boat to windward of the line can end up on the proper side quite fast.

Figure 106

Boat B can deprive both boats A and C of room at the committee boat before the starting signal.

Figure 107

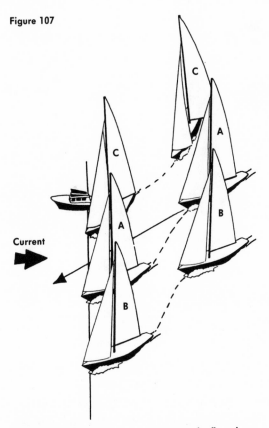

Barging is safer when current is setting the fleet down the line.

starting signal is made (at which time boat B must not sail above close-hauled—or above the first mark—to deprive boat A of room).

With current set (see Figure 107), however, it's far more likely that boat C will find room. Whereas boats A and B, being close-hauled, can't point any higher to adjust for the contrary current, boat C is far more flexible, and can head up from her reach right at the end of the line, leaving boat A with no chance to squeeze C out.

When current is running in the opposite direction (see Figure 108), carrying the fleet *toward* the starting line, the reverse is true. There can be an awful mess of boats near the line, all being pushed over early by the current and by leeward boats reaching down the line in an attempt to avoid going over early. In this case, the most leeward boat can get, if not the best, at least the safest start.

There are various methods for determining the velocity and direction of

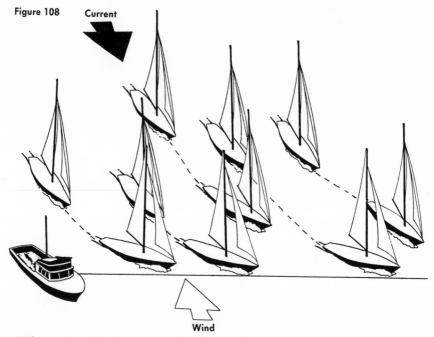

With current carrying the fleet towards the line, many boats are early and luff up or bear off. Don't try a barging start.

the current. Observe the committee boat or other anchored yachts to see if they are heading straight into the wind. If not, there is some current running. This observation is fine in light winds, but will not be discernible when the wind is heavy. A better alternative is to sail near the buoy end of the line, and to observe the water flowing past the mark. The mark will appear as if it were being dragged upcurrent, and it will create a wake behind it when the current is strong. Look for debris in the water—bits of paper, twigs, or even bubbles flowing past. To be more scientific, drop a "current stick" into the water next to the buoy. A current stick is a piece of wood or aluminum tube weighted to float vertically. It is preferable that it be equal in length to the draft of the boat so that it will be affected by the same current affecting the boat. The weight should be heavy enough to allow only a very small portion of the stick to be above the surface of the water. Thus, the wind will not affect its travel very much. After dropping the stick, sail around for about a minute, and then pick it up, noting how far and in which direction it drifted from the buoy. Knowing that a nautical mile is roughly 6,000 feet and a knot is the speed necessary to cover one nautical mile in one hour, we know that a knot of current will carry the stick 100 feet in a minute. If you are sailing a 30-foot boat and judge that you're about three boat lengths (90 feet) from the mark when you pick up the current stick a minute later, you know that the current is almost one knot. Moreover, you also know the rough distance you will have to allow for to be on the line at the starting signal if the current is carrying you away from the line. This knowledge will also help you at the weather mark to judge the layline accurately.

So far we have discussed only windward starts. Timing leeward (running or reaching) starts so that you hit the line at the gun is slightly different and, in a way, more difficult. The difficulty is that sometimes it can be hard to slow down if you're early, yet it's deadly to be late. Sailing upwind you can recover faster from a bad start by tacking for clear air and playing wind shifts better than your competitors. When reaching or running it can take "forever" to get past other boats, even if they're smaller, when they had a better start than you did.

When the wind is in the direction shown in Figure 109, my general tactic is to choose a point on the line where I would like to be at the gun. I then time it to be at that point on a beam reach at roughly two minutes to go, providing there's a good breeze. Since it's a reach, we pick up speed very quickly after the turn to return to the line, so a shorter time sequence can be used. With light winds I would use a longer time sequence, because it takes longer to pick up speed. I would also sail more downwind, more parallel to the line, in order not to diverge very far from it and to make our approach

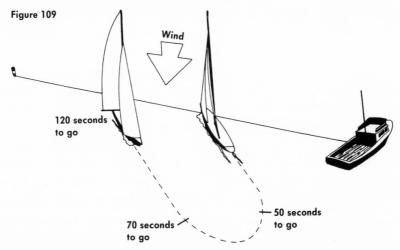

Figure 109

Wind

120 seconds to go

70 seconds to go

50 seconds to go

Vanderbilt start: 120 seconds remaining. *Add* 20 seconds for tacking = 140 seconds. Divide by 2 = 70 seconds. When this time remains on your watch you'll have sailed 50 seconds away from the line (120–50 = 70). After the tack takes 20 seconds, there's 50 seconds left to get back to the line.

when returning a tighter reach for greater speed. After reaching away from the line something less than a minute, we jibe or tack and head back for an equal amount of time.

The Vanderbilt timing system shown in Figure 109 could well be used in this instance. We cross the line at two minutes (120 seconds) going away. We add the time it takes to jibe or tack, say 20 seconds, and divide by two $(120 + 20 = 140; 140 \div 2 = 70)$. At the moment our watch says there is a minute and 10 seconds (70 seconds) left before the start, we begin our tack or jibe. When we complete it, the time remaining on the watch (50 seconds) is the same as the time elapsed to the start of the jibe or tack. Figure 109 shows the time remaining at various stages.

As we approach the line, we might find ourselves early. Falling off towards the buoy helps eat up the time remaining. If the time is badly misjudged, we can luff up. As long as we have an overlap on a boat to windward, we can luff up to close-hauled, and they must respond. If our mast is forward of their helmsman, we can luff head-to-wind. The windward boat can only curtail my luff if an obstruction, a third yacht or other object, restricts her ability to respond. Because of the anti-barging rule, the committee boat doesn't qualify as an obstruction or "other object."

This brings us to the danger involved with our approach if early. If we have chosen a point on the line too close to the committee boat, and we have a number of boats to leeward of us which are also early, we could run out of line before the gun. We can't bear off across the line, because we will foul the leeward boats. Possibly we can luff up behind the stern of the committee boat, but there's bound to be some "spoiler," such as boat A in Figure 110, who is trying to mess up the port-tack starters by approaching on starboard. Boat B is in big trouble, and I'll leave the reader to figure out how she gets out of it unscathed. The only answer I have is: Don't get yourself into that position in the first place.

When the wind is far enough aft so that the starboard tack can be easily carried to the line (see Figure 111), yet the port tack is the desired course after the start, a good approach is that of boat A. As the starboard tack vessel, boat A has right-of-way. She converges with the other boats, and, if necessary, she can head up to avoid being over early. Just before the starting signal, she can jibe to port, placing herself advantageously to windward of all the others.

Figure 111

Figure 110

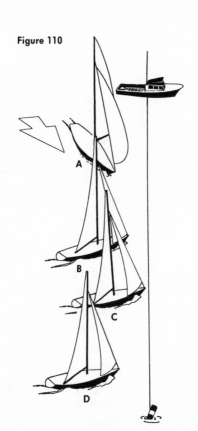

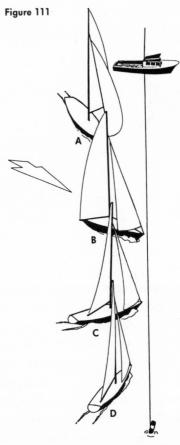

Watch out for starboard tack spoilers on broad-reaching starts.

On running starts, make use of starboard tack rights.

Choosing a Starting Location

We have covered the first rule for getting a good start: Be on the line at the instant of the starting signal. The second is: Be at the best location on the line.

With a few exceptions, it pays to be at the favored end of the line. By "favored" I mean the upwind end of the line for windward starts. Most sailboats start a race on starboard tack, which gives them right of way over any boat on port tack. When the line is absolutely square to the wind direction, as in line A, Figure 112, a windward boat with slightly better timing than a leeward boat should have no trouble driving over the top (passing to windward) of the leeward boat. This gives a slight advantage to the windward boat, and means more boats will bunch up at the starboard

Figure 112

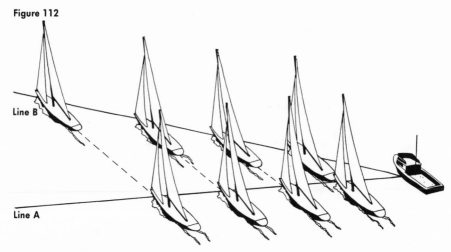

Line B

Line A

A slight favor to the port end spreads the fleet out along the line better.

end of the line to secure a windward location. By moving the buoy up to position B in Figure 112, the leeward boats are less overlapped by the windward boats and thereby less disadvantaged. A slight cock of the port end of the line to windward will tend to spread the boats more evenly along the full length of the line, and will limit congestion in any one area.

However, if the port end is well upwind, as in Figure 113, any boat starting at the buoy will have a great advantage over one starting at the committee boat. Assuming two boats can sail within 45 degrees of the wind at the starting signal and they start sailing upwind on opposite tacks toward each other, Fig. 113 shows how far ahead the port-tack boat will cross the starboard-tack boat. The line is only 13 boat lengths long, the wind is 30 degrees off of square, and boat A already has a five-length lead over boat B. In this case, the buoy end is "heavily favored."

Figure 113

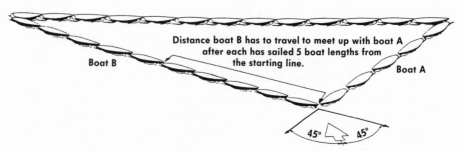

Distance boat B has to travel to meet up with boat A after each has sailed 5 boat lengths from the starting line.

Boat B

Boat A

45°   45°

The starting line is 13 boat lengths long. The wind is about 30° off of square. Boat A already has a 5-boat-length advantage over boat B.

What happens if the windward mark is way to the right, and there is a shorter straight-line distance to the mark from the starboard end of the line than from the port—the upwind—end? In Figure 114, an arc described from the windward mark through the committee boat clearly shows that the buoy end is farther away from the windward mark, but the wind still favors the buoy end so much that when boats A and B have sailed equal distance, boat A has retained a commanding lead. A few assumptions are made here: that there is no difference in the speed of the boats; that there are no wind shifts and that there is at least one tack involved in the weather leg. If it were just a reach from the starting line to the weather mark, then the shortest geometric distance would be the fastest route to take.

Assuming that we want to be at the favored end, how do we tell which end of the starting line is favored? My preference is to determine the compass bearing of the line as we did in Figure 99 by lining up the buoy with the starting line flag on the committee boat. Let's say we get 135 degrees for the line. If the wind were absolutely perpendicular to the line, as in Figure 115, it would be 90 degrees from the line direction or from 45 degrees. I call this our "magic" number. Just recall that number every time we shoot the wind to determine the favored end. If, when we point the boat into the actual

Figure 114

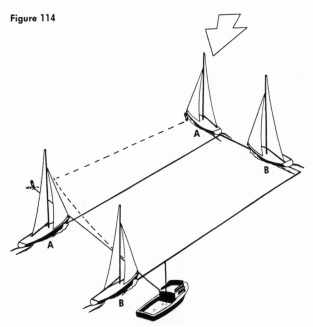

Boat B is physically closer to the mark than A, but since the buoy end is so upwind, boat A retains the advantage.

Figure 115

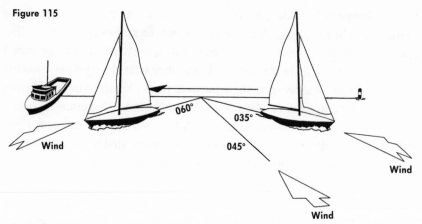

Remember the "magic number" of 045° as a perfectly square line and compare it with wind readings each time you shoot the wind.

Figure 116

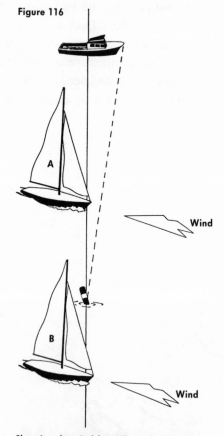

Shooting the wind from the end of the line gives you a range to judge the line, allows you to look one way only, and doubles any bearing compared to the middle of the line.

wind, and the compass reads 035 degrees, the port end is 10 degrees favored. If it reads 060 degrees, the starboard end is 15 degrees favored. Some sailors add or subtract 90 degrees from the actual wind direction and compare it with the compass course of the line. That calls for a calculation every time you shoot the wind rather than recalling one number.

When you shoot into the wind to check its direction, make sure the boat comes to a complete stop. In light air, the boat's momentum will carry a long way, and the wind will appear to be dead ahead while the boat is moving forward. Only when this forward movement has ceased can you accurately determine the true wind direction. The sails, particularly the jib (if it doesn't overlap the mast), will luff right over the centerline of the boat when the wind is dead ahead.

The advantage of the compass system is that you can check the wind direction a distance from the line in undisturbed air, away from other classes that are starting, and still know which end of the line to play when it's your turn to start.

This also has advantages over another system commonly used: checking the wind when right on the line and noting toward which end your bow points. Since the bow of the luffing sailboat A in Figure 116 is pointing more toward the buoy than the committee boat, the buoy end is upwind and favored. Boat B does the same thing from an extension of the line and sights abeam. Since the committee boat is aft of abeam, the starboard end is favored; if forward of abeam, the port end is upwind. The advantage B has over A's system is that B knows when she is right on the line and has to sight only in one direction. Boat A has to guess when she's on the line, and has to sight in both directions. If the wind's angle from square is very slight, B is more apt to pick it up accurately.

If you shoot the wind and find one end of the line very much favored, consider the possibility that the race committee might be doing it on purpose. For example, there may be a known geographical wind shift near some land on the right side of the course, as depicted in Figure 117. Most sharp competitors know that if they tack immediately after the start, they will be gradually headed on port tack as they approach the shore. After tacking they will get a starboard-tack lift along the beach. Because the race committee doesn't want a lot of hot competitors sailing at their transom at the start, they place the buoy end way upwind in order to coax a large portion of the fleet to start at that end. It is very tempting, because, at least initially, a boat at the buoy end has a decided advantage over one at the other end. However, as the boats sail into the new wind, that advantage is lost, and

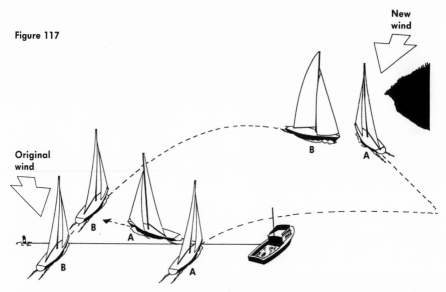

Figure 117

New wind

Original wind

B   A

B   A

B   A

The initial advantage B has over A at the start disappears if A stays on port and gets into the header first.

the boat that gets into the new wind first gains the most distance. Note that boat A on starboard tack in Figure 117 crosses boat B near the shore. She never would have crossed boat B if she had taken starboard tack from the starting gun.

If it looks as though there will be several boats starting at the starboard end, and it's necessary to get on port tack to reach the wind shift, only the one or two boats nearest that end will get a good start. The others will have to sail on starboard away from the lift until the windward boats tack. This being the case, the boat that approaches the line late, but right behind the boat nearest the mark, will get the second or third best start in the fleet. She will be clear to tack as soon as she passes the committee boat, assuming it's at the starboard end of the line.

Another time you might not select the "favored" end of the line is when the wind is shifting back and forth. Let's say the buoy end is currently upwind, but, by testing the wind before the start, you have noticed that the wind is as far to the left as it's ever been, and is due to shift back now. In other words, the boat with the perfect start at the buoy on starboard tack is sailing in a header rather than a lift and, worse yet, is pinned on that tack by other starboard-tack boats.

Figure 118

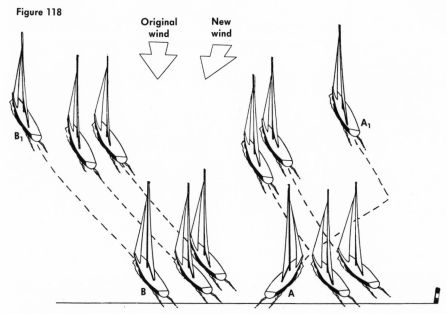

Boat B, at the favored end, is sailing in a header and is pinned by other boats. Boat A, on port tack, is on a lift. When the new wind comes, she tacks and is well to windward of boat B, who is sailing on the outside of a lift.

In Figure 118, boat A approaches the line on port, sailing in a lift in clear air. As soon as the heading shift comes back, she tacks to starboard and has the rest of the fleet beaten. Boat B, with what appeared to be the best start in the fleet, is on the outside of a lift, and every boat to windward has her tucked away.

There are some excellent sailors, like Peter Barrett, Olympic gold medalist, who use port-tack approaches on almost every start. Whereas the starboard-tack boat has to hold her course, except to assume a proper course to start, the port-tack approach is fairly common and reasonable. It works best when the port end of the line is so favored that boats can barely cross it on starboard tack. Note Line A in Figure 119. The port-tack boat will have a little trouble crossing the starboard-tackers because they are almost in a straight line bow to stern. The port-tack boat in line B where the wind is almost square will have major problems crossing and will probably have to tack.

Weigh a port-tack start very carefully. Instant disqualification isn't a very good way to start a race. Moreover, the port tack may be taking you away from a more desirable area. In one recent race, I considered a port-tack start

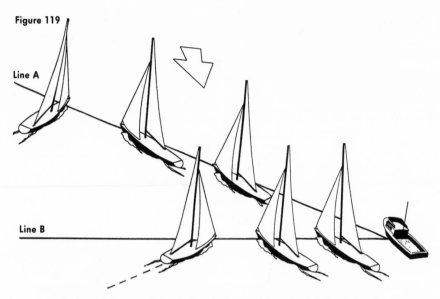

A port-tack start works best when the port end is well upwind as in line A.

because the port end was well upwind. However, there was a nearby shore with shallower water, less current, and usually a port-tack lift. Since we had to get to that shore on starboard anyway, I decided to save a tack and to start on starboard (see Figure 120). Also, the committee boat was at that end, which makes a port-tack start there more dangerous. If you are forced to tack by a starboard-tack yacht, you can't avoid hitting the committee boat. *Aries,* with Lowell North steering, made a perfect port-tack start, and barely squeaked across *Sleuth,* who was on starboard. *Sleuth* carried into the shore, got slightly headed and tacked. When she converged with *Aries* again, she crossed her handily, having taken a short-term disadvantage for a later gain. Buddy Melges, Olympic medalist, Star and Soling world champion (among other championships), says, "Put your head one hundred yards in front of your boat." In effect, that's what we were attempting to do.

In Antigua Race Week, *Sleuth* and *Aries* seemed to have somewhat comparable speeds upwind. At the start of another race, I elected not to try for the ideal position right at the committee boat, because the starting line was closer to shore than in the preceding example (see Figure 121). I estimated that we would have to tack so early after the start to avoid going aground that we wouldn't be able to clear starboard-tack boats, and we might be forced back in toward shore. So we played the start a little farther down the line. As we approached the shore, *Aries* called for water. She had

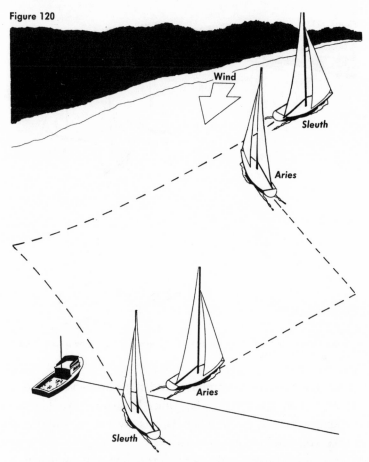

Figure 120

Wind

Sleuth

Aries

Aries

Sleuth

Don't try a risky port tack start if starboard takes you to the new wind first.

to tack to avoid going aground, and couldn't without fouling us. We tacked at her request (as required by the racing rules) and she tacked immediately (also as called for by the rules). This put her right in *Sleuth*'s backwind. As we both came out on port tack, *Aries,* slowed by our dirty air, failed to cross *Fandango* on starboard (just the position I was worried about getting into at the start), and was disqualified. This is another example of how possible future situations may affect your decision as to where to place yourself on the starting line.

Sometimes it's important to decide not only where on the line you will start, but also where you will practice. Arthur Knapp once found that novice racing sailors were often watching him and starting where he started. This was getting tiresome, so he began to make practice starts at the wrong end of the line, thus drawing all the neophytes to that area. Then, at the last

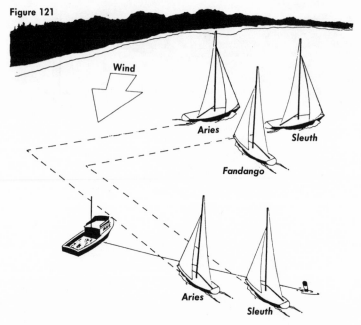

If you're heading for shallow water try to be in a position to be advantaged after both boats tack.

moment, he hightailed it to the preferred end of the line where he could start with less congestion. Naturally, he had timed how long it would take to sail from one end of the line to the other. This is always good information to have in case you need to change ends.

Another reason it's beneficial to know the length of the line is to help in your judgment of distances. The two ends of the line are the only fixed points around the starting area that can give a time-distance reference. Suppose it takes three minutes to sail from the buoy to the committee boat. If you're one-third of a line length away from the line as you approach to start, you are approximately one minute away. You just have to make allowances for boat speed, which could have been faster reaching along the line than on the final approach.

Starting With Clear Air

The third rule for a good start—to have clear air—has been covered in part by some of the previous examples. It is a vital factor. Figure 122 shows the disruptive air patterns from one boat and how they affect other boats in nearby positions. Boat A is said to have a "safe leeward" position on boat B.

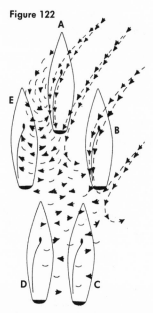

Figure 122

Safe leeward, backwind, and blanket zones.

The wind is bent aft by A's sails so that the wind direction to windward of A is slightly more parallel to her course. Thus B is sailing in a header and is unable to bear away to fill her sails because of the proximity of A. It's highly unlikely that B will be able to pass A, even if she is a larger yacht.

The wind leaves the mainsail of boat A in a turbulent form called "backwind." Boats C and D are in A's backwind zone. Since the efficiency of a sailboat's sails depends in large part upon the smoothness of the air flowing past them, this turbulence causes the sails to lose their lift. Boats C and D will gradually drop back.

The worst position to be in is that of boat E. This is aptly called the "blanket" zone. A's sails are blocking the wind from getting to E in any usable form. What wind there is will be turbulent, and boat E is in an untenable position.

Just after the start only the boats that are not affected by others will move out. It's obvious from Figure 122 that for every boat with clear air there are quite a number of others being hurt. The tactic required is usually either to tack away, as boat C should do, or foot away to leeward, which boat E might consider doing. A boat in D's position must do something drastic such as luffing her sails and dropping back fast to tack. It's slow death to just "hang in there."

The first few minutes after the start are crucial. It's important then to hike out hard and build up speed as fast as possible. As Ian Bruce says, "Speed begets speed." The lift off your keel, rudder and sails is proportionate to the square of your speed, and as your speed doubles, your lift quadruples. This can give you a great advantage over boats that haven't accelerated as fast.

Also, be sure to have good boom vang tension before the start. Then, when you trim in your luffing mainsail, the whole sail comes in like a barn door, resulting in instant acceleration. Otherwise, when you trim the lower part of the sail the upper section falls off and acceleration is slower.

Starting Rules

All racing skippers should be well aware of those rules that apply and are in common use before the start of a race. We will paraphrase some of the rules and omit any portions that are of no immediate interest to this discussion, so refer to your rule book for the full text.

One of the more confusing pre-start rules is that which refers to "luffing before starting," because it ceases to apply after a boat has started and cleared the starting line. A yacht "starts" when, after the starting signal, any part of her hull, crew, or equipment first crosses the starting line in the direction of the course to the first mark. She hasn't "cleared" the line until

Figure 123

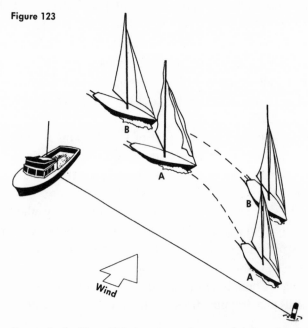

Boat B's mast is aft of boat A's helmsman, so she can only luff to close-hauled.

every part of her has crossed the line. Only then does the "luffing after starting" rule apply.

Before the start, the leeward boat cannot luff a windward boat above a close-hauled course if her mainmast is aft of the windward boat's helmsman. In Figure 123 boat A is luffing along the line. Boat B overtakes her to leeward and initiates a luff. (To luff means to alter course toward the wind.) Boat B's luff forces boat A to alter course to avoid a collision. The luff must be carried out slowly and in such a way as to give boat A room and opportunity to keep clear. If boat A turns upwind to avoid B and her stern swings down and hits the leeward boat, she has some justification in claiming that she wasn't given enough room and opportunity to keep clear. In this example, boat B is unable to luff above a close-hauled course since her mainmast is aft of boat A's helmsman.

In Figure 124, when boat A's helmsman sights abeam from his normal station, it is obvious that he is aft of the leeward boat's mainmast. Here, boat

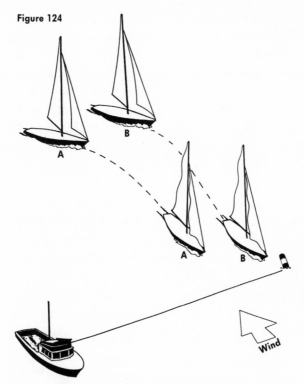

Figure 124

Boat B can luff *slowly* head-to-wind because her mast is forward of boat A's helmsman.

B can luff right up to head to wind as in the diagram, but she still must luff slowly and give room and opportunity for the windward boat to keep clear. After the starting signal, boat B can continue to luff boat A as long as the leeward boat is not depriving the windward boat of room at a starting mark (the anti-barging rule). In the incident depicted in Figure 124, the anti-barging rule does not apply.

The ease with which a leeward boat can control you as the windward boat makes it crucial that you protect your lee quarter as you approach the line on starboard tack, unless you are late for the start. If you are killing your speed and a boat attempts to get an overlap to leeward, trim in your sails get out in front of him, and duck off to leeward. However, if you feel you have the start timed well and you expect the leeward boat to charge on through and run down the line without bothering you, just let him go. If you expect to be early and you have room to luff head to wind, keep in mind that no boat can luff you any farther if you are head-to-wind already. Any boat to windward has to keep clear because you are the leeward boat. Mast position is not a factor unless you are altering your course toward the wind. If you have already arrived at your head-to-wind position, you are no longer in the process of carrying out a luff, and windward boats (i.e., boats on your starboard side, since you are still on starboard tack) have to keep clear.

As mentioned before, many skippers approach the bulk of the fleet on port tack, find a hole to leeward of a group of starboard tack boats, and tack into it. As you sail toward the line on starboard, watch for any port-tack skipper who has his eye on that patch of open water to leeward of you. Without breaking the rule on altering course, head down at him. This will force the port-tack boat to sail even farther off the wind, closing the distance faster between the two boats. If he still intends to tack, he will have to do so earlier. Since you are reaching with good speed, you should be able to drive over the top of the leeward boat, which is going slowly after the tack. The altering course rule provides that the right-of-way boat shall not so alter course as to prevent the other boat from keeping clear, or to obstruct her while she is keeping clear. If the starboard-tack boat changes course early enough and then holds a steady course, she is not in contravention of this rule. This alteration of course is one risk the port-tack boat is taking and should be aware of.

There are some rules that specifically do not apply at starts. One is Rule 42: "Rounding or Passing Marks or Obstructions." A leeward boat on starboard tack that is squeezing to round the port-end buoy, as in Figure 125, cannot call for buoy room to the windward boats if the starting mark is

Figure 125

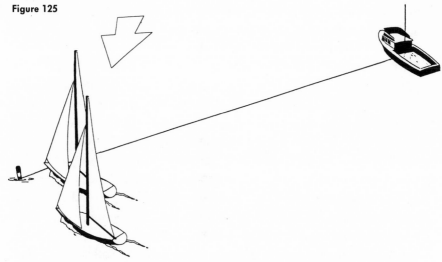

Leeward boat cannot call for buoy room, but could luff if she had rights (not in this example).

surrounded by navigable water. If she has luffing rights, she could make room for herself by luffing the windward boats. But in the diagram as drawn, the leeward boat only has an overlap (her mast is aft of the windward boat's helmsman), so she can luff no higher than close-hauled, a course she is already on. Being squeezed out, her only choice is to pass on the wrong side of the mark, make a circle, and try again.

Let's place the leeward boat in the position shown in Figure 126. Here, boat A can presumably luff boat B head-to-wind since her mast is forward of B's helmsman. However, the helmsman of boat C is forward of A's mast, so A cannot luff above a close-hauled course if the luff will affect C. Rule

Figure 126

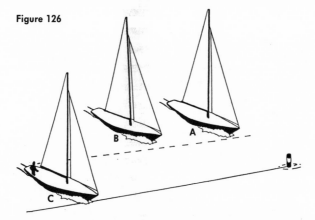

Boat A could luff B head-to-wind in the absence of C. But since she doesn't have the right to luff C, she cannot luff B if such luff will affect C.

38.6 states that a boat shall not luff unless she has the right to luff all boats that would be affected by her luff.

The rule about hitting a mark applies at the start also. A boat that touches a starting mark after she begins racing, which is from the time of her preparatory signal, or causes a mark or mark vessel to shift to avoid being touched, must retire immediately, unless she alleges that she was wrong-fully compelled by another boat to touch it or cause it to shift, in which case she must protest. (If the other yacht accepts an alternative penalty as prescribed in the sailing instructions, the protest is not necessary.) She also has another choice. She can exonerate herself by doing a 720-degree penalty turn. The boat in Figure 127 has touched the buoy at the port end of the line two minutes before the starting signal. Since she is racing from her prepara-tory signal, generally five minutes before her starting signal, she is liable tothe provisions of the rule. Had she hit the mark earlier, before her preparatory signal, she could have ignored it.

Another rule reads, "When code flag 'I' has been displayed, and when

Figure 127

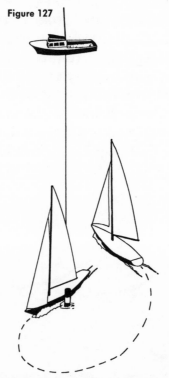

Having hit the buoy after the preparatory
signal, the boat must do a 720° penalty turn
to exonerate herself.

any part of a yacht's hull, crew or equipment is on the course side of the starting line or its extensions during the minute before her starting signal, she shall sail to the pre-start side of the line across one of its extensions and start." This code flag is often displayed after general recalls.

General recalls occur when so many boats are early over the line that the race committee is unable to identify them all. The only fair thing is to have another start. To reduce the possibility of a second, third, or even fourth general recall in a particularly aggressive fleet, the above rule was devised. Commonly known as the "Round the Ends" rule, it effectively keeps most of the competitors away from the starting line before the start, particularly near the center of the line. There, a boat that was over early would have quite a long distance to sail to get around the end of the starting line to start. This rule also precludes doing a dip start, so be aware of it after a general recall. Tactically, a conservative center-of-the-line start can be an excellent one after a general recall because all your competitors are bunching up at the ends of the line to reduce the distance they have to sail if over the line before the starting signal.

WIND SHIFTS ON THE WEATHER LEG

After you start and clear the line, the first weather leg is crucial. Boats are still relatively close to one another, and the wind is chopped up by numerous sails. Other than boat speed—which we are not including in our discussion of tactics—the major difference between skippers is how they play the wind tactically.

There are two basic types of winds. One tends to shift back and forth, but maintains one mean direction. We call this an oscillating wind. The other wind makes small shifts back and forth, but the mean wind travels either clockwise (veering) or counterclockwise (backing). We call this a continual shift. A study of meteorology will tell you what type of wind to expect from a given weather pattern. The oscillating shift is symptomatic of an unstable air mass—cold air over a warm body of land or water. The warm air near the surface rises and the cold, heavier air falls to the surface. Because of surface friction and the rotation of the earth (Coriolis effect), in the northern hemisphere the upper air is usually more veered than that at sea level. In a typical cool northwest wind, the upper air hits the surface in gust cells that fan out as they travel along. On some days the wind shifts caused by these gusts are quite regular and can almost be timed. The skipper who tacks on

Boat A tacks on every header and is always on the lifted tack. Boat B sails through lifts and headers on the same tack. It doesn't take long for boat A to build a commanding lead.

every header will easily outdistance those who sail through the shifts or who are "out of phase" and tack on the lifts. Boat A in Figure 128 tacks every time she is headed, and is always sailing on a lifted tack. Boat B sails on one tack through a lift, a header, a second lift, and a second header before she tacks. We are assuming both boats sail within 45 degrees of the wind, the wind shift is 20 degrees each time, and they are sailing at the same speed through the water. It is clear that boat A has gained a commanding lead over boat B in a relatively short distance.

The continual shift can be just as impressive if played correctly. We touched on it briefly in choosing the end of the starting line nearest the expected shift. The continual shift is associated with a stable air mass. Southerly winds bringing warm air over cooler water or land cause a stratified condition as evidenced by smokestack emissions flowing parallel to the land rather than rising.

In Figure 129, boat B starts off in the direction toward which the wind is expected to shift, and boat A sets out on the other tack. Boat A gets lifted, feels good about it, and continues on. At position 3 they both tack. Now boat A is sailing in a header and boat B in a lift. The difference is that A's header is much worse than when boat B was sailing in a header and B's lift is much better than A's original lift. If A had gone much farther before tacking, she would have lost far more distance. When you find yourself sailing what we call "the great circle" in a continual lift, the sooner the decision is made to tack to get over to the good side of the course the more the losses are cut. It takes a great deal of fortitude to do this, because it's easier to hope that the wind will shift back again, head you, and give you a lift on the other tack.

Many sailors know the foregoing theory of wind shifts very well, but have trouble spotting them on the race course and remembering how to use them properly. There are various ways to spot and to use wind shifts. After

Figure 129

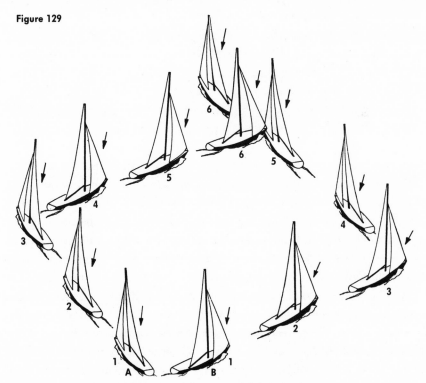

Boat B sails toward the expected shift and makes out.

long experience some of the best sailors can tell a shift direction by the gust on the water. I've heard that Paul Elvstrom and Hans Fogh (in preparation for the Olympics) worked long and hard at guessing whether an approaching gust (as outlined by dark ripples on the water surface) was a header or a lift. After much practice they could determine the expected wind direction with great accuracy.

Most of us rely almost exclusively upon the compass to show us wind shifts. One crew member, usually the tactician, is assigned the job of watching the boat's heading while the skipper concentrates on keeping her in the groove upwind. Some skippers like to hear "up five" or "down ten," meaning that they are sailing five degrees higher or ten degrees lower than the agreed-upon mean course. Others prefer to hear the actual compass headings. If they are sailing 260 degrees on the starboard tack and hear the number 265 degrees and 270 degrees called out, they know they are being lifted. While higher numbers are good on starboard tack, they are generally bad on port since they indicate a header.

There are times when good skippers will ignore the indication of a header. For instance, when the wind velocity decreases, the apparent wind goes forward. The skipper will have to sail a lower course and has apparently been headed. The true wind direction, however, has remained the same. The best skippers, like Buddy Melges, have the wind velocity totally cranked into their mental computers, and don't necessarily tack on headers if they are created by wind velocity changes.

A change in velocity can completely disorient the more inexperienced skipper. The scenario is as follows: the boat sails into a hole in the wind, and the apparent wind, created by the boat speed, goes forward. Being "headed," the skipper decides to tack. As the boat turns into the wind the sails fill because the apparent wind comes aft due to the boat's rotation. The skipper decides the header was temporary and aborts the tack. By the time the boat settles down on the original tack, the boat speed has diminished considerably, the apparent wind is no longer forward, and the skipper's decision to abort appears vindicated. Yet the true wind has never changed direction. Only the velocity changed.

Another way of spotting headers and lifts, one that doesn't depend on the compass, is to observe the heading of other boats. Boats A and B are abeam of each other in Figure 130, position 1. Along comes a big header, as in position 2, and boat B forges ahead. When a large lift comes, as in position 3, it benefits the "inside boat," boat A, the most. The boats have won or lost great distances, but have been moving through the water at exactly the same

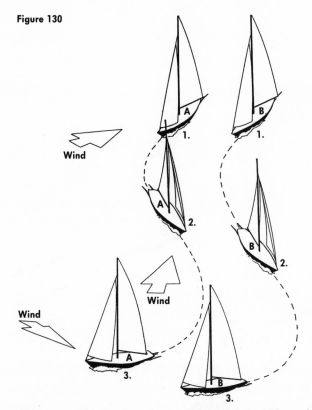

Figure 130

You can call headers and lifts from your "gains" and "losses" alongside another boat.

speed. It's obvious from the diagram that one wants to be the leeward boat in a header and the windward boat in a lift. But how is that possible? If, when headed, boat B tacks while boat A continues on in an extended header, they may very well change places. Then boat B is in position to take advantage of the next lift, and boat A has ended up on the outside of the lift, a very poor position indeed.

When the crew of boat B notices that suddenly in position 2 they are looking very good on boat A, as if their speed has greatly increased, they figure that something's fishy. Since such a jump in speed isn't likely, they determine they've been headed and tack. So without looking at the compass they have been able to play the wind shift well.

Dinghy sailors learn to understand wind shifts from boat relationships very well. Once I was sailing a two-man dinghy with Peter Barrett, an Olympic medalist in the Finn class, and we were in the position of boat B in Figure 131. We were coming up to a windward finish ahead. I felt we could just about cross boat A if we tacked at position 1. I suggested to Peter that

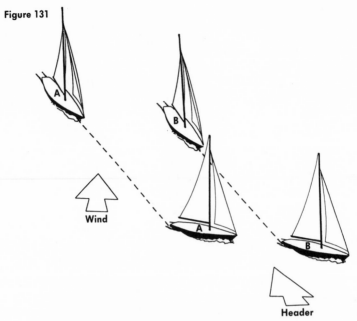

Figure 131

Wind

Header

Consolidate over your competition on a header, not on a lift.

we consolidate our position by getting to windward of boat A and covering her. We both were laying the finish, but boat A, with a lightweight crew, was moving much faster in the prevailing light air. Peter kept on sailing on starboard for a few moments, and then said, "Now let's tack." At that time, in position 2, I looked back at boat A, and saw we could cross easily. Since we were still laying the finish line (a layline is an imaginary line indicating the last tack to the windward mark) I wondered why Peter had chosen to cover at a time when we looked so good. It hardly seemed necessary now that we were handily beating boat A. Even if she caught up, she would have trouble breaking through our backwind. In retrospect I realized that we both had been slightly headed, and Peter was consolidating our lead by utilizing the lift on port tack. By our getting to windward of A, any future lift would not work to our disadvantage as before and there would be no chance of our competitor passing us to windward.

Watch boats to windward of you on a beat. Headers and lifts will hit them first, and as the shift is traveling down to you, quite a bit of distance can be gained by using the proper tactics. Boat A in Figure 132 sees that a boat to windward of her has been lifted, but A is still sailing in the original wind. If A keeps on sailing, she will be in position A1 when the lift arrives. If she tacks twice, she'll be in position A2 when the shift gets to her. By drawing

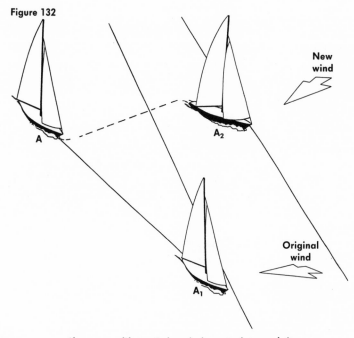

Figure 132

New wind

Original wind

A

A₂

A₁

If you see a lift to windward of you, tack towards it.

lines perpendicular to the wind direction, we can see that A2 is farther upwind than A1. To the best of my knowledge Peter Barrett originated these lines back in the sixties, and calls them "lines of equal position." Any boat on a beat that is on the same line (perpendicular with the wind direction) with another boat or boats, is the same distance upwind as the others. Boat A, by noting that a lift is expected, realizes that she is sailing in a header vis-à-vis the course she will be sailing when the shift reaches her. Thus, the prudent rule of "tack in headers" still holds.

Often, distance can be gained by observing a boat to windward that is being severely headed. In one Rolex Cup race at St. Thomas the race course ran through a pass between two islands with high terrain. A boat ahead and to windward of us held high through the pass, expecting the wind to veer and thus head her. We noticed she was being headed, and though we were not closehauled and could have squeezed up 10 to 15 degrees, I decided to reach off for speed. What happened is shown in Figure 133. The position lines in the original wind are much farther apart than the position lines in the new wind. This indicates how much distance we caught up.

The tactic is apparent: When you expect a header, foot (sail fast) for it. Figure 134 shows three boats equal to one another in the original wind. Boat

Figure 133

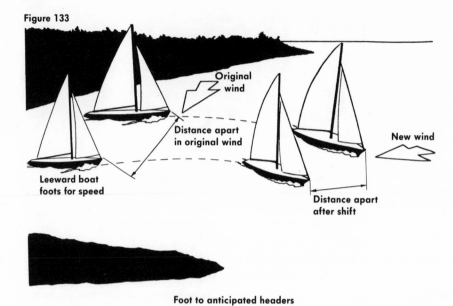

Original wind

Distance apart in original wind

New wind

Leeward boat foots for speed

Distance apart after shift

Foot to anticipated headers

Figure 134

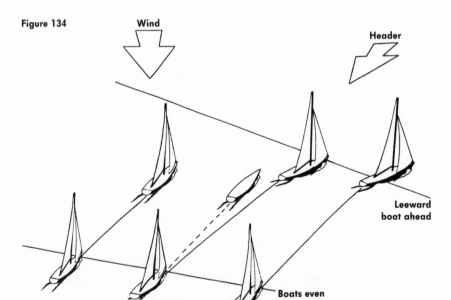

Wind

Header

Leeward boat ahead

Boats even

A sails close-hauled while B foots off for speed. When the heading shift arrives, the new lines of position show that boat B has gained considerably over boat A. Even if B remains close-hauled (the dotted lines in Figure 134) she would gain on A when the shift arrives because she is closer to the side of the race course from which the new wind is expected to come. Boat C, being the farthest to the right, gains the most. So if you expect the wind to veer, play the right side of the course. If you expect a backing wind, play the left side. My experience is that more than 50 percent of the time in the northern hemisphere it pays to play the course for a veer rather than a back. If you know nothing about the weather or the geographical wind patterns for a certain area, playing the right side of the course pays off slightly more than the left.

Computer studies show that if you are sailing in an oscillating wind, it is best to foot when you are in your greatest lift. In Figure 135, you are lifted on starboard tack, position 1, and should be footing. As you get headed towards position 2, the course you steer on starboard tack in the mean wind, you reduce the footing and change to a tight sailing mode. At position 2 you tack and end up on port tack at position 3, again in a tight mode. As you get lifted up to position 4 on port tack, you return to the footing mode. You will reach the windward mark faster with this method of playing shifts.

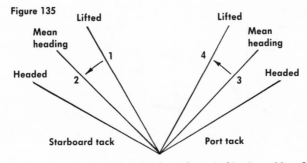

Foot slightly in positions 1 and 4. Sail tight, without pinching in positions 2 and 3.

COVERING, BREAKING COVER, AND LUFFING

Often a skipper is concerned about only one other competitor. On the last windward leg to the finish, it may be the nearest boat. In the last race of a series, it could be the competitor who is closest in points. Or perhaps it's just the perennial foe who is always nearby and forever hard to beat. Many races are lost because skippers do not cover opponents when the chance exists. A typical example occurs when a boat on starboard tack crosses an opponent on port and fails to tack to cover. If the finish line is nearby, sailing farther before covering ("splitting tacks") is a very risky business. Any little wind shift can cause positions to change. The proper tactic is to stay between your opponent and the finish line, sailing in the same direction and, therefore, in the same wind.

The desired spot on a beat is dead upwind. Although you actually lose distance on any wind shift, as shown in Figure 136, you are still ahead and in a position to keep your opponent from passing. In position A, one boat is dead upwind of the other, and the leeward boat will have to sail six units of distance to be in the same position as the windward boat. A large header comes, as in position B. The leeward boat tacks immediately, and has only five units to sail. In position C a large lift again puts the leeward boat closer, this time by a little over five units. Smaller wind shifts make the loss smaller, but it's still there. It's possible to anticipate and to minimize the loss if you are fairly sure what the next shift will be. If a header is expected, the windward boat might tack a little earlier. By so doing, more is gained by being more in front, rather than dead upwind, of the leeward boat. However, you are vulnerable to being hurt more if a lift occurs instead of a header.

Figure 136

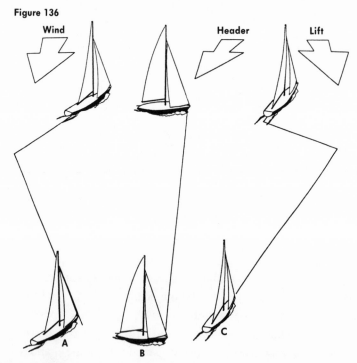

Though every wind shift represents a loss, stay between your competition and your destination to minimize the loss.

Covering an opponent must be done with full knowledge of his reactions. When you tack close to dead to windward of another boat, he has no other choice but to tack away to avoid the bad air from your sails. This means you have to tack again to cover and possibly again after that, assuming your opponent keeps on tacking to get clear air. There are many situations when such a tacking duel does neither of you any good. It is useful if you are match racing, but in most other races you will lose places to other boats by spending too much time covering your prime competition. That's when a "herding" type of cover is appropriate. You want to go in the same direction as the bulk of the other boats, for instance, so you cover your opponent tightly, hurting his air when he is sailing away from the others. When he tacks back toward the others, cover loosely, allowing your opponent clear air. In Figure 137, boat A has a loose cover on B as port tack is desired.

Figure 137

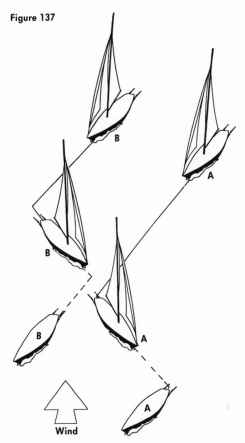

A loose cover gives the leeward boat clear air.
A tight cover gives leeward bad air and forces a tack.

When B tacks, A tacks right on his wind, forces him back on port and again institutes a loose cover on port tack.

Covering an opponent too closely is also a disadvantage is when you are both sailing in a lift. A tight cover will force him to tack, and by covering you will also end up in the header.

To place a tight cover on another boat properly takes timing and precision. The tack after crossing the opponent must be made just at the right location and moment so that you're dead on his wind by the time you have picked up momentum after the tack. Tack too late, and the other boat will have a safe leeward position on you. Tack too early, and, although you'll be giving him some backwind forcing him to tack, he will have a clear safe leeward on you when he does.

The covered boat has a number of options open to break the cover. One is to initiate a tacking duel, which can end up in one of three ways: (1) the covering boat is worried about losing to others in the fleet and breaks off; (2) the covered boat tacks and accelerates faster, so the covering boat loses ground and decides not to continue tacking; or (3) the covered boat loses ground for the same reason and sees no future in continuing the duel.

The covered boat has the advantage of having the choice of when to tack, whereas the covering boat can only react to an opponent's tack. By watching the wave patterns, the covered boat can choose an intermittent smooth patch of water in which to accelerate rapidly after tacking. The covering boat simply tacks upon seeing the leeward boat tack, and is often in worse wave conditions.

Dick Stearns, a well-known Star sailor, once worked over Tom Blackaller in an interesting manner during a Bacardi Cup Star series. Though Dick had good boat speed, Tom was well upwind and covering in the normal way. They had a shifty offshore breeze of 15 knots. Dick watched the hull of Tom's Star closely. When Tom appeared to be lifted, Dick tacked. When Tom tacked to cover, he was now sailing in a header. Since the wind shift took a few moments to travel down to leeward, Dick had a few degrees of heading advantage until the new wind reached him. By repeating this procedure over and over, Dick ate up Tom's lead.

Sometimes you can cover from ahead and to leeward, such as when there is less adverse current along a lee shore. Bruce Goldsmith "covered" Gordon Lindemann during a Soling Midwinters in Ft. Lauderdale, Florida, by footing toward the shore out of the current. Gordon's style was to point high, but pointing just kept him in the current longer. By sailing fast but low, into less current, Bruce ended up to windward and ahead of Gordon every time around the course. Just as you should foot to headers, foot also to areas of less adverse current.

Once a covering position has been established, the boat being covered generally tries to break the cover—to get free air and even to turn the tables—to become the covering boat. One way already mentioned is to initiate a tacking duel. If this tactic isn't helping, try a false tack. If the covering boat is starting his tack at the instant you start yours, a false tack can sometimes work. Act just as though you are planning to complete the tack, but abort it when head to wind. The windward boat has completed his tack, and has to gain speed before tacking back to cover. For a short time you are on opposite tacks, which should be sufficient to break the cover. Frankly, the false tack rarely works in top-flight competition because the covering boat will delay tacking just long enough to force you to complete your tack.

On a free leg of the course, a false jibe sometimes works. You're both on port tack with your competition slightly abaft abeam to leeward. A jibe will give you right-of-way. Your opponent will have to quickly jibe to avoid fouling you and is anxious to cover you by jibing the minute you do. Give every indication of a jibe—square the pole back, perhaps even yell "trip" (as long as your crew is clued in that it's a false jibe), but don't complete the jibe. Your opponent will probably complete his jibe and you will have broken free.

Another method is to lead the covering boat into an obstruction. The covering boat's skipper is concentrating more on the boat he wants to beat than on his surroundings. The skipper of the leeward boat can look around for solutions to his problem because he is calling the shots as to when the tack occurs. I saw a beautiful example of this in the 1963 Pan American games. Pat Duane was the American Flying Dutchman National Champion. As the series was drawing to a close, she and the Brazilian entry were way out front of the other Flying Dutchman skippers. Pat was being closely covered by the Brazilian to windward in light air on the final beat to the finish line. They were on starboard tack when Pat noticed the tail-end boat of the Snipe fleet they were about to lap. He was on the port tack, to windward and ahead of her opponent. Knowing that the Brazilian would tack to cover her, Pat timed her tack so that when he covered, he'd be sailing right down the transom of the Snipe (see Figure 138). What happened next couldn't have been foreseen by Pat, but it clinched the lead for her. The Brazilian decided to pass to windward of the Snipe, who at the same instant tacked to get out of the way of the two leading contenders for the Flying

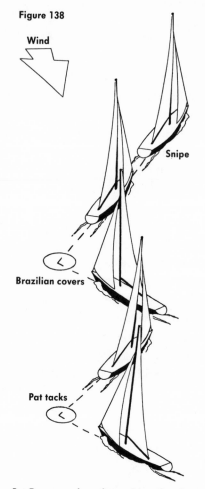

Figure 138

Wind

Snipe

Brazilian covers

Pat tacks

How Pat Duane used an obstruction to break cover.

Dutchman Gold Medal. The Snipe was now on starboard tack, which forced the Brazilian to tack over on to starboard also to avoid fouling the Snipe. The two Flying Dutchmen were now on split tacks, which broke the cover. When Pat came back over on starboard tack later, she crossed the Brazilian and won the race.

I was once crewing on a boat that was being covered by another when I noticed that a tug towing a barge far astern was approaching from windward. We tacked over and sailed across the bow of the tug. Our opponent, well to windward of us, was blocked by the towline and had to tack away. The key is to be observant. Look for any obstacle or occurrence into which you can sail the covering boat.

Watch the windward boat carefully for opportunities to tack away when the skipper or crew is preoccupied. For instance, they may be changing jibs, or may have fouled up a jib sheet. If they are unprepared, or unable to tack, that's the obvious time to break the cover. It's a simple tactic, but one often overlooked. Many opportunities to get away are lost forever when not seized at the moment.

One can even break the cover from a boat behind with a little thought. A few years ago I was crewing on *Carina* in Long Island Sound. Toward the end of a two-day race, we were "rock hopping" along the shore shortly after dawn to pick up the light offshore breeze. We noticed that *Baccarat,* about a half a mile to leeward, matched every tack we made to stay as close to shore as we were. The tacks weren't random. They were covering from behind. When we tacked toward shore, they tacked at the same instant. Feeling we could put such predictability to good use, we started poring over the chart. We noticed in one area that the ten-foot bottom contour took a long passage toward the shore (Figure 139), so we sailed out on port tack until we judged that *Baccarat* was opposite the channel. We tacked and, true to form, so did she. We then sailed in as far toward shore as possible, and tacked when our centerboard touched bottom. *Baccarat* tacked and promptly went hard aground on an outgoing tide at the "X" in Figure 139. We sailed away until she was out of sight astern, still aground. Lest readers feel we were somehow playing with danger, let me reassure them that going aground in mud along the Long Island shore is a commonplace occurrence, and no danger or damage is possible on light days.

Dr. Stuart Walker, well-known author of sailing books, told me of a tactic

Figure 139

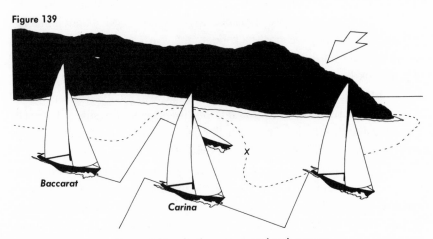

How watching depth contours can break a cover.

Figure 140

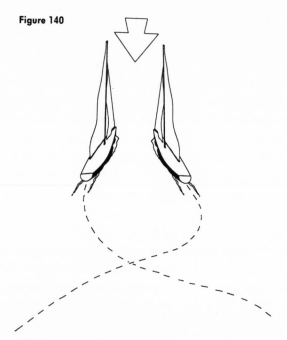

If both boats are tacking at the same time, the one on the
other's port side shall keep clear.

he has used successfully to break a cover almost before it happens. He
worked this tactic sailing his International 14 dinghy in a team match. A
port-tack boat in a team match expects a crossing starboard-tacker to tack
and to cover—either on her lee bow or on her weather quarter. Stuart, in the
port-tack boat, bears off early to go under the starboard-tack boat. This
forces the starboard-tacker to cross because a safe leeward is unobtainable.
To avoid obstructing the port-tack boat, the starboard-tacker can't start
tacking to cover until the port-tack boat's bow crosses her stern. Stuart, in
the port-tack boat, tacks immediately after she passes astern to meet the
starboard-tacker tacking simultaneously. When two yachts are tacking at
the same time, rule 41.4 says the one on the other's port side shall keep
clear. By using this tactic, the port-tack boat may force the other back onto
starboard tack, as in Figure 140, and drive over her.

This tactic seems to work best with dinghies, but has been tried on boats
as large as 12-Meters. Dennis Conner, skipper of *Freedom* in the 1980
America's Cup trials, while sailing on port tack ducked under *Clipper* on
starboard tack near the layline. As Tom Blackaller, helmsman of *Clipper,*

tacked to pin *Freedom,* Dennis Conner started to tack simultaneously. However, Tom just did a sweeping, slow tack and cleared *Clipper*'s bow. Tom knew the rules, recognized the trap Dennis was trying to lure him into, and adjusted his tactics accordingly.

Luffing is a common defensive tactic to prevent another yacht from passing to windward. Because this tactic is rarely used when beating, it tends to be forgotten as an option. There are times when a good luff on a beat can be tactically rewarding. For instance, you are approaching the layline to the weather mark, and cannot tack because of the proximity of a boat on your weather quarter. You have a safe leeward position on the boat and normally the skipper would tack away to avoid sailing in your bad air. This time, however, you are pinned and can't tack for the mark until the weather boat does. If you bear off to gain tacking room to leeward, so does your opponent to keep you from tacking. Only when he can be sure of laying the mark will he tack, and then there is no way for you to lead to the mark.

The situation can be saved by a well-timed luff short of the layline. I was once crewing in the Mallory Cup eliminations in Ensigns. We found ourselves in just the situation described above. Brit Chance, also crewing, suggested a luff. The late Palmer Sparkman was skippering and agreed. Knowing that the luff would be almost head-to-wind, I released the jib. The windward boat was caught by surprise. Their crew failed to release the large overlapping jib, which backed, forcing the boat over to starboard tack. We kept on sailing a few boat lengths to the layline, tacked and met the other boat on port tack at the mark. Since the latter had to tuck under our stern, we rounded ahead.

There are those who consider such a luff bad sportsmanship. I disagree when it's for a defensive purpose such as to avoid being pinned to the layline. I don't particularly like the skipper who luffs in an attempt to "tag you out." The rules allow a sharp luff without warning, and if there's contact, the windward boat is usually either disqualified or penalized. Some skippers use the rule to luff all over the course without any apparent purpose except catching the windward boat unawares. Generally, if you are the skipper of a windward boat that is luffed and tagged by a leeward boat, you should be annoyed at yourself for putting your boat in such a vulnerable position, rather than at the leeward skipper for exercising his rights.

The one spot where the proximity of boats makes it difficult to avoid a sharp luff is right after rounding a mark. Let's say you have an inside overlap at a mark. The outside boat gives you just enough room to allow you to round safely. This puts you in closer than you would normally be in case of a luff. Since you are placed in this vulnerable position through no fault of your own, you must be particularly wary.

It was just such a situation that was the impetus for me to learn the racing rules well. I was about sixteen years old, and had borrowed my father's Atlantic class sailboat for a Saturday afternoon race at my local yacht club. I was approaching the leeward mark on a port tack run, and my bow was almost overlapped with the stern of an older member's boat on starboard tack. He sailed right past the mark without jibing. I swung inside and hardened up around the mark, whereupon he jibed, luffed head-to-wind, hit me near the stern about a boat length past the mark, and yelled, "You're out!" I disregarded the call and kept on racing. Two weeks later the race committee chairman said to me, "Stevie, an incident happened on the race course a while ago, and the club cannot condone such behavior." I was taken before a protest committee and thrown out of the race. I knew nothing except the basic right-of-way rules, so I couldn't defend myself. That night I started studying the rule book and found that (1) the protesting skipper hadn't jibed at the first reasonable opportunity; (2) he had luffed without luffing rights; (3) he had failed to fly a protest flag; (4) the protest was not in writing; (5) the protest was not made within two hours of the finish of the race; (6) a reasonable time was not allowed for the preparation of a defense, and so on, and so on. I swore never to be so unprepared again.

I soon learned, in regard to luffing after starting, that a leeward boat can only luff a boat that is passing to windward. A leeward boat cannot overtake to leeward and then luff. If, at any time during an overlap, the helmsman of the windward yacht is abeam or forward of the mainmast of the leeward yacht, the latter shall not sail above her proper course while the overlap exists.

When a boat does attempt to pass you to windward, you can luff that boat head-to-wind if you desire. As two boats turn toward the wind, however, the outside leeward boat has farther to turn and so loses ground on the inside windward boat. If the leeward boat's mast comes abeam of the windward boat's helmsman, he calls "mast abeam," and the leeward boat has to fall off to her proper course to the mark. There are a few tricks that have been outlawed. Windward's helmsman must be in his normal steering position, and cannot lean way forward so as to call mast abeam earlier. Nor can he point the boat higher than the leeward boat to get the same result. If leeward's helmsman feels the call of mast abeam has been premature or otherwise improper, the only recourse is to protest. Furthermore, leeward's helmsman can luff only if he has luffing rights on all boats affected by the luff. Keep this in mind the next time you are being luffed. I've often stopped a leeward boat from luffing me because the helmsman of a boat to windward of me was forward of leeward's mast.

There are other ways to avoid being luffed, but one of the most interesting can be attributed to Jim Mattingly aboard *Tenacious*. Many race circulars for long-distance races have a rule that limits luffing. The wording varies a great deal in each circular, but it's common—although not exclusive—to allow luffing up to one hour after the last class starts or, alternatively, between the hours of sunrise to sunset. At other times the International Rules of the Road at Sea prevail. The idea is to prevent boats from having dangerous luffing matches at night or out at sea.

Jim was tactician on *Tenacious,* and they were being legally luffed by another boat. While the crew of the other boat was yelling and screaming at *Tenacious,* Jim politely asked if they had read their race circular. This distracted them enough to send a man below for it and by the time they figured out they did indeed have the right to luff, *Tenacious* had slipped on through.

LAYLINES

A basic tactical rule of sailboat racing is "avoid the laylines." (The layline is an imaginary line indicating the last tack to the windward mark.) If you make your last tack for the mark a long distance from it, many of your options to take advantage of wind shifts are lost. If you get lifted, you've overstood the mark. This means you have sailed above the new layline, and you will have to reach off for the mark. If you get headed, you can no longer lay the mark and must tack. Every boat closer to the mark gets a greater advantage from a header than you do. In Figure 141, boats A and B were even in the original wind direction. When headed, they both tack and B has gained. Moreover, A has only a short distance to sail before she arrives at the new layline, and has to tack for the mark. If the wind hasn't shifted back, she will be sailing for the mark in a header while B is still on a port-tack lift. Boat D was on the original port-tack layline. But when the shift arrives, boat C is now on the layline while D has overstood.

Another reason to avoid the layline until a few boat lengths from the mark is that each boat on the layline is feeding bad air to the boat behind it. Unless you overstand a little, the backwind from the boat ahead could be sufficient

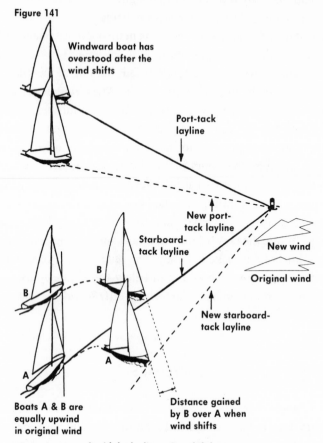

Figure 141

Windward boat has overstood after the wind shifts

Port-tack layline

New port-tack layline

Starboard-tack layline

New wind

Original wind

New starboard-tack layline

B

B

A

A

Boats A & B are equally upwind in original wind

Distance gained by B over A when wind shifts

Avoid the laylines. Any shift hurts.

to slow you substantially. A slow boat makes more leeway, which could result in failing to lay the mark. Many skippers start to pinch the boat when this occurs, which results in more leeway and virtually guarantees a problem at the mark. The correct tactic is to sail fast and, if it's close, shoot dead into the wind to get around the mark. Release the jib, especially a genoa, to avoid backing it.

When it becomes obvious that because of current, another boat's backwind, or whatever, there is no way to lay the mark, look for a spot to tack early. Even if it's necessary to slow the boat down to let a windward boat pass, it may be better than continuing on into an impossible situation. A windward boat will usually bear off for speed in an attempt to take the leeward boat's wind (to blanket her) even if, by doing so she fails to fetch the mark. This guarantees the windward boat the lead at the mark. If they had allowed the leeward boat to pinch or to shoot to fetch the mark, the latter would have an inside overlap, and would probably maintain the lead.

For many reasons, therefore, it's important to avoid reaching the laylines too early. About the only disadvantages in arriving at the starboard-tack layline very close to the mark are: (1) congestion, and (2) the short distance on the starboard tack to set up for a spinnaker. The first depends on the size of the fleet, the length of the weather leg, and the type of boats. A large, evenly matched fleet of identical boats can result in a mammoth pack of starboard-tack boats approaching the weather mark for a port rounding. A port-tack boat may have to take fifteen or twenty sterns before finding a hole in which to tack. On the other hand, a boat in a class of cruising boats that have finished a five-mile beat may find no other boat within 100 yards.

The second disadvantage is more important to the cruising boat. Because of the more cumbersome equipment, such as heavy spinnaker poles, more time is needed to prepare for a spinnaker leg than on smaller boats. One has to approach the layline at a distance from the mark to allow the crew time to set up, but not so far out that one either overstands or otherwise misjudges the layline.

This brings us to the tactics involved in determining when the layline has been reached. One common method is to observe how other boats are heading on the opposite tack as you pass their sterns. At the instant you cross an extension of their centerline, you can determine if they are pointing at the mark or not. Beware of the cagey skipper who, knowing you'll be checking, heads off 10 degrees or so below the mark just as you pass his stern. His change of course is imperceptible to you, and it appears he is unable to fetch the mark, which misleads you into sailing farther and overstanding.

A variation on this theme occurs when the port-tack boat is crossing ahead of the starboard-tack boat. Since the latter is on the layline and doesn't want the port-tack boat to feed her bad air all the way to the mark, she heads off about 10 degrees and maintains a constant course so as not to obstruct the port-tack boat. When the opponent tacks in a safe leeward position or dead in front of the starboard tack boat, the latter heads up to close-hauled and drives over the top of the boat that just tacked.

By remembering your compass course the last time you were on star-board tack, you can take compass bearings on the mark, and tack when it bears the same as your last reading on starboard. This assumes no wind shifts or current, but these can be cranked into your calculations. For instance, if you're sailing in a 10-degree header on port tack, add 10 degrees to your last heading on starboard tack and use that for a bearing.

Skippers of many boats paint laylines on their decks based on their normal tacking angles. Let's say your boat sails within 40 degrees of the wind and tacks in 80 degrees. A line painted almost abeam (80 degrees from the center line of the boat) indicates the layline. When the mark is on an extension of that line, a tack will place you right on the layline. Often other lines are added 50 degrees from the centerline, as in Figure 142. The

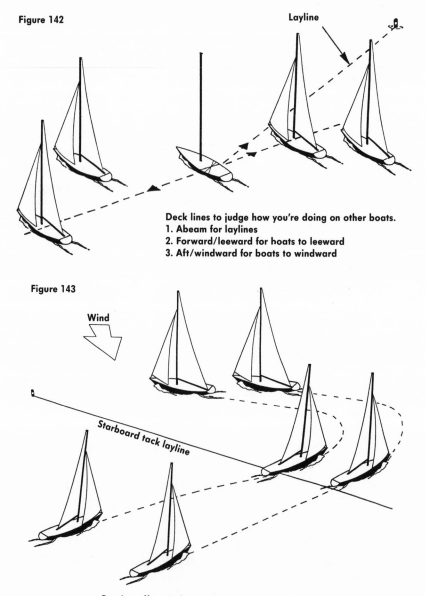

Figure 142

Layline

Deck lines to judge how you're doing on other boats.
1. Abeam for laylines
2. Forward/leeward for boats to leeward
3. Aft/windward for boats to windward

Figure 143

Wind

Starboard tack layline

Bearing off to pin leeward boat. Only legal upwind

forward line shows whether you are ahead or behind a boat to leeward. The aft line gives the same information on a boat to windward. Of course, these lines only work if there are no wind shifts, if you are steering an accurate close-hauled course, and if you have calculated your tacking angles correctly. Since these are very big ifs, such lines are used as rough aids rather than absolutes.

There are times when you may want to overstand the layline. If a boat is ahead and to leeward of you on port tack as you approach the starboard tack layline, you must make sure she is unable to tack without fouling you (see Figure 143). To that end, you bear off for speed, and get close enough to windward of her that she can't tack. With her pinned in that position, you drive her past the layline to the point when you can fetch the mark easily. Then, when you tack, you will be able to sail full and fast enough to keep her from passing you. If you had tacked right on the layline, she would be past it due to her relative position, and could possibly drive over you at the mark were it necessary for you to pinch near the end of the leg. The defensive tactic on the part of the leeward boat, as mentioned before, is a sharp luff short of the layline. This will work only if the windward boat is caught unawares. The windward boat should keep enough

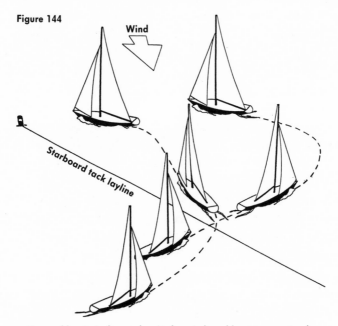

Figure 144

Wind

Starboard tack layline

Covered boat pinches and waits for windward boat to overstand.

open water between her and her opponent to negate the effectiveness of a luff.

Another overstanding tactic is used when a leeward boat is being covered by a boat to windward and ahead, as in Figure 144. The leeward skipper is banking on the hope that the windward crew will be totally engrossed in covering him. As the leeward boat approaches the layline, the skipper pinches and slows the boat. This results in the windward boat's sailing farther past the layline while the leeward boat sails slowly. It further allows the leeward boat to inch up closer to the mark. The leeward boat keeps on going slowly past the layline until the windward skipper comes to his senses, realizes he has overstood, and tacks first, and then will cover. Figure 144 shows the desired result. The leeward boat should at least maintain an inside overlap at the mark and come out ahead.

Pete Conrad of Sobstad Sailmakers mentions a tactic that can often be used to advantage. He was sailing in a Finn class National championship and was just about laying the weather mark on starboard tack in a breeze that was gradually lifting him. The lead Finn was close to crossing him, and the last thing he wanted was for the leader to tack and to feed him bad air all the way to the mark. So Pete shouted something to the effect of, "Go ahead across, you have it made," whereupon his opponent took the bait, thanked Pete, and crossed his bow. Pete slowed down intentionally, and ducked the port-tack boat. The competitor sailed another 10 to 15 boat lengths, tacked, and realized he had overstood the mark. Pete rounded in the lead and won the race. Pete's competitor had become so captivated by the boat-to-boat confrontation that he lost sight of the overall view. As you can see with many of these tactics, that's the aim of the initiator. When a boat that has right-of-way waves you across, immediately start wondering why. Am I sailing in a header? Is the breeze lighter where I'm going? Is the water shallow? Could I lay the mark on the other tack? Take the cynic's viewpoint that altruism is hard to find on the racecourse.

Dick Tillman used a tactic in the Snipe Nationals that is effective when worked with precision. He was short of the layline on starboard tack, close to the weather quarter of his major competitor. His plan was to pin the leeward boat to keep her from tacking until he could lay the mark. He initiated his tack for the mark at a point where his crew had to back the jib to swing the bow over fast enough to avoid hitting the buoy. This necessitated the leeward boat's sailing past the mark before tacking and returning on port tack. In the meantime, Dick had rounded to port, and had established a starboard tack on the next reaching leg, just as his competitor was returning to the mark on port tack. Not caring to add injury to insult, Dick elected to take his transom and not to protest. After all, Dick had placed him in that situation in the first place.

I saw another interesting weather mark tactic in the Pan American games. Peter Barrett was sailing a Finn, and had only one competitor giving him trouble. Peter was on starboard tack, just barely laying the mark, with his competition about half a boat length dead to leeward. There were no windows in the sails, so Peter couldn't see the other boat. His competition banked on this blind spot, and sailed right past the mark. He expected Peter to bear off to a reach around the mark and to foul him since Peter, as windward boat, had to stay clear of a leeward boat. However, no such thing happened. Peter kept on going close-hauled until his competitor realized after 50 yards or so that there was no future in continuing. Peter obviously wasn't taking the bait, and the leeward boat still had to jibe, sail all the way back, and round the mark. Peter won the race easily. Later I asked Peter how he had figured out what his competition intended to do. Half of it, he said, was knowing his competition. The other half was sensing something amiss when he had reached the mark, and could still see nothing of the other boat. Iain Murray on *Kookaburra III* tried the same tactic in the last race of the 1987 America's Cup series against Dennis Conner on *Stars and Stripes*. Again, it didn't work.

I sometimes approach a layline on port tack, deliberately using another port-tack boat to leeward and ahead as a spoiler. If a starboard-tacker comes along that could give me trouble, the other port-tack has to tack first, which can slow the starboard-tack boat down and allow me to cross them both. It is sometimes the edge needed to reach the layline, tack on both of them, and round the mark ahead.

WEATHER MARK ROUNDINGS

The first weather mark rounding in a sailboat race is second only to the starting line as an area of congestion and confusion. The boats that can spurt out of the mess at the mark in good order stand a good chance of lengthening their lead on the bulk of the fleet. When the second leg is a spinnaker reach and there's a cluster of boats close behind you, consider delaying the spinnaker set and reaching high to avoid having them on your wind. When they fall down to course and set spinnakers, do the same. When there's a large space of open water between you and the boats behind you, the opposite tactic is usually the best: turn right down to course, and set the spinnaker quickly to lengthen the distance between you and your pursuers. They will probably luff each other up high of the course and, along with having to sail a longer distance, they will have to sail on a slower point of sail to get down to the mark.

Years ago Bill Cox (*American Eagle*'s helmsman in the 1964 Cup trials) told me about a tactic he used which is now fairly common: the delayed spinnaker set. When rounding a weather mark close behind another boat, sail across the wind on a close reach for a few moments with main and jib trimmed properly. Assuming the boat ahead falls right down to course, her speed will be markedly slowed by the crew's bouncing around and the windage of the spinnaker going up. Meanwhile the weather boat gets on her wind, which makes leeward's spinnaker more difficult to fly. Once in such a controlling position, the windward boat sets her chute. That the process also slows her down doesn't affect their relative positions, since the leeward boat is being blanketed. The obvious defense is for the lead boat to sail on a close reach to discourage such a maneuver.

Hans Fogh once played the "delayed spinnaker set" in reverse. In a 1965 Flying Dutchman race in Italy, a Swiss boat was leading and Hans was in second place, with the rest of the fleet way behind. The two remaining legs on the race were close reaches, and to pass the lead boat would be close to impossible. He figured that if he set a spinnaker, so would the Swiss. If he luffed to pass to windward, so would the Swiss . . . a virtual stand-off. So, rounding the last weather mark to begin the last two reaches, Hans's crew made all kinds of commotion, yelling and screaming as they set the spinnaker. As soon as the Swiss saw the spinnaker going up on the boat astern he turned his back and began setting his, whereupon Hans pulled his down. When the Swiss's spinnaker was full, Hans sailed right around him to weather (since the reach was so close) and went on to win the race.

Most race committees attempt to set a 45-90-45-degree right triangle course. If the windward leg is perfect—meaning the wind is blowing directly to the starting line from the windward mark, then the apparent wind on the first reach will be sightly forward of abeam, and it will be the same for the second reach. Seasoned racing sailors become accustomed to the reaching wind angle, and often even the best become disoriented after a wind shift. If the wind veers and they reach off with the apparent wind slightly forward of abeam, they will be well high of the reaching mark. I've heard that even Paul Elvstrom sailed to the wrong reaching mark in the 1968 pre-Olympics. Inevitably, the fleet follows, since the best sailors are usually in front, and most of the others think the leaders must be right. It's interesting to look at what talented sailors do when they realize they've made a mistake or discover the mark isn't where it ought to be.

Jim Mattingly had a similar problem in the 1971 Half Ton Cup Worlds championship. He was leading the fleet on a reach, realized the mark was to leeward, but noticed a fog bank to windward. He pretended to see the mark to weather, and hardened up under the spinnaker. The fleet followed him into the fog bank. As soon as Jim's boat was well hidden from the rest, he jibed and finished the race hours ahead of the other boats.

Hans Fogh found himself in a somewhat similar situation on a weather leg. He was directly to leeward of several boats and no one could find the mark. Hans knew that the mark was still to windward, but he took advantage of the uncertainty of the others to pull off a little ruse. He spotted a mark (of a similar type to the true weather mark) directly in front of him. He rounded it and, much to his pleasure, all the boats to windward bore off to round the same mark. He slowed the boat down, and waited for them all to round. Then he tacked, beat up to the real weather mark, and ended up winning the race.

The common denominator in all these cases is a fertile imagination and an indomitable spirit that snatches victory from the jaws of defeat.

REACHES

Perhaps less dramatic, but nevertheless helpful to a winning effort, are some of the other tactics used on reaches. Since an inside overlap at the jibing mark can mean a difference of many places, you sail the leg with that in mind. If a boat luffs up to pass you to windward, you must protect your position by luffing also. Once, on a tight spinnaker reach during an Olympic-course race, *Sleuth* was just ahead of *Running Tide*. The air was light and, although *Running Tide* was a larger boat than *Sleuth,* we had beaten her to the windward mark. Early in the reaching leg we luffed *Tide* very high of the course to the jibing mark when she attempted to pass us to windward. This discouraged her from trying again, so she tried sailing through our lee, which didn't work. Later in the leg, nearing the jibing mark, she tried to break through to windward again. This time I luffed far less. Ideally, I wanted her to be overlapped to the outside of us, so I could head at the mark with an inside overlap. When it became obvious that she could power over us, I no longer luffed. *Running Tide* passed us and, when she was clear ahead, we held a course that would take us past the buoy outside the two-boat-lengths circle. If we had headed for the mark when we were within two boat lengths, we would not have been overlapped and would not have been entitled to room. We would have just followed her around the mark. The crew on *Running Tide* obviously wanted to jibe for the mark but couldn't without fouling us in the process. When we reached the spot shown on Figure 145—well past the mark—we jibed, and had an inside overlap at the mark with *Running Tide* tucked away in our bad air.

This incident indicates the thought processes that must go on when racing. Many skippers luff any boat passing to windward indiscriminately, without considering the desired end result. If you luff hard on the first reach to avoid being passed, you work up to weather of the mark and when you bear down to round it, your angle will create an overlap for the trailing boat on the inside (See Figure 146). On the second reach, luffing a boat hard has the opposite effect. As you head down for the mark, you break the overlap the weather boat may have had on the inside.

Whether to sail high or low of course on a reach depends a great deal on the anticipated wind strength and direction. When the breeze is fresh early in the leg and you expect it to soften, sail low initially. This allows you to harden up to a faster point of sailing as the wind dies. Do the opposite when you expect a light breeze to freshen. Head high first, and come off as the breeze strengthens. With a wind that is steady in direction but changeable in

Figure 145

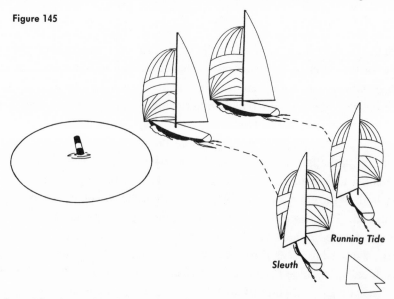

Running Tide

Sleuth

By avoiding the two-boat-lengths circle you avoid the rules that apply to mark rounding.

strength, fall off for speed in the puffs and head up in the lulls. This will also keep you in the puffs longer as they move downwind.

Current is also a factor on reaches. Generally, in a contrary or cross-current situation, the best course is the shortest distance and thus the shortest time spent in the effect of current. You often know roughly the strength and direction of the current from *Current Tables* studied before the race. Just how much it is affecting you can be seen after you've sailed down the leg for a while. Steer your boat directly at the jibing mark ahead and glance astern. If it's more to the starboard side of the boat, you've been set to the left of the course and vice versa. When the jibing mark can be easily distinguished against a shoreline, try to steer your boat so the shore doesn't

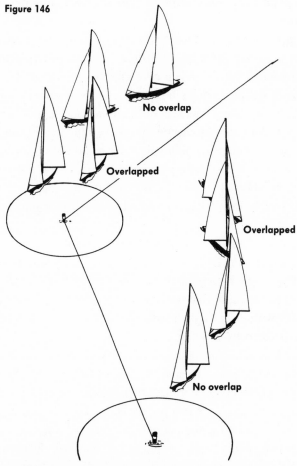

Figure 146

No overlap

Overlapped

Overlapped

No overlap

Luff with caution first reach, luff with abandon second reach.
Inside at the mark is the place to be.

move behind the buoy. If the buoy moves to the right along the shore, you are being set to the left of course by the current, and must steer more to starboard to offset it.

JIBE MARK

We are finishing the first reaching leg, and approaching the jibing mark. When the first reach is broad, the next reach will be quite tight, and an early jibe is indicated. If possible, complete the jibe before arriving at the mark so you are free to harden up to the new course right at the mark. In this way you will lose nothing to leeward. The opposite is true if the first reach is tight, but it doesn't take much to realize you shouldn't start jibing before arriving at the mark.

Although it's beneficial to be the inside boat at the mark, there are many times when it just isn't possible to get the required overlap before reaching the two-boat-length circle. When many boats are overlapped, the outside boats squeeze the inside boats fairly close to the mark. This prevents the inside boats from playing it wide at the approach and tight at the turn. When you know you don't have a chance for an overlap, a good tactic is to slow down the boat by collapsing your spinnaker or luffing your mainsail. Then swing out wide, and do an early jibe. Harden up for the mark past the sterns of the overlapped boats, and go for the opening between the mark and the stern of the inside boat. It's risky and takes excellent timing, but it can be done.

If you round in front of a number of boats, luff sharply after the mark to discourage any of them from attempting to pass you to windward. It doesn't hurt to end up a little high of course on the second reaching leg of a marks-to-port triangle, because that will put you inside at the leeward mark. So, while we luff with discretion on the first reach, we luff with vengeance on the second to keep from being passed.

Knowing that such will be the tendency of an opponent ahead of you, any luff on your part to get to weather of him should be done very early and sharply. Don't climb up his stern and then decide to pass, because you'll be luffed right off the course. When you are still a few boat lengths back, go up sharply. If you're lucky, the skipper of the boat ahead won't notice your move until it's too late. When there are one or two boat lengths of open water to close before the leeward boat can effectively luff a windward boat, leeward may not even try. By the time she gets up to you, you may very well have a

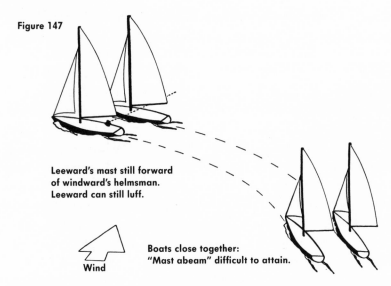

Figure 147

Leeward's mast still forward
of windward's helmsman.
Leeward can still luff.

Wind

Boats close together:
"Mast abeam" difficult to attain.

mast-abeam position, and the leeward boat would be unable to luff legally. By closing the gap in attempting to luff, the leeward boat is now sailing slower, in a more disturbed area of your wind shadow.

Most skippers who have experienced these problems won't luff unless they have a good chance of holding off the windward boat. They realize that the greater distance the two boats are apart, the quicker the windward boat's skipper attains a mast-abeam position. In Figure 147 two boats are close together. Leeward luffs and windward responds, but still hasn't reached mast abeam. In Figure 148 there is more space between the boats. The same

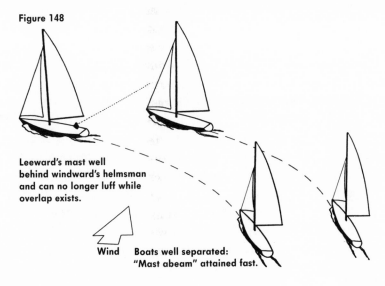

Figure 148

Leeward's mast well
behind windward's helmsman
and can no longer luff while
overlap exists.

Wind

Boats well separated:
"Mast abeam" attained fast.

luff and the same response results in windward's helmsman's being far ahead of leeward's mast as he sights abeam. Leeward can no longer luff, and must fall back to her proper course.

There are times when the tactical interplay between boats on reaches is done at long distance. Chris Bouzaid, former president of Hood Sailmakers (U.S.A.) Inc., recounts what he calls his favorite ocean racing maneuver. He has used this tactic during two One Ton Cup championships and it is very effective. Two boats are on a tight spinnaker reach. The lead boat is eight to 10 minutes ahead, and the objective in Chris's trailing boat is to close the distance. Chris first establishes very clearly where the turning mark is. At this point the mark is not within sight. Because both boats have been reaching for some time, they have sagged below course, and eventually will have to douse their spinnakers to reach up to the mark under jibs.

With about 10 miles to go, Chris starts sailing the boat as high as he can to windward, losing speed while doing so. Although Chris may be gaining a little weather ground, the lead boat is assuredly opening the gap between them. This situation continues for the next five miles, by which time Chris has made a considerable distance to windward, but is far behind. When the turning mark is spotted, it becomes obvious that both spinnakers will have to be doused for the boats to fetch the mark. At this stage, the combination of being way behind and well to weather creates an easy reach to the mark for Chris. The lead boat, being so far ahead and downwind of the mark, has to go close-hauled to fetch it, and often has to tack. The distance between the mark and the two boats is almost the same, so Chris has closed the distance between the two boats considerably with this maneuver.

LEEWARD MARK

As you approach the leeward mark on the second reach, it's again desirable to get an inside overlap. In Figure 149, boat A is trying to get to weather of boat B for an inside overlap at the mark. But B luffs sharply and, as she approaches the two-boat length circle, she falls off toward the mark. Often this turn can break the overlap and place the windward yacht in a "clear astern" position, defined in the rules as "when her hull and equipment in normal position are abaft an imaginary line projected abeam from the aftermost point of the other's hull and equipment in normal position." As the leeward boat turns toward the mark, this imaginary line swings forward, and the overlap is broken.

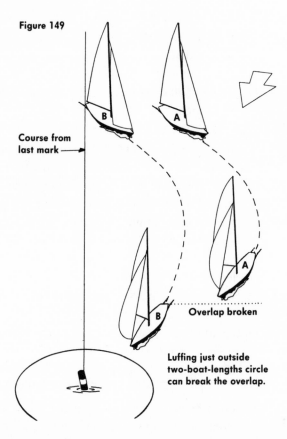

Figure 149

Course from
last mark

Overlap broken

Luffing just outside
two-boat-lengths circle
can break the overlap.

A good tactic at the leeward mark when the spinnaker is to be doused is to leave it up until the last possible moment and sail to leeward of a bunch of boats. We did this once when racing *Sleuth*. We were vying with *Intuition* for the lead when we both fell into a hole. The rest of the fleet sailed right up to us with a light breeze, and their momentum took them right through us to the mark. The tables had turned on us completely, and we were almost last. The mass of boats stalled at the mark when they doused their spinnakers. I saw a stronger breeze filling in from windward. A couple of the leaders had broken free from the group, and they were moving out close-hauled in the freshening wind. I elected to stay well low of the jumble of boats and, with the pole on the headstay, to sail with the spinnaker on as tight a reach as possible. We broke through the lee of the largest group, doused the spinnaker well past the mark, and hardened up. We then tacked onto starboard, which took us directly toward the new wind. Most of the boats that were stalled at the mark took our stern on port tack, and we were back in decent position, having gained back about 10 to 12 boats.

When there is a strong current against you in light air, consider a later spinnaker douse. The boats ahead that have doused too early now find themselves with too little sail area to stem the current, and the rest of the fleet is catching up under spinnaker and blanketing the boats ahead. To avoid this situation, assuming that you are either leading or have a clear shot at the mark, carry your spinnaker right up to or even past the mark if the current could set you onto the mark as you round. When you reach a position where the current will just about set you to the proper side of the mark if you lose your way, douse the spinnaker. For the small amount of delay going to windward, you are at least sure of having cleared the mark.

Normally, if current and other boats are not a worry, the proper mark rounding is to swing wide at the beginning and thus be close to the mark at the point where you are close-hauled. Boat A in Figure 150 has made a smooth, even rounding, and is on the wind right next to the mark. Boat B has approached too close to the mark, drifts out on the turn, and ends up on the wind well to leeward of boat A. Since it is doubtful she could tack without fouling boat A, boat B has gone from a winning position to a losing one. Naturally, boat B could make a much tighter turn if her spinnaker were down, and she were prepared for it. However, since a tight turn results in a large loss of speed, the result would be the same.

If you do a decent rounding, as does boat A in Figure 150, but it's right behind a number of other boats, a common maneuver is to shoot almost head-to-wind to gain some breathing space. Quite often the crew of a boat ahead hasn't finished cleaning up after the spinnaker leg, the boat is heeling too much because the crew isn't hiking, or the skipper may not be on the

Figure 150

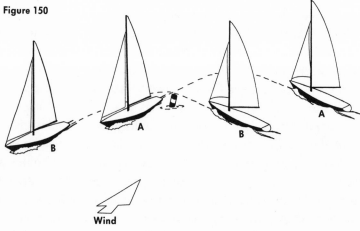

Wind

A smooth, close rounding can overcome an outside position.

wind because of other distractions. As long as you aren't heading dead at the stern of the boat ahead, you have a good chance of passing. The luff barely slows you down if it's part of a continuing turn around the mark as the centrifugal force of the mast and sails shoots the boat to windward. With just half a boat length of open water to windward of the boat ahead, concentration on accurate steering and crewing can ensure success.

A luff sometimes doesn't work if the boat ahead has also luffed to avoid the backwind of another in front of her. A tack away from the bad air is often the answer, but will not be successful if the boat ahead also tacks and covers you. This is the time to watch carefully for an opportunity. On some larger day-racing keelboats, a crew member has to get on deck to clear the spinnaker pole. Sometimes the crew forgets to get out the out-haul on the mainsail. Wait until the skipper or crew of the boat ahead is distracted by some problem that will delay her from tacking immediately to cover you; then tack. This is an excellent way of breaking cover.

AFTER ROUNDING THE LEEWARD MARK

When you are in the enviable position of having a commanding lead on the fleet, and neither side of the course is advantageous, standard practice dictates the use of a tactic called "splitting the distance." After rounding the mark and hardening up to close-hauled, check how far back your nearest competition is. When they have covered half the distance to the mark, tack. By the time they reach the mark, you should be dead upwind of them. This places you squarely between your destination and your competition. To beat you they have to go "through" you, which is very difficult.

Some of the greatest gains and losses occur shortly after rounding the leeward mark. It is essential to know whether you are sailing in a header or a lift, and to judge which way you expect the wind to shift. A shift may have occurred on the second reaching leg, where it's more difficult to detect. The apparent wind would go forward, but this also happens if the breeze lightens, so the skipper may not have noticed. After rounding and sailing close-hauled for a while, as in Figure 151, he suddenly notices that other boats, which have rounded long after, are well up inside of him. While he was sailing on a header, the other boats were on the reaching leg. When they reached the mark, the wind backed, lifting all boats on port tack. This put the boats at the mark in an instantly favorable position vis-à-vis the skipper who sailed in a header. If he recognizes this fact, he may keep on sailing on

Figure 151

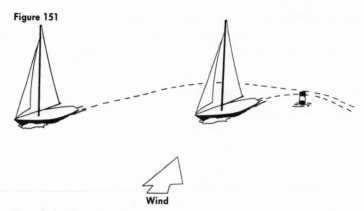

Wind

Beward of sailing off in a header after rounding the leeward mark while others, rounding much later, are in a lift.

the lift, and wait for the next header to come before tacking. If he doesn't realize what has happened, he may feel this bad position was the result of poor crew work, or perhaps that there is more wind where the other boats are. This might prompt him to tack, whereupon he would again be sailing in a header when all the others are sailing in a lift—a bad move.

This solution is to avoid getting into the position before it happens. If you haven't been able to determine any wind shift on the reaching leg, check your compass course after rounding and sailing close-hauled. You should know your heading on port tack from the last beat, and compare it with your present heading. If lifted, hold on; if headed, tack. Remember, however, that the other tack will take you toward the other boats that haven't rounded yet. Their sails can chop up the wind severely and you will be sailing through their bow and quarter waves. Although you have right-of-way (being leeward boat on starboard tack), the amount gained from the shift is offset somewhat by the bad sailing conditions.

When you round the mark and find yourself in a lift, but hurt by other boats, consider laying off below them. In one 5.5-Meter Nationals, we found ourselves in that position. The reach became quite free near the end of the leg, and we realized the wind had shifted aft (a port-tack lift). We were behind and outside a number of boats at the turn, and normally would have tacked away to clear our air. But starboard tack was headed. It was imperative that we stay port tack so, instead of tacking, we reached off to leeward and broke through the lee of the boats to windward. When the header returned we were in an ideal position to make use of it: ahead and to leeward. We tacked, and crossed a number of the boats that had beaten us to the mark.

THE BEAT TO A RUN AND THE RUN

The second beat isn't much different from the first, except that the competition is more spread out, and one starts thinking about staying between the competition and the mark, covering, and avoiding taking flyers. Often the wind has shifted more to one side of the course, making one tack the long tack to the mark. Generally, the proper tactic is to take the long tack first. This is in keeping with the premise of avoiding the laylines, as the short tack will take you to the laylines faster.

As you can see in Figure 152, a boat that sails a port tack from the leeward mark in the new veered wind (indicated by dashes), will soon reach the starboard tack layline, and will overstand if she continues on. Since she will be spending so little time on port tack and so much more time on starboard, she must play the wind shifts differently from the first weather leg. The skipper will generally tack on a small header when on port tack, but will absorb a much greater header on starboard, because he must remain on starboard tack for a greater distance.

The approach to the weather mark for rounding to a run demands different tactics from those used when rounding to a reach. It usually does

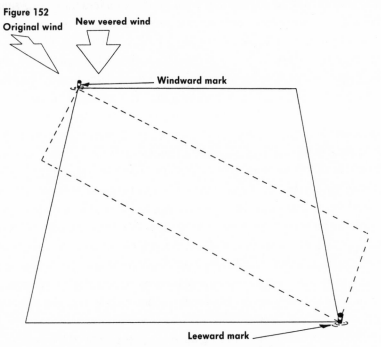

Figure 152
Original wind **New veered wind**

Windward mark

Leeward mark

All else being equal, sail the long tack first.

not pay to hold high after rounding, except to clear your air, because you lose so much distance by not heading directly downwind at the mark. This is particularly so when the course to the leeward mark necessitates a jibe. If we're leaving marks to port and the wind has shifted, as shown in Figure 152, the long tack upwind will on starboard, and the run will be on port. Just remember "starboard tack up, port back," and vice versa.

As you approach the weather mark, a decision must be made as to which tack to run on. If the wind is fairly parallel to the course and the next leg is almost directly downwind, the starboard tack makes the most sense for port roundings. Since you are approaching on starboard, it's easiest to set up the spinnaker pole for that tack. A jibe set is usually slower, and on larger yachts there's more that can go wrong (e.g., the spinnaker wraps around the jib stay during the jibe).

Another disadvantage to having the pole and spinnaker all set up for a jibe to port occurs when you have ended up outside of other boats at the mark. I have seen boats in this position, held off by inside leeward boats unable to jibe to port because the leeward boats were on starboard tack. The outside boat has to wait until the others have cleared out ahead before she is able to jibe past their sterns to set her own spinnaker.

A boat that takes the port tack after rounding sails into the congestion of sailboats approaching the weather mark, whereas starboard tack takes the boat away. The congestion can cause two problems: (1) all the close-hauled boats, whether on port or starboard, have right-of-way over the boat running free on port tack; and (2) all the close-hauled boats on the starboard tack layline, to windward of the running boat, disturb the wind terribly. In light air the running boat's spinnaker can be well blanketed by these close-hauled boats.

Once around the mark, it's crucial to keep away from the blanket zone of another boat. In light winds the zone of disturbed air carries for several boat lengths downwind from the windward boat. The helmsman of the windward boat will try to stay "on the wind" of the leeward boat by keeping his masthead fly pointed right at the leeward boat. At times it may be necessary to reach up a little for extra speed to get the leeward boat in your blanket zone. Doing so makes the distance between the boats greater and your blanket less effective. But some blanketing is better than none, and you should still be able to slow the leeward boat enough to start gaining back the lost distance.

It's often best to stay out of luffing matches on the leeward leg. When you and another boat are in a luffing match on a reach, the luff is still somewhat in the direction the fleet is sailing. A luff on a run may take you at right angles to the course. While the fleet is sailing toward the mark, you are making zero progress toward it. Furthermore, when you curtail the luff and fall back down to course, you will have to sail lower than the rest of the fleet, which will have a better point of sailing.

On a run, you use the benefits of blanketing mainly to close the distance and to catch the lead boats, but it usually takes a jibe or two to get through safely. In Figure 153 the trailing boat has gradually cut down the lead of the leading boat by disturbing her wind. At position 2 the lead boat luffs up to protect herself, whereupon the trailing boat jibes and the lead boat follows suit a few moments later. At position 3 the trailing boat is still on the lead boat's wind, and has an inside overlap at the mark. The mistake the lead boat made was in not anticipating the jibe of the trailing boat. By either jibing first or being prepared to jibe at the same instant, the lead boat would be to leeward with luffing rights, and could protect her position by luffing.

Figure 153

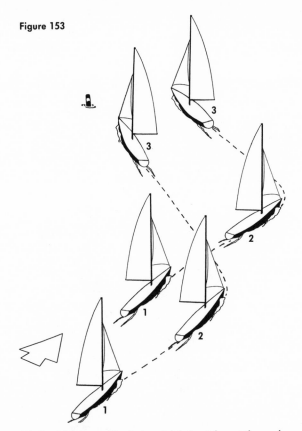

The lead boat must jibe first or risk being taken at the mark.

Luffing can only be done by a leeward boat to prevent a windward boat from passing. When a boat catches up from behind to leeward, the reason she cannot luff during the existence of the overlap is that the helmsman of the windward boat was forward of the mainmast of the leeward boat when the overlap was established. The overlap begins when the boats, one of which is no longer clear astern, are within two overall lengths of the longer one. If, as they converge and an overlap is established, the mast of the leeward boat is forward of windward's helmsman, the right to luff is also established.

Another way luffing rights can be established by a boat that is catching up to leeward is by a couple of jibes. A new overlap begins after a jibe has been completed. In Figure 154, position 1, a boat has caught up from behind, and has established an overlap to leeward. Because her mast is behind windward's helmsman, she cannot luff while that overlap exists. At position 2, she jibes to starboard tack and back to port at position 3. A new overlap is established at that point. The leeward boat now has luffing rights, because her mast was forward of windward's helmsman when the new overlap was created.

Figure 154

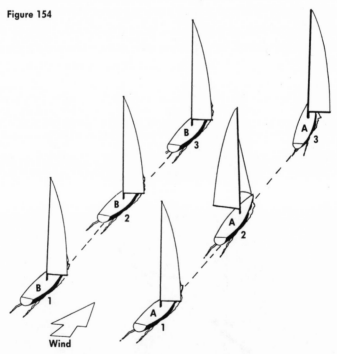

Wind

A new overlap starts when boat A jibes from starboard tack to port. Now she has luffing rights.

Bob Johnstone, who builds and successfully races the J/24 and other J class sailboats designed by his brother Rod, uses a subtle tactic to shorten the lead of a boat in front of him on a run. He teases the skipper ahead into sailing a longer course to the leeward mark. When his competitor looks back to check on Bob's position, Bob steers a little high. The competition steers higher yet. Bob immediately resumes his previous course to the mark, but his competitor, having gone higher, takes longer to get back down to course. Then Bob will exaggerate going low for a moment while the competitor sails low for 15 to 30 seconds. Bob claims this tactic, done repeatedly, is usually good for three or four boat lengths, or even more, if you can blanket the boat ahead.

Wind Shifts

One of the most important tactical decisions on a run is how to play the wind. On a beat we almost always tack in heading wind shifts. On a run it's the opposite; we jibe in lifts. Whereas failure to play the wind shifts properly on a beat can result in startling losses, the results are not as dramatic on runs. You will still be heading roughly toward the leeward mark. In Figure 155 boats A and B are sailing dead downwind toward the leeward mark on starboard tack. A new wind that is a lift comes in. It allows boat A to head up, which she does. Now boat A is no longer heading directly at the mark. She is sailing a longer distance on a dead downwind run. Boat B has jibed to port, and is heading at the mark on a much faster point of sailing.

Let's say the course to the leeward mark is 195 degrees, and we know that the reciprocal of the true wind was 200 degrees when we rounded the

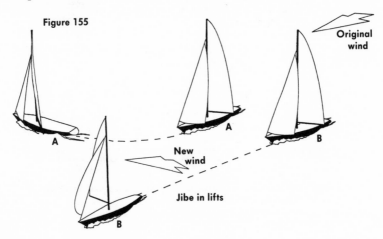

Figure 155

Original wind

New wind

Jibe in lifts

weather mark (See Figure 156). We are sailing on port tack 20 degrees high of the true wind (180 degrees) in light air to gain more boat speed from a higher velocity apparent wind. We watch our compass, and keep the apparent wind angle constant by observing the angle of the masthead fly or our apparent-wind direction instrument. Since we head off in gusts and up in lulls, we have to be careful not to make decisions based on the different apparent-wind velocity. Our compass shows we have been lifted to 170 degrees with the apparent-wind direction and velocity unchanged. This indicates that 190 degrees is dead downwind and, since we desire a course of 195 degrees, the starboard tack is closer and therefore faster.

If the wind shift is continual, you again play it the opposite of a beat. On a beat you sail toward expected headers; on a run you sail away from them. In Figure 157 boats A and B are sailing at equal speed toward the leeward mark. Boat A has sailed toward the new wind direction, and when it arrives, she has to sail dead downwind to the leeward mark. Boat B has sailed away from the new wind direction. She jibes and is on more of a reach, a much faster point of sail, when the new wind arrives. This tactic is satisfactory if the wind shifts only a few degrees. However, if the wind continues to veer so much that boat A is beam-reaching on port tack, and boat B can't carry a

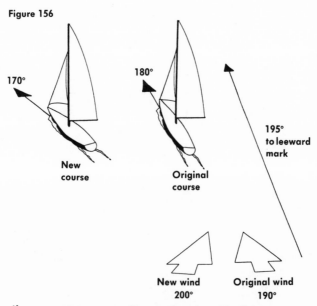

Figure 156

170°

180°

195°
to leeward
mark

New
course

Original
course

New wind
200°

Original wind
190°

If your compass course confirms you have been lifted and the other tack takes you closer to your destination, jibe.

Figure 157

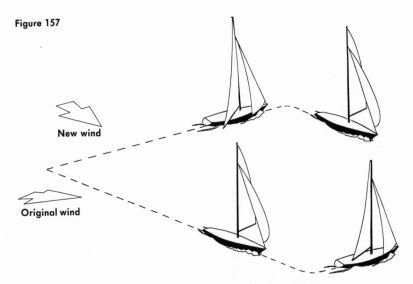

Downwind, sail *away* from the expected wind shift.

Figure 158

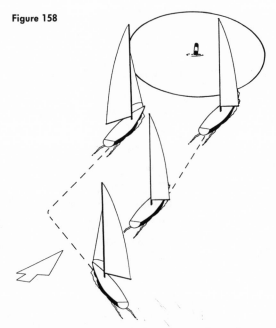

Attempt to get the inside position at the mark.

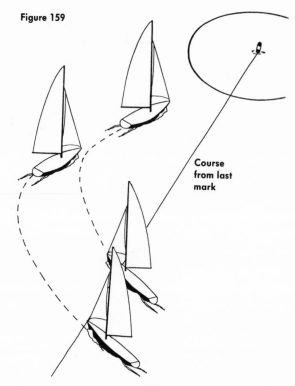

Figure 159

Course
from last
mark

Don't allow the competition to get inside.

spinnaker to get to the mark, the benefits of sailing away from the shift are lost.

As you approach the leeward mark on a run, it's very important to get to the inside of the fleet. It may be that the right side of the leg was the place to be for wind, but that won't be much help if you find yourself outside a stack of ten boats at the mark. Consider the problem early to avoid getting caught in the wrong spot. Even if you have to harden up very sharply and cross a few sterns, it can be of benefit. In Figure 158 boat A has crossed B's stern, jibes, and returns on starboard tack with an overlap at the mark. Boat B's defense is shown in Figure 159. She jibes and also heads high of the mark to retain the inside position.

ANCHORING AS A TACTIC

There are times when the breeze is so light that the current overpowers it. Rather than lose precious distance to the mark, anchor your boat. If you are the first to anchor, you will stay in one place while the rest of the fleet is moving backward. I've anchored at night and seen us "passing" running light after running light, just as if we had doubled the boat speed of the others. To press the advantage of being the first to anchor, no one else should realize you've done it. Quietly slip the anchor over the leeward side near the shrouds. One crew member should do it while the others pretend to be racing the boat for all they're worth. An anchorline running along the hull is hard to see, so it's possible no one will notice that you're anchored. Arthur Knapp says this tactic was pulled on him by Cornelius Shields way back in 1933. It's been used a lot since then.

An anchor can be used for purposes other than actual anchoring. Once when I was sailing as tactician on *Carina* in an Admiral's Cup race during Cowes Week in England, the start was in drifting conditions with a three-knot current carrying the fleet across the line. Owner Dick Nye asked for my suggestions about starting under such conditions. There was only one way, in my mind: power to a location where, when the five-minute gun sounded and the engine had to be turned off, we would have five minutes of drifting with the current to the line. We judged the distance quite accurately, but failed to get turned around. We were drifting stern-first toward the starting line. The Class 1 fleet was also drifting in a mass toward the starting line, bouncing against one another and fending off. There was only one boat heading in the proper direction that had been able to pick up the slightest zephyr. We *had* to get the boat turned around. I called for the anchor to be lowered over the stern just far enough to drag along the bottom, but not enough to hold. Immediately our bow swung down-current. We lifted the anchor, and were second out of the mess.

THE FINISH

The choice of which end of the finish line to cross is the critical decision that consistently accounts for the most places won or lost in an upwind finish. Just as the upwind end of the line is favored at the start, the downwind end is favored at the finish.

In the 1968 Olympics, I saw Buddy Friedrichs, the U.S. skipper in the Dragon class, take four sterns and still finish first. Buddy was on port tack laying the starboard end of a long finish line. He met four other Dragons on starboard tack, one after another, and ducked under the stern of each. Rather than tacking on him, they all continued toward the port (buoy) end of the line. By choosing the downwind end, Buddy went from fifth to first in a couple of hundred yards and won the gold medal.

Unfortunately, it's very difficult to determine which end is downwind. You don't have the same opportunity as at the start to take the bearing of the line and to compare it with the wind direction. However, there are a few tactics that can help.

As you approach the finish, you have four laylines to deal with: port and starboard tack laylines to the port end and both laylines to the starboard end. The four laylines are shown with the wind square to the line (Figure 160). You never want to sail past the first layline you reach. A starboard-tack boat will tack on the port-tack layline to the starboard end. A port-tack boat will tack on the starboard-tack layline to the port end, as shown in Figure 160.

In Figure 161, the wind has veered, making the port end downwind by a good margin. As two boats approach the intersection of the two laylines, it is obvious that boat B will have a much shorter distance to sail than boat A. The buoy will seem closer than the committee boat.

Distances are deceiving when you are comparing two objects of such disparate size as a buoy and a yacht. Furthermore, you will rarely find yourself precisely at the intersection of both laylines. You are sailing

Figure 160

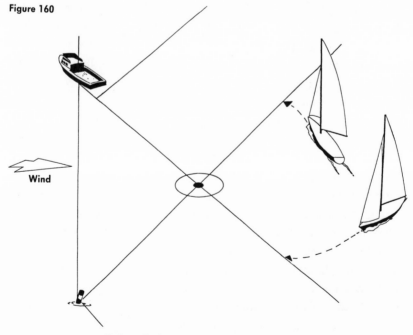

Wind

Tack on the first layline to the finish you reach.

Figure 161

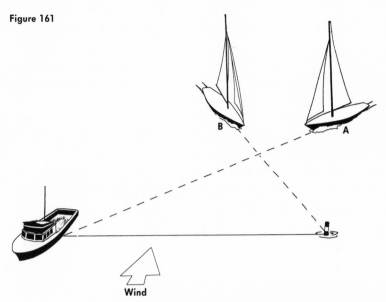

Wind

Sail for the downwind end of the line.

tactically among other boats that you may have to cover or to break away from. This determines your approach to the line, which may be quite different from the course you would have taken in the absence of other boats. Try to judge whether you are sailing more parallel to the line or more across it. It sounds like a simple-minded tactic—sail across the line, not parallel to it—but it's amazing how many skippers take the course of boat A in Figure 161 until they reach the middle of the line and then tack. They should tack immediately when they can lay the buoy on starboard tack.

Harry Sindle, many-time national champion in a number of classes, had the following comment about the finish at the completion of the second weather leg of an Olympic course. Often the committee boat has moved from the leeward mark—where the race started—and has set a finish line at the weather mark. As Harry tacks to go around the weather mark for the run, he is crossing what will be the finish line two legs hence. When head-to-wind during that tack, he observes whether either end is abaft abeam. That end will be the downwind end at the finish, barring any major wind shifts.

If you know the ability of the race committee, you may be able to tell which end is favored simply by the wind direction. If the wind is essentially straight down the course line from the windward mark to the leeward mark, the finish line will be perpendicular to the course, and neither end will be favored. If the wind has veered, and the finish line is still perpendicular to the course line, the port end will be downwind as in Figure 161.

Race committees are now expected to adjust slightly for the wind direction by splitting the difference between the finish line's being square to the wind and being square to the course from the last mark. In the past, the line was always supposed to be square to the course regardless of wind direction. Although this change cuts down the amount one end of the finish line can be favored over the other, it doesn't alter the fact that if the wind shifts to the right of the course, the port end should be downwind and vice versa. As you sail up the last weather leg, therefore, keep in mind the true wind direction. If the port tack takes you closer to the finish (the long tack), then the wind has backed and the starboard end is downwind.

Head reaching, shooting into the wind across the line, is a useful tactic in trying to nip ahead of a close competitor. It works only in boats that carry a great deal of momentum, such as large displacement keelboats. It also works best on light days rather than heavy. When the wind and seas are high, the boat is stopped quickly by the windage of the rigging and the force of the seas against the hull. When you're about one boat length from the line, shoot dead into the wind as boat B does in Figure 162. Boats A and B are equidistant upwind. By shooting the line, boat B slows down, but sails such a short distance compared to boat A that she wins. The timing has to be perfect: shoot too late and its value has been lost; shoot too early and you may lose all momentum before reaching the line. Of the two errors, the latter is more prevalent. Just as skippers think they are right on the starting line well before they reach it, so do finishers seem to believe they have

Figure 162

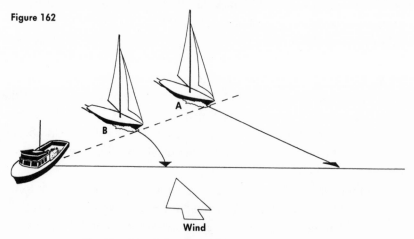

Shoot head-to-wind at the finish to shorten the distance.

crossed the line well before they actually have. Sail a little farther than your instincts tell you before shooting. If your timing is off and you find yourself losing speed without having crossed the line, tack. Don't fall back onto the same tack; it's too slow. Consider your head reach as a slow tack that you will complete if you don't hear a finish horn in time.

The racing rule "Definitions" state that "A yacht is racing . . . until she has . . . finished and cleared the finishing line and finishing marks. . . ." Clearing the finishing line means the boat is no longer touching any part of it. Since you finish when any part of the hull, crew or equipment in normal position crosses the finish line from the direction of the course from the last mark, your boat doesn't have to cross the line entirely to be legally finished. You can drop back on the course side of the line and sail home. This is a common occurrence when finishing in very light air against a current. To avoid penalty or disqualification, be careful not to use your engine until you have cleared the line.

ECCENTRIC TACTICS

Following are some innovative tactics that have used during races at night. In the 1980 Southern Ocean Racing Conference Lipton Cup Race, Harold Cudmore was skipper of *Mistress Quickly*. He was close on corrected time to *Kialoa,* which was ahead of him close-hauled on starboard tack, and to *Ondine,* which was slightly behind and to leeward of *Kialoa* and *Mistress Quickly.* Harold doused the light that illuminates the jib. Anyone watching from *Kialoa* and not seeing any light from *Mistress Quickly* as *Ondine* passed (they were too far apart to see running lights), would have assumed that *Mistress Quickly* had also tacked, and was blocked from view by *Ondine.* So *Kialoa* tacked to cover, and *Mistress Quickly* secretly sailed on toward the Florida shore still on starboard tack. By being able to break cover, she was able to beat *Ondine* boat for boat and *Kialoa* on corrected time.

Another (not too legal) use of lights to outfox an opponent originated on the Great Lakes in the 1950s. One boat was equipped with a rheostat that regulated the brilliance of her stern light. When the crew had their arch rival tucked behind they would gradually diminish the intensity of the light so their competitor would think he was being left behind. The crew of the lead boat would then see many flashlight beams on deck and could hear winches turning, indicating that all sorts of sail adjustments were being made on the boat astern. Since the latter were actually messing up their sail trim instead of improving it, the lead boat would in reality start moving out. The intensity of the stern light was then adjusted upward. Their competition now believed the adjustments made were helping them gain back lost distance, when actually the opposite was true.

The best tactic I've ever heard of I've saved for last. It might have some trouble with the Fair Sailing rule, but that's not for me to judge. Dick Tillman was sailing in the Brigade Sailing championship at the U.S. Naval Academy, Annapolis. He could win the series only by putting a boat between him and the boat immediately behind him, which otherwise would be first overall by finishing second to Dick. The third-place boat was too far behind for Dick to use the most common tactic of dropping back to camp on the wind of the second-place boat, thereby slowing the boat sufficiently to allow the third-place boat to catch up and to pass. Some other tactic had to be initiated. The idea struck Dick to finish on the wrong side of the committee boat, and to lure the second-place boat along. The possibility of this happening seemed good, since the course included numerous mark roundings, and the finish line was not clearly defined. In any case, he had nothing to lose. So Dick "finished" while still covering the second boat close behind, and as they crossed the incorrect line Dick congratulated him for taking the series. He then chatted with the "winner" from leeward and closer to the committee boat until the third boat was close to "finishing." Dick then sheeted in, and returned to the course. He shouted to the third boat that he (Dick) had finished incorrectly and that they should follow him to the correct side of the committee boat. They did so before Dick's real competition realized what was happening. This tactic gave Dick the required boat and the series.

Fascinating tactics like these make the sport of sailboat racing a varied and interesting one. However, until the racer starts thinking in terms of besting his competition actively and aggressively with tactics, he isn't really racing.

Chapter VIII

MEDICAL PROBLEMS, ACCIDENTS, SAFETY

Medical problems are like accidents—they happen to the "other guy" on "other boats." You never expect them to strike home. Because of this attitude, sailors are often blasé about preparing for them.

Probably the best preparation is at least a basic layman's knowledge of what to do when medical emergencies arise. If you've never taken a first aid or cardiac pulmonary resuscitation (CPR) course, take one. Thereafter, in an emergency medical situation, even if you're not current in the procedure, you will probably remember enough to make a difference when the adrenalin is pumping. As a case in point, Earl Kegler, an Offshore Sailing School instructor, once happened to be on the scene when a heart attack occurred. He recognized the symptoms and was able to apply CPR technique quickly, which no doubt saved the victim's life. Earl never thought he would ever have to use the procedure, but he had taken the course and was able to react correctly in a critical moment of need.

In another instance, a year or so after the Heimlich maneuver (for dislodging food from the windpipe) was discovered, my wife choked on a piece of roast duck. I quickly applied the maneuver and dislodged it. A year earlier, knowledge of the procedure had not existed; it would have been necessary to get her to a hospital to dislodge the meat and it's very doubtful that that could have been done in time to save her life. I had never expected to need to use the Heimlich maneuver; it seemed just another bit of interesting but useless information I picked up from Frank Field, the weatherman and science reporter on TV. But I am very thankful that I had listened and did know what to do when the need came.

I raced in the 1988 Newport to Bermuda Race on Larry Huntington's *Denali*. A crewman on our boat—Larry's son, Matthew—came down with abdominal pains. Another piece of "useless" information I had picked up at school in my teens was the location of McBurney's Point (midway between the navel and the starboard hip bone) for diagnosing appendicitis. That spot was tender to pressure, so we made an early diagnosis of possible appendicitis and immediately made radio contact with a doctor aboard *Kittiwake,* another participant in the race. He confirmed the probability of appendicitis. At that point, the yacht *Karyatis,* owned by Christos Kritikos, agreed to drop out of the race, power back to us and take the stricken crew member to Bermuda. *Karyatis* was much faster under power than we were and could get to within helicopter range of Bermuda by the following afternoon, if one were needed. The crewman did have an acute appendicitis and was successfully operated on in Bermuda, thanks to Mr. Kritikos's sportsmanship and timely assistance.

That incident gave us further insight into three particular requirements for good medical practices aboard.

First, always have handy a good medical diagnostic book. Larry, an amateur mountaineer, had an excellent text aboard called *Medicine for Mountaineering,* edited by Dr. James A. Wilkerson. This text outlines reasons for abdominal pain, and as our crewman's symptoms progressed, appendicitis was clearly indicated. Just as mountaineers are in the wilds for weeks at a time with no chance of immediate professional medical help, so sailors have to be medically self-sufficient when offshore. (At Offshore Sailing School, we like the book so much, we now sell it in our retail stores, On and Offshore, Inc. Call [813] 454-1700 to order.)

Second, the ship must carry a well-supplied medicine kit. *Denali*'s kit had been professionally prepared and included a powerful antibiotic recommended for appendicitis called Methoxin. My understanding is that this drug delays the bursting of the appendix and fights the infection if it does burst. Administered every four hours until the patient reached Bermuda, this antibiotic made a great difference in his condition and chances for recovery, according to the doctors there. We were extremely fortunate that Larry's medical preparations had been so thorough.

Another treatment for the same condition is also worth mentioning here: Once, in the days before refrigeration aboard yachts was common, an owner with whom I sailed many transatlantic races suddenly found that he apparently had an appendicitis victim aboard. He dealt with the situation by packing the painful area in ice from the icebox, thus keeping the appendix from bursting until they could reach port and a hospital.

Third, every yacht should have a good radio. VHF is line-of-sight and is adequate for contacting nearby ships or for coastal cruising, but single sideband (SSB) radio has the much greater range needed for offshore use, and it offers the possibility of reaching an ocean marine operator and having your call patched to just about anywhere in the world. Also, with this equipment you will be able to contact the various medical services for yachtsmen that are on radio call 24 hours a day, should you wish to sign up beforehand for the service.

Less dramatic, but very painful medical problems afloat that you must also be prepared to cope with include sunburn, which can be incapacitating in its worst form. As we are now often warned, the sun's ultraviolet rays are very damaging to the skin, not only in direct sunlight, but when reflected from the water as well. However, today protective creams and lotions with high sun protection factors (SPF), if used properly, can all but eliminate bad sunburn. Every boat should have a good supply of such preparations aboard and crew members should be required to use it during long exposure.

Also with reference to sun exposure, it is important to be aware that some medications you might be taking increase your sensitivity to sunlight. Once, while cruising in the Virgin Islands, I felt nauseous. It seemed like seasickness, but I was sure it could not be. I was taking tetracycline, which had been prescribed for a skin condition. I immediately stopped taking the drug, and the nausea disappeared. Crew on special medications should discuss this possibility with a doctor.

Another debilitating condition that frequently occurs aboard boats is dehydration, which can result from too much sun, seasickness, strenuous activity, and insufficient consumption of water. Both wind and sun are constantly at work removing body moisture, and it doesn't take much fluid loss (two percent of your body weight) to reduce your effectiveness as a competitive crew. Greater fluid losses can lead to nausea, heat exhaustion, or heat stroke. The onset of thirst may not be a good indicator of the body's need for fluids, because you can lose as much as four percent of your body weight before feeling thirsty, and when you do drink, your thirst is quenched long before the fluid has been totally replaced. Since it is best to drink chilled water, which is absorbed faster than room-temperature water, keep a bottle of it in the fridge or icebox if possible. Drinks with a high sugar concentration are not absorbed as quickly as plain water, and coffee, tea, and alcoholic drinks should be avoided in hot weather because they are diuretics and increase the desire to urinate and therefore promote dehydration rather than impede it.

Seasickness is not a lethal medical problem, but in some cases it's so bad the victim would prefer "the alternative." There are some people who are totally incapacitated by seasickness and others who can continue to function and just toss it off, so to speak. As soon as they vomit, they feel better for a while. Seasickness can hit just about anyone. We sailed a transatlantic race one time with a crewman named Steve—not me—who claimed he had never been seasick and never would. Now that's quite a claim. Never is a long, long time, but such was his confidence. We went through a heavy storm one night and the following day there was no wind, but there was a sloppy sea left over from the storm. As the sails slatted in the slop, we lost a pin from a shackle. Steve volunteered to get a replacement from the shackle box under the floor in the forward cabin. Ten minutes later he emerged with the pin. He was white as a sheet and made a single comment: "I'm a believer."

Let's look at the lessons Steve learned.

Normally, you will have less tendency to seasickness on a sailboat than on a powerboat because a sailboat's motion is steadier. It pitches with the bow driving up and down over waves, but does very little yawing (slewing side to side) because the keel helps it track in a straight line with very little rolling, except when sailing downwind. When there is no wind to keep the boat heeled at a constant angle, and the sea is rough, you are tossed in all directions. Steve aggravated the problem by going up to the bow of the boat where the motion is worst. If you are feeling queasy and have to be below, stay just aft of the center of the boat—where the motion is least—and if you're sleeping below, berth in the quietest part of the boat in the same area.

Also, Steve's eyes were focusing on an item up close while the background was moving around unfocused. This is deadly, as any kid knows who has tried focusing his eyes on the tip of a broom handle held at arm's length and then spinning around in a circle. The close-up focus increases dizziness. I experienced this once when splicing the painter of a dinghy to its bow eye while lying on my stomach at the stern of an anchored sailboat.

As I leaned over the side of the boat in a calm harbor, the water was the background of the splice. The dinghy bow was rising and falling six inches or so. By the time the splice was finished, I was feeling green. I couldn't believe it—the water was so calm. Obviously, focusing on the splice against a moving background had caused the problem.

When sailors suggest that a seasick victim stay on deck where he can see the horizon and breath fresh air, they know what they're talking about. Another tip: Let the queasy person steer. It often helps to be doing something active that necessitates looking up at the horizon; steering also provides anticipation of what the next movement of the boat will be, which can be helpful.

When I was indoctrinated into the Air Force we were given rides in a jet trainer to test our adaptability to flying. A number of us were taken up, one at a time, by a top-gun type who had a record of making five consecutive passengers sick with his high-speed acrobatics. My turn came. The trainer had dual controls and I held onto the second stick lightly as he dove, looped and rolled. I had a split-second anticipation as the pilot moved the stick and I felt it in the duplicate controls before the jet responded. To his disappointment, I broke his chain of sick passengers, although he tried mightily, thanks to my sailing experience. The same is true to a lesser extent when steering a sailboat. Being able to anticipate boat movement helps to reduce the queasy feeling.

Among the other causes of seasickness, what you eat is high on the list. If you drink too much alcohol the night before sailing, you will be more prone to getting sick. If you eat greasy, hard-to-digest foods, you also increase your chances of getting sick. Some of the first signs of the onset of seasickness are burping and indigestion. I recommend eating Saltines and drinking Coke or Pepsi. These two drinks help reduce the chances of getting sick because they contain phosphoric acid, which is an ingredient in Emetrol, a drug to control vomiting. That's the medical explanation I received from a doctor when I asked the reason a Coke seems to settle the stomach.

There are other seasickness cures—some good, some not so good. One of the "nots," in my estimation, is gingerroot. This has been a traditional cure for queasiness for centuries, and may be effective for some people in mild sea conditions. I bought some gingerroot pills and offered them to a number of Offshore Sailing School graduates on a recent Tahiti cruise. The passage from Bora Bora to Raiatea was a beat in reasonably brisk winds and steep seas. Of those who tried the gingerroot pills, they all swore "never again." Not only were they sick, they were burping ginger, which made them feel worse.

One of the good remedies for some people is a product called Sea Bands. There's a pressure point on your wrist three finger thicknesses from the bend of the wrist and between the two tendons that, when pressed, seems to reduce queasiness. To make this work you have to press both wrists at the proper point. Sea Bands are simply elastic wrist bands with a button on each to put pressure at the proper spot. A similar product, Accu-Band, uses a Velcro wrist band to press the button on the wrist. The Chinese discovered this and call it acupressure. We have found that it works for quite a few people, and since there are no drugs or side effects, the bands are ideal for health-conscious sailors.

As for drugs, Scopolamine behind-the-ear patches, which can be obtained only with a prescription, work well for many people. There can be side effects such as drowsiness, dry mouth, and in some cases double vision. The instructions indicate those who should not use them. The patches allow a slow release of the drug into the bloodstream, which minimizes side effects, but they still may occur.

For that reason I prefer a combination of prescription drugs called Ephedrin and Promethezine. One is an "upper" and the other a "downer." They work so well against each other that I have no feeling that I've taken any drug—no drowsiness, no jag, no dry mouth, or any other effect, except that it kills any feeling of seasickness. For me, they are very effective and unlike other drugs, I can wait until I feel sick before taking them. Again, these are available through prescription only. There are people, such as anyone with a heart condition, who should not take them.

Other anti-seasick tips include the following: Stay in fresh air if there are alcohol, diesel, or gas fumes below. Sleep on your back rather than on your stomach. This makes it more difficult to throw up. Clean your ears before sailing. I understand this allows the balance mechanism in the ears to work better. Keep busy on deck rather than just sitting and thinking about it. If you feel really terrible, tickle your throat over the lee side of the boat and get rid of it. You'll feel much better once you do.

I'm not a doctor, but I believe every medical kit should have some type of sleeping pills. I learned this lesson when I was in the Fastnet Race at the age of 20 on the 72-foot *Mare Nostrum*. We had just won the transatlantic race from Cuba to Spain, and the doctor aboard had to return to his practice in the U.S. When leaving, he turned his medical kit over to me with the scantiest instructions.

The coffee grinders in use at that time were a menace. Sometimes the drum backed off when you changed gears, causing the handles to spin in the opposite direction from the one in which you were cranking. When that happened, you could only jump away from the spinning handles. It happened and I jumped, but the guy cranking with me was whacked across the back of the hand by a spinning handle. He was a wonderful, stoical Spaniard named Angel, with whom I had sailed over 5,000 miles and who never complained, no matter how bad things got. He had already been hit once by a spinning winch handle earlier in the summer when someone tried to lower the mainsail by putting a winch handle in a wire reel winch and backing it off. Although Angel had chipped a bone then, he completely ignored the pain and kept on crewing. This time, however, it appeared that every bone in the back of his hand was broken. We were a day and a half from the finish and the owner of the boat, to whom Angel was an old family retainer, turned to me, saying, in effect, "Steve, you're now the doctor. What are you going to do for Angel?" My only solution was to get him into a bunk, immobilize the hand and feed him sleeping pills. Whenever he woke up and started moaning, I gave him another. It was a crude remedy but it kept the patient relatively comfortable until we reached the finish at Plymouth, England. I've been a believer in having some sort of strong sedative in the medicine kit ever since.

MAN OVERBOARD

There has been a great deal of study recently by several groups, including the U.S. Yacht Racing Union, the U.S. Naval Academy, the Cruising Club of America, and the Sailing Foundation of Seattle, as to the best way to retrieve a person who has fallen overboard. At Offshore Sailing School we have also studied the various suggestions and along with the above committees, believe that on larger boats, the "Life Sling" method is the best. Sometimes called the "Seattle Sling," it was developed by a group in Seattle for sailboats cruising with as few as two people aboard. Regardless of the retrieval method you use, always have a buoyant cushion ready to toss to the victim immediately and have a spotter keep constant watch on the victim's position.

The Life Sling consists of a buoyant sling that sits in a case attached to the stern pulpit ready for instant deployment. The sling is attached to the boat by a long, unsinkable line. When a person falls overboard, a nearby crew throws the sling over the side and the helmsman sails the boat in a circle around the victim. Care must be taken not to turn so sharply that the boat runs over her own "tail." The loop formed by the floating line decreases very quickly so the person in the water can grab the line, letting it run or feeding it through his hands until he reaches the sling. Just before the sling gets to the victim the crew aboard stops the boat by turning head-to-wind and lowers the jib. They then pull the victim in the sling up to the stern quarter of the boat using a jibsheet winch. When the victim is alongside, they attach a block and tackle to the main halyard at one end and the sling at the other and haul the person up on deck. This system has been tested by numerous couples with only the wife left aboard, and in all cases she was able to "save" her husband.

The advantages of the sling are numerous. By immediately maneuvering in a circle around the victim, you keep him or her in sight. Moreover, it isn't necessary to maneuver so close that you might run over the victim in heavy seas; the contact is made at a distance. People seldom fall overboard in fair weather, good visibility, and calm seas. It usually happens when conditions are at their worst, and it takes a calm, experienced crew to maneuver alongside a person when the seas are 10 feet and the winds 35 knots. The Life Sling solves that problem.

The Sling also solves the problem of getting the person back aboard the sailboat. If the water is very cold, the victim may be unconscious by this time. The Life Sling keeps the victim afloat and connected to the boat. With the Life Sling and enough crew you just attach a halyard to the top of the sling and hoist away. With a shorthanded crew you use the block and tackle system.

On smaller cruising boats we recommend the "quick stop" method of rescue. This should also be used on larger boats if a Life Sling is not available. The method is just as its name implies. The fastest and most foolproof way to save a person is to be stopped right near him or her. A sailboat stops when heading into the wind, so that's the direction we turn. No matter what point of sailing you are on, you tack. If the jib is up, don't touch the jibsheet. Let the jib back, forcing the bow over. Continue the turn with the jib backed until the wind is abaft abeam. After two or three boatlengths, alter course to dead downwind and drop the jib. Then make a complete circle by jibing and sailing roughly close-hauled until you are alongside the person. Then turn head-to-wind to stop the boat, toss the person a heaving line, and pull the victim aboard. If a spinnaker is set, ease the pole as the boat rounds into the wind and release the halyard when head-to-wind. The spinnaker will fall to the foredeck and the boat continues the circle.

While the quick-stop system works well on cruising boats, it has drawbacks for some smaller boats. On the 27-ft. Solings used by Offshore Sailing School, we find that a fast tack—even backing the jib—takes you too far upwind of the victim when sailing close-hauled, and a jibe produces faster results. The reason is that the Soling is much more responsive and maneuverable than a cruising boat. On even smaller boats that are lightweight and capsizable, a fast tack with the jib backed would end up with the remaining crew in the drink also. A capsize would be unavoidable. Of course, if the boat is easily righted and self-bailing, this is the ultimate "quick stop" and might even save time. But since a capsized sailboat might be difficult to right, we recommend rounding up and luffing the sails completely for centerboarders and catamarans. They will drift down within reach of the victim very quickly.

Luckily, a man-overboard situation is a rare occurrence. In all my ocean racing, I've been aboard only one boat that lost a person over the side. It was in Sydney Harbor while practicing for the Sydney-Hobart Race. We threw the various lifesaving paraphernalia over the side, but by the time they hit the water the victim would have had a long swim. We took the spinnaker down and sailed a reciprocal course, but fortunately a photographer's boat in the vicinity had picked up the injured crewman and taken him ashore. That experience has made me a believer in the quick stop and Life Sling systems for rescuing man-overboard victims.

Although such an accident rarely happens, you must be prepared for it. How often, for instance, have you ever needed to use an oxygen mask in a commercial airliner? Yet you are "trained" before each departure. How often have you ever had to take to the lifeboats on a cruise ship? Yet, you are trained in the procedure within an hour of leaving the dock. You may never have to pick up a person who has fallen overboard, but your crew should be drilled frequently in the procedure. Even experienced crew can be stunned to inaction by the shock of seeing someone go over the side; training helps the rescue operation to be started automatically, overcoming the shock.

COLLISIONS

Nothing is more terrorizing than a collision at sea. I have been on a sailboat during a close call with a ship at night or in fog, and I'll never forget it. On

one occasion, while sailing down Manila Bay at the end of the South China
Sea Race from Hong Kong to Manila on the 81-foot maxi *Nirvana,* we
encountered an approaching ferry at night. She made no attempt to slow
down or alter course when she saw us. She just sounded her horn and kept
on coming toward us. I was steering and had to spin from close-hauled on
starboard tack to a dead run parallel to the ferry with about half a boat-
length of open water between us, to avoid being run over. We were moving at
about 10 knots and the ferry at about 15 as we passed. At night with low
visibility it was far too close for comfort. A few years later, U.S. newspapers
had an account of an overloaded ferry colliding in Manila Bay with a ship,
resulting in the loss of hundreds of lives. I now understand how it could
happen; ferry skippers there seem to have no regard for the Rules of the
Road.

There is no way of knowing how many sailboats are lost due to collisions
with ships, but there may be several. Years ago, well-known East Coast
sailor Harvey Conover disappeared while cruising off the Florida Keys with
his wife, son, and other crew aboard his yacht *Revenoc* (Conover spelled
backwards). Speculation was that she was run down by a ship because the
weather was not bad enough to bother a well-found sailboat that was being
sailed by such an experienced crew. We'll never know for sure because the
boat was never recovered. It's doubtful that she collided with a whale, as has
happened in numerous other cases, because of her location.

I was sailing the Bermuda Race one year when two very large whales
headed right at our bow from dead ahead, swimming side by side. I ran to
the foredeck with another crew member for a better look and then my
curiosity turned into fear as they kept on coming rather than veering off. At
the last possible moment they both sounded, exhaling from their spouts and
flipping their mammoth tails out of the water. It was a miracle that they
never touched us, but the incident was very frightening, considering the
damage they could have done. As it was, we were splashed by their tails and
engulfed by a rancid, awful smell from their exhale.

The newest hazards at sea are containers lost overboard from container
ships. They are 40 feet long, float almost completely submerged, and thus
are hard to see and hard to miss. They are thought to have been responsible
for the loss of a number of sailboats.

Many collisions can be avoided by an alert crew, but when the crew is a
lone voyager—as on a single-handed race—a certain amount of risk is
inherent. One year I raced the Vineyard Race that passes the entrance to
Newport (Rhode Island) Harbor. We were close-hauled on port tack and

were closing on a smaller, starboard-tack boat. I noticed a flag flying off the stern, so I assumed the boat wasn't racing. A racing boat should not be flying an ensign. We were definitely racing and the common courtesy is to not force your right-of-way on a racing boat if you are cruising. As the starboard tacker got closer, she bore off as if to go under our stern. This confirmed my opinion that she was allowing us to cross her rather than forcing us to tack. Then, at the last moment, she headed up again, giving me a start. We passed with little room to spare, and, now to windward of her, we could see that there was nobody in the cockpit. Then, a head popped up from the companionway and looked around. It dawned on us that this was one of the entries in the single-handed around-the-world race (BOC), and he had activated his self-steering only a few miles from the start in heavily trafficked waters. It could have been a short race for that competitor.

When boats are on converging courses, the boat with the right of way is the "stand-on" vessel. The boat that has to avoid the collision is the "give-way" vessel. The stand-on vessel must maintain her course and speed to avoid misleading the vessel giving way, but must, nevertheless, avoid a collision when it appears the give-way vessel is unable to fulfill her obligations to keep clear.

However, the important thing—no matter which boat you are aboard when converging with another boat—is to determine very early whether the chance of a collision exists. To do this, we quickly take a bearing on the other boat by maintaining a steady, constant course and lining up something on board—a shroud, for instance—with the converging boat. If the shroud continues to line up with the other boat minutes later, a collision can occur. Or, if we take a compass bearing—a more accurate method—and the bearing doesn't change as the boats get closer together, watch out for a collision. Even if one boat is sailing faster than the other, as is boat A in Figure 163, a collision will result if the bearing doesn't change, because boat A is covering more distance in the same amount of time as boat B. Each time the crew of A takes a bearing on B it remains 30 degrees relative. Collision is imminent unless the give-way vessel—the port-tack sailboat—changes course and speed as required. The starboard-tack sailboat—the stand-on vessel—has the right-of-way, but shares the responsibility of avoiding a collision in case the port-tacker fails to take evasive action.

A handy tip: If there is land a mile or so behind the other boat, as you converge, watch the relationship between the other boat and the land. If the other boat appears to be moving forward past the land, she will cross you; if she remains stationary against the land, you are on a collision course; if she

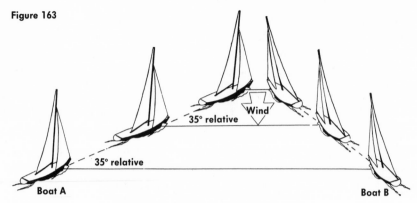

Figure 163

35° relative

Wind

35° relative

Boat A   Boat B

If the bearing doesn't change, a collision is imminent.

is sliding back relative to the land, you will cross her. Your crew can watch the other boat and tell you whether you are gaining ("making land") or losing it relative to the other boat.

The most frequent cause of collisions and near misses at sea is inattention. Sailors are notorious for being lulled into a sense of solitude; even in fairly crowded waters the sea gives a feeling of spaciousness. Sailboats travel very slowly compared to the high speed we're used to on highways, so we don't have the same feeling at sea that we have on the highway that we must always be alert. Yet two boats a mile apart, each sailing at six knots, can hit each other in five minutes. An all too common comment after a near miss is, "Where the devil did he come from?" The boat was always there, but just unnoticed. This is a very good reason why drinking and sailing don't mix. Save the drinking until after the hook is down for the night.

Most near misses occur at night when it's hard to judge closing speeds and angles. Obviously, it's imperative that anyone who sails at night be able to recognize navigation lights on other boats. The basic lights that almost all vessels carry are red and green sidelights. These can be seen from dead ahead to two points abaft the beam.

To review, there are 32 points in the 360 degrees of a compass, eight in each quadrant, or 11¼ degrees in each point. Two points abaft abeam translates to 112½ degrees. The red is on the port side, green on starboard. A sailboat carries only side lights and a white stern light, although under power she has to carry a bow light. Larger powerboats carry red and green side lights, a stern light, a bow light, and also a higher range light aft. The relationship between these last two lights tells the observer which way the boat is turning.

Which boat has right-of-way is determined by the Rules of the Road. After many years of substantial differences, the inland and international rules of the road are now, for all intents and purposes, identical. Thus, in any confrontation on the water, we have three possibilities: sail vs. sail, sail vs. power, and power vs. power.

When you are sailing and meet another sailboat you are either 1) on opposite tacks; 2) on the same tack; or 3) overtaking or being overtaken. On opposite tacks, the starboard-tack boat has right-of-way. On the same tack, the leeward boat has right-of-way. In an overtaking situation, the overtaking boat must avoid hitting the overtaken boat.

When you are sailing and meet a boat under power, you have right-of-way in almost all cases. The few exceptions are when the motorboat is anchored or not under command, is fishing, is being overtaken by the sailboat, or when the motorboat is a large vessel restricted in her ability to maneuver.

When you are under power and meet another powerboat, the one in the other's "danger zone" has right-of-way. The danger zone is the area from dead ahead to two points (22.5 degrees) abaft the starboard beam. Any sailing vessel has to stay out of the way of a commercial vessel in a narrow channel when the latter can safely maneuver only in that channel.

At night, a motorboat in your danger zone could be showing one of the following combinations of lights: (1) red and green side lights with the bow light and range light in line, which indicates she's heading right for you or that you are crossing in front of her; (2) a green side light, indicating that there's little risk of collision because she's going to pass your stern, is running parallel with you, or has crossed your bow and is running away from you (depending on the relationship of the bow and range lights); (3) a low white light (her stern light), indicating that she's steaming ahead of you or you're overtaking; or (4) a red light, which means "watch out." She may be on a collision course (depending on the angle of her range lights and her bearing) and have right-of-way over you since she's in your danger zone.

Here we've only described what the lights of another powerboat *might* look like in your danger zone area at night. Of course, you can see her red side light at many other times. If, for instance, you were sailing toward each other on parallel courses to pass port-to-port, you would see her red side light. There's an infinite variety, but the whole idea is that by seeing those few key navigation lights and knowing their relationship you can visualize the whole boat and her direction without really seeing her.

Probably the biggest hazard after dark is being run down by a commercial vessel such as a tugboat with a tow. Thus, it is extremely important that anyone operating a boat at night understand the lights such tugs carry. The tows are often far behind the tug and poorly lighted, and if you mistakenly sail between the tug and the tow you are out of luck. If not sunk or disabled by the towing cable, you will be hit by the tow which cannot swerve or stop to avoid you. It's even unlikely that there is anyone on the towed barge, and the crew on the tug, which is 300 yards ahead, will not see anything astern at night or hear anything over the throb of their own engines, so its possible no one on the commercial vessels would even be aware of an accident. Therefore, it is crucial to be able to understand the tug's lights and correctly establish whether or not the tug is towing a barge or whether or not she has one alongside.

The lights rule is simple. If the tow is more than 200 meters astern, the tug carries three 225-degree masthead white lights arranged vertically on a staff, and a yellow towing light above the stern light. If the tow is less than 200 meters astern, you will see two vertical lights and a yellow towing light. If the tow is alongside the tug, two vertical white lights are shown, but no yellow towing light. These lights are in addition to the normal side lights and stern light. Where there are no white lights arranged vertically, there is no tow and you can safely pass astern of the tug; there will be a masthead light forward and a higher one aft of it as in most other powerboats.

Let's say you see a boat on a collision course carrying the normal lights plus a green light over a white light vertically. This is a trawler dragging nets that has right-of-way over you. There are a number of other types of vessels with unusual lights you may encounter at night and if you can't identify them, the safest procedure is to immediately take compass bearings to determine whether you're on a collision course. If you are, make a large alteration of course to stay away from the other boat. There's a saying, "He was right, dead right, as he sailed along, and now he's as dead as if he'd been wrong." Don't push your right-of-way, especially at night.

When it looks as if there may be a close call developing, and the other vessel may not be aware of your existence, play your spotlight over your sails for several minutes so the other vessel's skipper can see them. I've found this works well in good visibility, but it's next to useless in bad weather (when you most need to be seen). It is more effective to shine the spotlight right at the wheelhouse of the other vessel. From this vantage point, the battery-operated spotlight will look like a pinprick of light, if it is seen at all. It certainly won't blind the helmsman—which you obviously want to avoid—but it will make him aware that there is a boat out there.

Your binoculars, which you use so frequently during daylight, can also be very useful at dusk or at night. I was in a situation not too long ago where we were converging with a number of commercial boats and it was hard to tell exactly what they were doing. The lights seemed close together and confusing, and no wonder. By checking with binoculars we found that we could cross one tug towing a barge and then safely sail between it and another tug towing a barge to windward of the first tug and tow. The binoculars made the situation very clear.

In another situation, we were converging at dusk with a ship that was lit up like a Christmas tree. We could not pick up the side lights and had no idea which way she was going. A check with the binoculars showed the boat to be a large sailing schooner (with a generator, which accounted for all the lights), and we easily set a course to avoid her.

Although a collision with a ship is of utmost concern, the more modern ships have excellent radar that signals a warning when a target enters a zone miles ahead. It also numbers and tracks a target, shows its course and speed and time of intercept. An officer of the cruise ship *Sithar Fairsea* recently demonstrated her radar to me and I commented that it should make collisions at sea a thing of the past. He agreed and said that to have a collision these days, you really have to be trying to mow a boat down. However, sailboats don't always show up very well on radar—which responds better to metal than wood or fiberglass—and it's a wise precaution for a yacht to hoist a radar reflector (a many-sided shape made of wire mesh or metal sheet) during periods of low visibility.

In the 1979 Fastnet Race, however, our major concern was other yachts. On large sailboats, side lights are usually positioned low in the bow, and in that storm the seas were so steep that you could only see a side light when both boats were on top of the waves. So, I'd see a light ahead for a split second and then it would disappear. Any course adjustment had to be decided in that split second and we were among lots of boats. Then, suddenly, instead of seeing a port side light of a boat crossing our bow, I saw a starboard one dead ahead. This meant, under the circumstances, either the boat was tacking or had momentarily rounded up into the wind and was going to fall back off on port tack. If I headed up from the starboard tack beam reach we were on, I would hit her if she tacked. If I headed down, I would hit her if she fell back on port tack. I decided to bear off dead downwind on the theory that even if she fell back on port, the most likely possibility—since a tack was unlikely from that location—was that we would cross ahead of her. After that first glimpse of the starboard side light, I never saw the boat again in the mountainous waves, so my decision was appropriate.

Reading lights correctly (determining course, speed, and type of boat from her lights) comes from experience. If you don't have it, you should not venture out at night without someone on board who has. Someone has to determine if you're on a collision course and if you have right-of-way in order to make the proper decision as to course change. A wrong decision could be disastrous, so don't take sailing at night lightly.

GROUNDINGS

Sooner or later anyone who sails will go aground. Though often embarrassing, it's usually not dangerous. Often the bottom is sand or mud in a bay or sounds and you've hit because you were sailing too close to shore in order to get out of the current, a sand bar shifted from its position on the chart, or you weren't following your course on the chart closely enough.

With a centerboard boat, getting off is easy. Once you bump, raise the centerboard and head for deeper water.

Getting a daysailer with a keel or a cruising boat off is a bit more difficult. The most important reaction when you first hit is to heel the boat immediately. Trim the sails in flat and get all your crew weight to leeward. More acrobatic crew members can walk out on the boom, as it's eased out over the water, leaning against the windward side of the mainsail. Others can hang on the leeward shrouds. Try to sway the boat by leaning in and then way out. By getting the boat to roll, the swing to leeward will be farther than by weight alone.

If this doesn't work, use the spinnaker pole to push off. This method is good if the bottom is hard, but with a muddy bottom, the pole just sinks (and fouls up the jaws and springs in the pole with mud, rendering them useless for later use).

Another answer in small boats is to get wet. Go over the side and start shoving. Try to rotate the boat by pushing the bow from one side while someone else pushes from the stern. For better purchase, take the anchor over the side and carry it out the full length of the anchor rode into deeper water. Even when the water is over your head, you can move the anchor out away from the boat or take it out with a dinghy if available. Rest the anchor on the bottom and with the line vertical, lift and swim. Wear a life vest to increase your buoyancy and for safety. Back in the boat, wrap the anchor line around a jib sheet winch and crank. You can achieve tremendous pulling power this way and may very well pull the boat off. This is commonly called "kedging off."

Obviously, another method is to accept some friendly assistance from a powerboat. I would suggest that you determine beforehand if there will be a charge and, if so, how much it will be. Some "helpful" people try to charge for their services afterward. Another hint: Use your own line rather than accept one from a strange boat. I understand that, under Admiralty Law, salvage can be more readily claimed and held up in court if you accept a towline from the assisting boat rather than tossing her yours.

When a couple of other boats are helping to tow your cruising boat off, it's sometimes practical to have one pull on a halyard to heel the boat farther while the other pulls on the hull. This may work, but don't try it on small boats with masts that may not be sufficiently supported to take the strain.

The most common reason for grounding is complacency. I know of one skipper who, having sailed his own boat to Bermuda, apparently regarded navigating a bareboat charter in the Virgin Islands an easy matter. In fact, he was so relaxed that he didn't tend to his piloting chores thoroughly enough when heading to St. John from the east into the late afternoon sun. His boat hit the only buoyed coral reef in the Virgin Islands on the windward side. The minute she bounced, the forward motion slowed and the boat made some leeway. In such a situation, if the boat is turned upwind and sails are trimmed, she will heel more, which may keep her from bouncing again and she might be able to claw her way off to windward and out of danger. However, in this case, it's more likely she hit again, was pushed sideways by wind and sea, ending up higher and higher on the reef with each wave. This was one of those times when the first bounce was too late. The boat was a total loss within hours.

This grounding was easily avoidable. It illustrates the importance of always navigating carefully. You should check the chart constantly, even if you think you know where the hazards are. A sudden squall, fog bank, unexpected current, or other surprise—such as an unexpected breakdown—may throw your bearings off unless you've been keeping careful track of your course right along.

For instance, consider the navigator who is aware of a dangerous shallow spot, sets a course to miss it, and then relaxes, confident of his own navigating competence. He never follows up with cross bearings to check that current, excessive leeway, or casual steering hasn't been setting him on the reef he so carefully plotted to miss. He may have been getting away with this type of navigation for years, but one big mistake will wake him up.

Many grounding situations can be avoided by using common sense. Once, when leading a cruise of four 41-ft. sailboats in the Grenadines, as we lowered sail to power through a channel to an overnight anchorage, I noticed a breaking reef to leeward. I then changed plans and led the boats the long way around to leeward of the reef. In case of an engine failure I did not want any of the boats to be to windward of the reef if that happened. Sure enough, just as the last boat got dead downwind of the reef, she had a fire in her starter motor and lost her engine. Luckily, she was not to windward of the reef.

Think ahead about what can happen, expect the worst, and you may avoid some unnecessary groundings.

It is also important to know the state of the tide—rising or falling and how much—where you are sailing. One can be far more adventuresome on a rising tide than on a falling one. In some areas in Europe, the tide rises and falls over 30 feet. Obviously, you can sail comfortably at certain times in areas that are complete dry at low water, but it's certainly safer to do so on an incoming rather than ebbing tide.

One of our fleet experienced this during a cruise of Offshore Sailing School grads in the Grenadines, when one of the boats powered into too-shallow water to anchor for the night. It was a quiet harbor, but the tide was ebbing and she couldn't get off. I took her anchor out in a dinghy and we tried kedging her off while the crew leaned out to leeward and I used the dinghy—tugboat style—to rotate the bow. The engine was in full forward, but nothing happened. She wouldn't budge. The wind was light and I didn't expect setting sail would help, but I suggested they unfurl the roller-furling jib and trim it tight. To my amazement, it worked like a charm. There's more heeling power in sails than you might expect.

In tropical waters where the bottom can be clearly seen, it's often hard to judge how far down the bottom is. With practice one learns to read the depth by the color of the water. Coral heads near the surface appear brownish in many areas. White, sandy bottom shows up clearly and if it's very white, the depth if quite shallow. A tinge of blue may give you sufficient depth, but be wary.

One of the best ways to pick your way through reefs is to put a lookout in the spreaders. From this high vantage point looking down, he can judge depths more easily and indicate a safe passage to the helm. He should either wear a harness and snap it around the spreader or shroud, or brace himself around the mast so that if the boat hits bottom he won't be thrown off the spreader. Also, he should wear sunglasses and take binoculars up with him; they will help him to read depth and distance far better.

It's also essential when picking your way through a reef that the sun be behind you. If your anchorage is to the west, don't ever try to enter a treacherous area late in the day. Plan to arrive earlier when the sun is high and you will be able to spot the reefs. The reverse applies for a morning departure toward the east. If you have to head out toward the rising sun, delay your departure until later in the day when the sun is high. Trying to thread your way through reefs when heading into the sun is courting disaster.

Grounding can become a serious problem in the case of the innovative winged keels. They are a mixed blessing, permitting a boat to have much shallower draft with little loss of performance, and they can sail waters where full-keeled boats cannot venture. However, once a winged keel goes aground, it can be much harder to get off. A full-keeled boat loses draft when heeled and can refloat by heeling, but the winged-keel boat increases draft when heeled. Thus, if you go aground in a winged-keel boat while sailing and heeled over, luffing or dousing your sails should free you to power out to deeper water, but if you go aground under power, there's not much you can do except kedge off and/or wait for an incoming tide.

STEERING FAILURE

We have previously discussed the worst kind of steering failure—loss of the rudder—but other failures occur more often. The hydraulics in the steering may lose fluid, something may get jammed in the steering quadrant, or the wire turning the quadrant may fatigue and break. Knowing what the problem is is one thing, but of more immediate importance is knowing how to cope with a lack-of-steering emergency.

Such an emergency occurred one year during a flotilla charter of Off-shore grads in Greece. The cruise was being led by our then operations director, Rob Eberle. He noticed that one of the boats appeared to be in trouble and was sailing toward shallow water off a point of land. He immediately raised her on the radio and asked the problem. The woman who responded was a fairly recent grad and she said they had lost their steering. Rob asked if she remembered from the "Learn to Sail" course how to tack a boat without using the rudder. She said, "Yes, luff the jib and trim the main," to which Rob replied, "Do it! Now!" He was delighted to see the boat tack and sail away from the shallow water. The point is, since it is possible to steer with the sails it is not a disaster to lose your steering. Every skipper should practice sailing without touching the steering wheel or tiller so that should a failure occur, he or she will know just how the boat handles when steered by the sails alone and would be able to guide her into safe water or to port. Unless you practice, it's easy to panic and end up in trouble.

However, if a steering loss occurs in shallow water, anchor, drop your sails, and fix the problem. Most cruising sailboats have emergency steering equipment of one sort or another. It's usually an emergency tiller that fits over the top of the rudder post, accessed through a plate-covered opening near the steering pedestal. If you can't fix the steering problem, just fit your emergency steering, raise anchor and head for port.

SAFETY

The 1979 Fastnet Race brought a number of safety factors relating to personnel into focus for me. We all were wearing a good sturdy harness (Lirakis) and we had jacklines or jackstays on either side of the boat running from the cockpit all the way forward. Jacklines are wires with eyes at each end that are lashed down to the deck at the bow and cockpit. They run inside of any sheets. This permits you to clip your harness on the wire before leaving the cockpit and thus have unobstructed travel all the way forward while remaining clipped to the wire at all times. Without a jackline, you have to unclip and reclip at various spots along the rail, leaving you vulnerable when unclipped to a sudden lurch or a wave throwing you off balance and over the side of the boat. It only takes a second. It's a good idea to leave a jackline rigged at all times when sailing offshore.

Another rule we observed in regard to harnesses (other than the obvious one of not snapping onto anything that might break (like a lifeline) or anything with a strain on it (such as a stay or shroud) was to pass our own clip to a crew member on deck before emerging from the companionway hatch. A crew member is vulnerable to being washed overboard during the few moments he is unclipped just as he comes on deck or is about to go below. When going below, you should leave your harness attached until you are safely inside the hatch and then ask a crew member on deck to unsnap it for you, and reverse the procedure when going on deck so that you are always clipped on when on deck.

The design of a harness is very important. The snaps should be easy to release and there should be snaps at both ends of the line. If the boat should capsize, you need to be able to release yourself from the harness. The snaps at the outer end of the line may be unreachable in such circumstances, so you must be able to release the end attached at your harness, and this cannot be done if it is spliced or sewn to the harness. The Offshore Racing Council has come up with complete standard specifications for safety harnesses. These are reproduced in Appendix I with the kind permission of the ORC.

Since it may take a few boat lengths to deploy a man-overboard strobe at night and the strobe may drift away from the victim, each crew member should have his own strobe attached to his safety harness at all times. Each crew should also have his own whistle for calling attention if in the water; this should also be attached to his safety harness. It is also useful to apply reflecting tape to the cuffs of foul weather gear (or buy the kind that has it sewn on), so that a spotlight can pick it up at night as an overboard victim waves his arms. However, I don't believe the color of your foul weather gear makes too much difference because most of it is underwater anyhow. A spotter will be more attracted by motion—and reflecting tape on the cuffs—than by the color of your gear.

The last safety requirement needing mention here is the life raft, an item it's hoped the reader will never have to use. Its use in extreme conditions—namely, the 1979 Fastnet Race—has indicated that it should be used only as a last resort. In the Fastnet disaster, some of the victims lost their lives when their life rafts flipped or broke apart, while many of the sailboats they abandoned weathered the storm without sinking. My own theory is that sailboats can float with a great deal more water in them than their owners realize. When the water is up to your knees belowdecks, most people quite naturally think the boat is about to sink, which actually might not be true at all. I would like to see designers inscribe an internal water-line in the cabin. When the water reaches that level, theoretically the boat should sink. I believe such a measurement indication would reduce premature abandonments.

Appendix II shows the Offshore Racing Council's minimum specifications for life rafts and the equipment they should have. It also lists items one should keep in a small waterproof bag to take aboard the raft; it's called, aptly, a "grab bag."

Appendix III lists safety and other equipment which should be carried by all racing boats. I consider it a good list for all cruising boats as well. The list was compiled by the Offshore Racing Council and is partially reprinted with their permission.

HYPOTHERMIA

A few years ago I decided to advertise for a person to produce classroom sailboat models for a couple of branches of our Offshore Sailing School. Among those who answered the ad was a young man in his late twenties, who gave me a very reasonable price. I asked him how he could afford to make the models at that price and he said, "I owe you one." He then explained that he was the teenager whose life I had saved about 15 years earlier.

That was my first experience with hypothermia. I was sailing an Atlantic class sailboat on Long Island Sound with a friend one cold September weekday when we were about 17 years old. The Sound was deserted and we thought we were alone—not another sail in sight. About four miles from shore we spotted some movement. At first we thought it was a seagull on a log, but since we weren't sure we sailed closer to take a look. We found a capsized Lightning with two young boys clinging to it. They had been returning from a weekend regatta, had set a spinnaker and made the mistake of cleating the lines while eating lunch. A sudden gust, and over they went. They had been in the water for over an hour and were cold and exhausted. We took them aboard, sent them forward under the foredeck out of the wind and wrapped them in a spinnaker.

At that point, we didn't know anything about hypothermia, but, as I later learned, these two were well on their way—they were pale, with blue lips, and shivering violently. We probably should have huddled with them for body heat transfer, but we didn't know enough to do that, and, besides, we had to sail the boat. At any rate, we got them home safely and, apparently, had picked them up before too much damage had been done. It is only in retrospect that I realize how serious their situation was.

In another accident, two men had a harrowing experience when their motorboat capsized near Boston in fall weather. The owner and his friend climbed up on the bottom of the turtled boat and were there for two nights and into a second day when found. His buddy died of hypothermia the second night. What saved the owner? Fat. He was a large man who weighed almost 300 lbs. The cold affects small, thin people much faster.

The Coast Guard explains hypothermia as subnormal temperature within the central nervous system. When a person is immersed in cold water, the skin and nearby tissues may cool rapidly. However, it may be 10 to 15 minutes before the temperature of the heart and brain starts to drop. When this core temperature reaches 90 degrees F, unconsciousness may occur. When the core temperature drops to 85 degrees F, heart failure is the usual cause of death, if the person hasn't already drowned.

Survival time is affected by activity in the water and whether the head is in or out of the water. A person treading water or swimming will cool about 35 percent faster than a person staying still, but a person who lowers his head under the water cools about 82 percent faster than if floating with his head out of the water. That's the importance of using a good life jacket. You can remain quiet with your head out of the water and the jacket helps you retain body heat. An average-size person may survive 2½ to three hours in 50-degree water under such circumstances. Since water conducts heat away from the body many times faster than air does, it's best to get out of the water or onto a capsized boat, like the fellow mentioned above.

If you can't get out of the water, assume a fetal position with your knees up to your chest and your arms hugging yourself. This is called "H.E.L.P." (Heat Escape Lessening Posture) and will reduce heat loss and increase your survival time. If there are a number of people in the water at the same time, body heat can be preserved by huddling side by side in a circle. Estimated survival times for the average person in 50-degree water is two hours when treading water or swimming; two hours and 40 minutes when holding still in a life jacket and four hours in the H.E.L.P. or huddle positions.

The old axiom "Stay with the boat" is particularly solid under hypothermia conditions. Some good swimmers have been able to swim 8⁄10 of a mile in 50-degree water before being overcome by hypothermia; others have not been able to swim 100 yards. Distances are deceptive and what looks like an easy swim may very well be too far to make. Also, rescuers can see an overturned boat, but they may miss seeing a swimmer. So, don't swim for it unless there's absolutely no chance of rescue by staying with the boat and you are absolutely certain you can make it. If you do swim, take a flotation device with you.

To avoid "after-drop" caused by improper rewarming, which allows cold, stagnant blood to return to the core of the body, causing death, the Coast Guard recommends the following:

1. Move a victim to shelter and warmth as rapidly as possible.
2. Gently remove all wet clothing.
3. Apply heat to the central core of the body (head, neck, sides and groin).
   a. Apply warm, moist towels to the core area. When the towels cool, add warm water (about 105 degrees).
   b. Use hot water bottles and electric blankets if available.
   c. An effective field measure is for one or two of the rescuers to remove their own clothing and use their bodies to warm the victim's naked body, using a sleeping bag or blanket to conserve body heat.

Coast Guard recommendations about what *not* to do.

1. Do not give the victim anything to drink—especially not alcohol.
2. Do not rub frozen body areas, especially not with snow.
3. Do not wrap a hypothermic person in a blanket without an auxiliary source of heat unless it is to protect against further heat loss before treatment.
4. Do not put an unconscious person in a bathtub.

UP THE MAST

Whether you need to go up the mast for emergency repairs or just for routine inspection and maintenance, be sure to do it the proper way. Avoid the urge to climb up hand over hand to accomplish the job. There's always some hero aboard who doesn't want to wait to dig out the bosun's chair—which is the only safe way to go up the mast—and shinnies up a halyard. I know of a man who did this and was holding on to the top of the mast when his hands cramped up and he could no longer hold on. He fell.

Normally the crew member is hauled up on a jib or spinnaker halyard. The jib halyard is probably safer because it's designed for heavier loads, and the sheave at the top of the mast is inside, so the halyard goes down inside the mast. If the sheave pin slips out, the halyard will jam, but you won't come tumbling down. Some spinnaker halyards are attached to blocks hanging from cranes on the forward part of the masthead. The problem with this arrangement is that if the block or pin breaks, the whole system comes down.

Not too long ago, a crewman I know went up a 70-foot mast using a spinnaker halyard. When he got there he was shocked to see that the screw pin of the shackle attaching the spinnaker block to the eye had backed out. The threaded end was canted down and the only thing keeping the block from falling out of the shackle was his weight jamming it against the threaded end. Moving very carefully, he supported his weight with one hand on top of the mast while he screwed the pin into the shackle (it should have been seized), with the other. He then came back down the mast, went below, and poured himself a stiff drink.

When going up the mast, select the halyard and shackle it to the bosun's chair. Now take a safety line and bypass the shackle. Tie it from the loop of the wire halyard through the shackle to the chair in such a way that if the shackle opens accidentally, you're still attached. If conditions are very rough, it's a good idea to tape the snapshackle closed because the pull cord could easily catch on something as you go up and pull the pin, opening the shackle. The safety line is a last resort, so you want to avoid its being used.

Your next problem is to assure that if you lose your grip on the mast on the way up you won't swing around like a paddle ball on the end of a rubber band. The mast describes a big arc in a rough sea, and it's not only hard to hold on, but if you let go you can swing wildly out of control. That happened to a friend of mine who went up in a blow to cut free a wrapped spinnaker. He ended up spinning around an upper shroud, all wrapped up in the halyard and unconscious.

I use two methods to avoid this mishap. First, I always have a downhaul line attached to the bottom of the chair, with someone feeding out slack in the line as I go up. Second, I snap a snatchblock to the same eye of the chair to which the halyard is attached. I then snap the block over any other halyard that runs all the way up the mast (so it doesn't have to be disconnected midway up). If no other halyard is available, I snap the block over the one that's taking me up. This is less desirable because there's no way to snub the halyard in tight since it is pulling me up.

The most important person in the whole process is the one hauling you up—the tailer. If he or she slips or the coils come off the winch, the chair makes a rapid unplanned descent. The tailer should sit on deck, well braced against boat movement. The direction of pull from the winch should angle toward the winch base rather than off the edge; thus, if the winch is on the deck, it should be tailed low. If it is on the side of the mast, the tailer should sit on the centerline of the boat. He always uses both hands. When the chair is at the desired height, the tailer adds a number of wraps around the winch and carefully cleats the halyard, finishing with a half hitch for safety.

To lower, the tailer takes the extra turns off the winch until there are one or two turns less than when he winched the chair up. When he eases the line, it should run out easily, not bind on the winch drum and jerk out.

Even with these precautions, the person going up the mast should never rely totally on the chair. There's a time-worn axiom: "One hand for the boat and one for yourself," which means *Hold on.* Wherever possible, the man aloft should accomplish the task to be done with one hand so he can save himself with the other in case the halyard or something else gives.

SAFETY BELOWDECKS

There are certain precautions that should be taken belowdecks, especially in regard to the dangers of fire, explosion, scalding, slipping, or falling, and improperly stowed items that can slide or fall or that could become projectiles with violent boat movement.

For fire protection, you should have several well-placed extinguishers, i.e., not stowed next to the stove or engine that might catch fire, yet within easy reach to be grabbed quickly. Also, every boat should have two easy means of egress from belowdecks in case one is blocked by the fire. On one of our flotilla cruises in the British Virgin Islands, the boat I was aboard suddenly developed a starter-motor fire. I pulled away the companionway steps and was on my knees spraying away with the fire extinguisher when I felt a lady's foot in the small of my back. With one bound she was out in the cockpit. We had a good chuckle about my qualities as a ladder. However, had she thought of it, she could have exited through the forward hatch.

The stove is a potential danger area only if you don't fully understand its operation and the type of fuel used. Anyone using the stove should be thoroughly schooled in lighting and extinguishing procedures for that particular stove and in the characteristics of the fuel it uses.

There are basically three types of stove fuel: alcohol, propane (LPG), and compressed natural gas (CNG). Their handling differs depending on which is used.

If yours is an alcohol stove, always keep a container of water handy to dump on it in the case of a flare-up. Water quickly puts out an alcohol fire.

If it's a propane gas stove, be aware that propane is heavier than air, and leaking gas will find its way into the bilge where any spark can cause an explosion. In the case of a leak, to remove the gas you have to bail out the bilge with buckets, etc., until it's gone.

If the fuel is compressed natural gas (CNG), it will dissipate quickly in good ventilation because CNG is lighter than air and will not collect in the bilge. Many people prefer this type of stove for this reason.

Naturally, it is imperative that stove fuel tanks be installed according to regulations. Gas tanks are always stowed on deck in an area that has no access to the inside of the hull except through the gas lines to the stove. A solenoid cut-off valve is often installed right at the tank so that the user, after cooking is finished, flips a switch that activates the solenoid cut-off valve while the stove is still lit. The gas remaining in the line below the tank is then burned off and the flame goes out. Then the stove burner is turned off. Luckily, gas used today emits quite an odor, so you usually know when there's a leak. Also, if you wish you may install a gas detector alarm on your boat which will warn of a leak in case you're sleeping and don't smell the gas.

The stern-mounted charcoal grill is a fourth popular type of shipboard stove, and because it involves open flame—always a fire hazard—it, too, must be used with care. In particular, it should be used only when the boat is at anchor and free to swing with the breeze, and only then if you are sure that the stern will swing clear of nearby boats with a wind shift. Obviously, the grill should never be used when the boat is tied up at a dock where a new wind or wind shift could spew sparks over sails, other boats, or even your own cockpit and start a fire.

A more frequent belowdecks hazard than fire or explosion is scalding. A friend of mine was boiling water while underway in a sailboat and had not thought that conditions warranted releasing the pins to allow the stove to gimbal. A powerboat wake caused the pot of boiling water to spill on his bare arm. He now has deep burn scars that look as though they had been caused by fire. To avoid such a problem, always let the stove gimbal when in use and secure the pots with the provided clamps. Some people wear foul weather gear during galley duty underway, but it's hot and I feel that's like wearing a helmet in your car on the highway in case you have an accident. The inconvenience outweighs the chance something will happen.

There's a greater possibility of scalding when pouring or spooning hot liquid from one receptacle to another. Do as airline flight attendants do— never pour into a cup someone else is holding. The same person should always hold both pot and cup, so the pouring and holding hands move in concert.

Slipping is another belowdecks hazard and it usually occurs when the cabin sole is wet. Thus, it's a good idea to make a rule that all wet clothing, boots, and gear be removed and stowed in one assigned area rather than allowed to drip throughout the cabin. Also, if the sole does get wet, it should be wiped dry as soon as possible. Bare feet also add to your chances of slipping; deck shoes should be the rule at all times.

Many people are injured by falls when the boat lurches during a knock-down or broach, but the boat-wise crew will always know just where the ceiling handrail is, particularly in the area of the companionway. If the bunks are fixed, lee cloths to keep you from falling out of the bunk are a necessity. Each lee cloth should be secured by a tie in the center to prevent the bunk occupant from being flung from the berth over the top of the cloth in case of a knockdown or rollover. Also, every object in the cabin should be secured to withstand a rollover. During the '79 Fastnet Race storm violence, many crew injuries were caused by flying batteries, stoves, anchors, and other objects, all of which should have been tightly secured in place.

OBSERVING WEAKNESSES

Safety is both the prevention of emergencies and the preparation for them. It may take years of experience, but some people are able to develop a sixth sense of when something is not quite right. For instance, one time I went for a one-hour sail to check out some new jibs for our 54-foot ocean racer *Sleuth*. It was my first sail in six months, yet I noticed that someone had shackled on one of the mainsheet blocks a quarter turn from lining up properly with the sheet pull. If it had been blowing harder and we had trimmed the sheet in tightly, we would have twisted, weakened, and possibly broken the bale to which the block was attached. We immediately corrected the problem. Not five minutes later I noticed someone had used a bolt with a non-locking nut on our starboard running backstay. If the nut had come off and the bolt popped out we would have lost the mast. These may seem like trivial problems and an untrained eye would no doubt miss them completely. But knowing what the end result might be if they were not corrected comes from long experience and the power of observation.

Some sailors never do develop this sixth sense, but it's important. You've seen something break before; you're aware of what to look for. A few years ago I advised an Olympic contender that he'd better change his spinnaker halyard shackle before competing in the final races. He didn't do it, and—sure enough—it broke the next day in a practice race. Then he fixed it. I just happened to know that it was a weak design.

I could give hundreds of such examples that have happened to me, but I doubt that would help the reader, because each boat and event is a little different. Suffice it to say many emergencies can be avoided if you are constantly observant. Following is a list of some of the things to look for:

1. Corrosion or hairline splits in shroud swage fittings that attach to the turnbuckles.
2. A broken strand in a shroud or stay.
3. Evidence of chafe on rope halyards, burrs on wire halyards.
4. Excessive water in the bilge, corrosion around through-hull fittings.
5. A captive pin halyard shackle that needs spreading to keep the pin from flopping around.
6. Lack of seizing wire on anchor shackles.
7. Sharp, untaped cotter pins that can rip sails.
8. Sharp edges on the boom that can also rip sails.
9. Loose steering.
10. Loose shackle pins on important items like hiking straps. If they let go, you can end up overboard.
11. No cotter pins in shroud turnbuckles (often forgotten by the person tuning the rig) make loss of the mast possible.
12. Note loss of cotter pins from any clevis pins you see.
13. Signs of weakness in the area of the main boom gooseneck. This is an area of tremendous strains and can be dangerous if the boom breaks free.
14. Make sure that the covers for any "watertight" compartments are securely fastened in case the cockpit fills with water.
15. Any loose deck blocks, travelers, or winches indicate that the nuts on some of the through-bolts have backed off. Any undue strain on the block might cause it to pop off the deck.
16. A bad lead on an anchor line or mooring line could cause chafe and the loss of your boat after you've left it for the night.
17. Broken stitching in a batten pocket, small tears in a sail.

Most of the above are found on small boats. On cruising boats there are myriad other things that can go wrong because we're introducing far greater strains. Also, there are engine and electrical problems, dinghy and propeller tangling problems, and many others.

The old adage, "an ounce of prevention is worth a pound of cure," is especially apropos on a boat. So, before you go out, try to spot the various potential sources of eventual emergencies and correct them.

HANDLING EMERGENCIES

Let's imagine that you have not noticed the signs of trouble before going out sailing for the day. Certain emergencies occur. How do you handle them?

The first situation occurs because you didn't notice the cracks in the swaged fitting on your starboard upper shroud. It breaks when you are on a starboard tack and the mast bends perilously to leeward. Immediately spin the boat into the wind dumping the air out of the mainsail and jib and flipping over to port tack. This puts the pressure on the unbroken port shrouds and saves the mast. If you can't go on port tack for some reason — such as proximity to shore — shoot into the wind, get your sails down and anchor. If a wire shroud breaks and the break is near the turnbuckle and you have some U-bolts aboard, you can make another eye and reattach the turnbuckle, assuming it's a small sailboat. Or, you can take both ends of the spinnaker halyard out to the edge of the deck and fasten them securely. If it's a double-ended halyard and one end is still attached to the mast, stretch can cause poor support, so attach both ends to the deck edge. If possible, shinny up the mast and pull the halyard out to the spreader tip with a looped line so the spreader can help support the mast as it does with the upper shroud.

Occasionally, the backstay breaks. If it happens on a run, the mast could fall forward over the bow because of the pull of the spinnaker and mainsail. The first thing to do is to throw off the spinnaker sheet and round up into the wind. This takes the pressure off the sails, and wind resistance pushes the mast and rigging toward the stern of the boat. Then trim the mainsail in tight. The leech of the mainsail on a small boat will have almost the same holding power as the backstay. Note the number of parts on the mainsheet and the strength with which you haul it in. Make sure the traveler is in the middle of the boat for maximum mast support. In moderate winds you can sail on most points of sail with the main trimmed in as if close-hauled. In heavier winds the main can be reefed down quite far and still give some support and allow you to sail to a destination. However, the support will only be to the point where the head of the sail is on the mast. To support the upper part of the mast, secure the spinnaker halyard aft at the stern (on boats where the spinnaker halyard runs to the top of the mast).

Another option in heavy winds is to douse the mainsail and run the main halyard either to the end of the boom or to the stern. By attaching the main halyard to the end of the boom, cleating the other end, and trimming the mainsheet tight we get excellent mast support. Attach the halyard to a boom bale, not the outhaul, because the latter can break. On larger sailboats with a main halyard winch, we would shackle the halyard right to the stern of the boat (or to an extra line if the halyard wasn't long enough) and tension it tightly with a winch.

Usually when a jib stay breaks the crew has a little time before the mast falls backward because the jib luff will support it for a while. The proper maneuver is to head downwind and ease the mainsail immediately. The force of the wind in the mainsail will push the mast forward and keep it standing. It's also fairly easy to find another unused halyard (either spinnaker or spare jib halyard on many boats) to attach to the bow for temporary support. When you get into the harbor, lower the mainsail first and then take care of the jib.

Sometimes the windward spreader breaks. The same procedures apply as when a shroud breaks. Tack or jibe immediately to put the strain on the good spreader on the other side of the mast. If you can sail on that tack back to the harbor you don't have to make repairs to get home. But if you must repair the broken spreader to be able to sail on that tack, search the boat for a piece of wood or tubing with which to splint the spreader. On small boats, remember there are the tiller extension, deck supports, floorboard supports, and other items that might be used. Use the tiller and then steer with the sails and a pair of pliers or vise grips attached to the rudder head. The key to survival in any situation is to be as inventive as possible.

Sinking is not a common emergency, but it can happen that the boat fills up with water to the extent that sinking is a possibility. If a small boat broaches on a spinnaker run and a crew releases the spinnaker guy, the spinnaker may lay the boat over flat and it's likely the cockpit will fill. With the forward and after hatches closed, there should be no problem. Get the spinnaker down and luff the sails so the boat straightens up. Then bail like crazy. I like to have at least one bucket on any boat I sail. A cruising boat should have several. Pumps do a good job, but they are unreliable as debris can clog the intake. Moreover, only one crew member can pump, but many can bail with buckets.

While sailing with the boat full of water, head for shallow water so the boat will be easily recoverable if it sinks. Under no circumstances should you make any violent alteration of course. I once saw a boat that was full of water sailing on a reach toward the shore. The helmsman decided to round up into the wind and stop the boat in order to bail more efficiently. The boat turned, but the water in the boat kept on going in the original direction of travel. The weight and force of the water rolled the boat over flat. It filled and sank.

In such conditions the crew should already be wearing life vests. When it's obvious that there's nothing that can be done to avoid sinking, try to tie a fender or some floating item to a long line—such as a spinnaker sheet—to mark the location of the boat for salvage later. You'd be surprised how much time you actually have. Air is usually trapped under the deck and the last throes are really quite slow as the bow or stern finally disappears beneath the waves. Make sure that the crew is well clear of the boat and in no way entangled in the various lines as she sinks.

Many daysailers have fore and aft flotation compartments. As long as they are tight, the boat will float. However, a collision with another boat might result in a hole in a compartment. During one of our racing courses, such a collision occurred, puncturing the after compartment of a Soling. On one tack the hole was submerged; on the other it was out of the water. The obvious procedure was to stay on the tack that would keep the hole out of the water until temporary repairs could be made. This particular crew didn't do that. One of the crew members then opened up the after compartment hatch to see if he could plug the hole from the inside. The effort was well-intentioned, but misguided. Water poured into the cockpit from the compartment and the crew barely got the hatch refastened. If the cockpit had also filled with water the Soling could not have remained afloat.

There are a few things that can be done about a hole below the waterline in a boat. First, stuff clothes or blankets in the hole. Next, cover it from the outside with plastic and then cover the plastic with a blanket or sails fixed in place with lines that go right under the boat and tie to either side. I have never had to resort to this and I hope I never will. The water pressure is said to hold the collision mat in place, but I'll believe it's a practical solution when I've had to try it. Nevertheless, it doesn't hurt to have some kind of solution in mind for emergencies that have never happened to you.

APPENDIX I

ORC Minimum Standard Specifications for Yachtsmen's Safety Harnesses

(Copyright Offshore Racing Council. Reprinted by permission of the Ocean Racing Council)

The Offshore Racing Council is not an approving authority and cannot be responsible for manufacturers' statements of compliance with these standards.

PREFACE: This standard was prepared by the Offshore Racing Council and is based on BS 4224–1975 and AS 2227–1978.

1) SCOPE

This specification sets out requirements for safety harnesses and lines for use by yachtsmen. It specifies general design requirements, constructional requirements, test methods, and requirements for individual components, together with a dynamic load test for the finished article.

2) GENERAL REQUIREMENTS

2.1 Safety Harness

The safety harness shall consist of an arrangement of webbing straps and shall be designed to locate the safety line at about armpit level. The safety harness shall be adjustable to permit it to be worn outside of light clothing or heavy sea clothing.

Alternatively, a garment is acceptable provided that it possesses an overall strength sufficient to meet the requirements of the performance test and the portion carrying the harness loads is manufactured from materials which will not rot or corrode in service at sea.

If a safety harness is manufactured in conjunction with any other garment such as a life jacket, the complete assembly shall comply also with appropriate standards for the combination garment.

The main load-bearing strap(s) of the safety harness (see clause 3.1) shall not be less than 38mm in width and brace straps shall not be less than 19mm in width.

The safety harness shall be designed so that it will not slacken during wearing as a result of body movement or as a result of accidental contact with other objects. Where the securing buckle and adjustment buckle are one and the same, this may be achieved by providing a keeper which should be permanently attached to the main belt. Other means of meeting this design requirement are acceptable.

2.2 Safety Line

The safety line (see clause 3.2) shall be designed such that: (a) the safety line shall be readily detachable from the safety harness by the wearer by means of a hook (see clause 3.5) attached to either the safety harness or the safety line, (b) the safety line is permanently attached to the safety harness. The safety line shall not be more than 2m in length from the wearer to the point of attachment inclusive of any fittings and shall be provided at the free end with a hook (see clause 3.5) attachment to a suitable anchorage point.

If the safety line incorporates an intermediate hook(s) to shorten the scope of the line, such hook(s) shall meet the load-bearing requirements of 3.5.

2.3 Securing Buckles

Where securing buckles are provided, they shall be designed so that either: (a) they can be fastened only in the correct manner, or (b) if they are capable of being fastened in more than one way, all methods of fastening will provide equal security. Means shall be provided for restraining the free end of any webbing that protrudes from a securing buckle.

3) MATERIALS AND FITTINGS

3.1 Webbing Straps

The yarn used for webbing shall be of bright, high-tenacity, continuous multi-filament polyamide (nylon)— or polyester fibers having a uniform breaking strength. The minimum breaking load of the webbing straps shall be 1,000kg per mm width.

3.2 Safety Line

The safety line shall be either:

(a) a polyamide filament (nylon) rope having a diameter of not less than 12mm and a breaking load of not less than 2,080kg; or,

(b) a webbing belt made from brighter, high-tenacity, continuous multi-filament polyamide (nylon) and having a breaking load of not less than 2,080kg.

3.3 Thread

Thread used for the sewing of components shall have similar properties to the materials being sewn. If pure natural fiber is used, it shall be treated to resist rotting and shall not be used to sew safety lines.

Note: Natural fiber may be used as a component of sewing thread.

3.4 Fittings

All metal fittings shall be smoothly finished and free from defects caused by faulty material or manufacture. Aluminum fittings shall be anodic-coated to comply with Grade AA15 or higher.

3.5 Hooks

Hooks shall be self-closing. The opening of the hook shall be sufficiently large to accept and close fully around a metal cylinder 12.7mm in diameter and shall withstand a minimum load of 1500kg without breaking or showing signs of flaws, defects or deterioration (i.e., normally not less than a safe working load (SWL) of 700kg).

3.6 Castings

Where metal castings are used as load-bearing components, they shall be made by the investment casting process.

3.7 Non-magnetic Properties

Not metal part or parts of the safety harness or safety line shall deflect a magnetic compass by more than 1 degree.

3.8 The main load-bearing buckles shall conform with the requirements of clause 5.

3.9 Keepers

A keeper is a device that provides a means of maintaining the tension of the main belt through the securing/adjusting buckle during wearing or a device that restrains the free end of any webbing that protrudes from a load-bearing buckle.

4) SEWING AND SPLICING

4.1 Sewing

All sewing shall be carried out in a lockstitching machine and be securely finished off by back-sewing for at least six stitches, except that where sewn by an automatic lock-stitching machine, the first and last stitches shall be sewn in such a way as not to provide a natural starting point for a break in the stitching. Exposed heat-sealed edges shall not be oversewn.

4.2 Splicing

Splices in the safety line shall consist of at least four full tucks and two tapered tucks. The length of the splicing tails shall be not less than one rope diameter from the emergence of the final tuck.

Splices shall be whipped with a suitable man-made fiber twine or shall be protected by other suitable means. Whippings shall cover the entire tapered portion of the splice and tails, and also at least half of the full tuck section. Other means of protection shall cover at least the tapered portion of the splice and the tails.

5) LOAD TEST

When tested, the safety harness with the safety line attached shall not break or otherwise fail. No component of the assembly shall show signs of flaws, defects, or deterioration after testing that would jeopardize the safety of the wearer. Webbing shall not slip and slacken by more than 25mm through any adjusting device or securing buckle.

6) INSTRUCTIONS

Each safety harness and line offered for sale shall be accompanied by printed instructions bearing words to the following effect:

(a) The wearer should locate strong anchorage points on the yacht capable of accepting the hook provided on the safety harness. Lifelines (guard rails) are not adequate.

(b) The safety harness and line should be kept clean, dry and free from oil or grease. Wash in clean fresh water after use.

(c) The safety harness and line should be inspected frequently for signs of deterioration.

(d) The safety harness and line should be replaced when they have been subjected to severe load.

(e) When it is intended to wear a safety harness and line in conjunction with a life jacket, users are advised to try them on together to ensure that one does not interfere with the function of the other and, in particular, that in use the line is not likely to foul the life jacket.

Instructions for adjusting and wearing the harness should be supplied when necessary. These instructions should include an appropriate phrase such as "Adjust to fit the wearer as tightly as possible."

APPENDIX II

ORC Minimum Specifications for Yachtsmen's Life Rafts

(Copyright Offshore Racing Council. Reprinted by Permission of ORC)
These specifications are mandatory from
1 January 1985.

GENERAL DESIGN:

Life raft(s) capable of carrying the entire crew shall meet the following requirements:

a) Stowage see ORC Special Regulations.

b) Must be designed and used solely for saving life at sea.

c) The life raft shall be so constructed that, when fully inflated and floating with the cover uppermost, it shall be stable in a seaway.

d) The construction of the life raft shall include a cover (which shall automatically be set in place when the life raft is inflated).* This cover shall be capable of protecting the occupants against injury from exposure, and means shall be provided for collecting rain. The cover of the life raft shall be of a highly visible colour.

e) The life raft shall be fitted with a painter and shall have a lifeline becketed round the outside. A lifeline shall also be fitted round the inside the life raft.

f) The life raft shall be capable of being readily righted by one person if it inflates in an inverted position.

g) The life raft shall be fitted at each opening with efficient means to enable persons in the water to climb on board.

h) The life raft shall be contained in a valise or other container so constructed as to be capable of withstanding hard wear under conditions met with at sea. The life raft in its valise or other container shall be inherently buoyant.

i) The buoyancy of the life raft shall be so arranged as to achieve a division into an even number of separate compartments, half of which shall be capable of supporting out of the water the number of persons which the liferaft is fit to accommodate, without reducing the total supporting area.

j) The number of persons which an inflatable life raft shall be permitted to accommodate shall be equal to:

   i) the greatest whole number obtained by dividing by 96 the volume, measured in cubic decimetres of the main buoyancy tubes (which for this purpose shall include neither the arches nor the thwart or thwarts if fitted when inflated: or

   ii) the greatest whole number obtained by dividing by 3720 the area measured in square centimetres of the floor (which for this purpose may include the thwart or thwarts if fitted of the life raft when inflated whichever number shall be the less.

k) The floor of the life raft shall be waterproof (and shall be capable of being sufficiently insulated against the cold either

   i) by means of one or more compartments which the occupants can inflate if they so desire, or which inflate automatically and can be deflated and re-inflated by the occupants; or

   ii) by other equally efficient means not dependent on inflation *

* Section in brackets optional.

EQUIPMENT:

All the following equipment must be secured to the raft!

a) one buoyant rescue quoit, attached to at least 30 metres of buoyant line

b) one safety knife and one bailer

c) two sponges

d) one sea anchor permanently attached to the life raft

e) two paddles

f) one repair outfit capable of repairing punctures in buoyancy compartments

g) one topping-up pump or bellows

h) one waterproof electric torch

i) three hand-held distress flare signals in accordance with SOLAS regulation 36, capable of giving a bright red light

j) six anti-seasickness tablets for each person which the life raft is deemed fit to accommodate

k) instructions on a plastic sheet on how to survive in the life raft

l) The life raft shall be inflated by a gas which is not injurious to the occupants and the inflation shall take place automatically either on the pulling of a line or by some other equally simple and efficient method.

Means shall be provided whereby a topping-up pump or bellows may be used to maintain pressure.

MARKING OF LIFE RAFTS

Each life raft at, or before its next service, shall be clearly marked with the yacht's name or sail number or an identification code on:
a) the canopy
b) the bottom
c) the valise or container
d) the certificate

Numbers and letters on the life raft should be as large as possible and in a strongly contrasting color. From 1.1.87 retro-reflective material shall be fitted.

GRAB BAGS:

A grab bag containing the following is recommended:
a) second sea anchor and line
b) two safety tin openers
c) a first aid kit
d) one rustproof drinking vessel graduated in 10, 20, and 50 cubic cm
e) two "cyalume" sticks or two throwable floating lamps
f) one daylight signaling mirror and one signaling whistle
g) two red parachute flares
h) three red hand flares
i) non-thirst provoking food rations and barley sugar or equivalent
j) watertight receptacles containing fresh water (at least ½ litre per person
k) one copy of the illustrated table of life-saving signals nylon string and polythene bags

N.B. Equipment in the grab bag may be counted as part of the general equipment required under the ORC Special Regulations.

Note: The Offshore Racing Council may in the future adopt the detailed specifications for life rafts currently being defined by the International Council of Marine Industry Associations and the International Organisation for Standardisation (ISO).

APPENDIX III

Offshore Racing Council Special Regulations Governing Offshore Racing

4.0 CATEGORIES OF OFFSHORE EVENTS

4.1 The International Offshore Rule is used to rate a wide variety of types and sizes of yachts in many types of races ranging from long-distance ocean races sailed under adverse conditions to short-course day races sailed in protected waters. To provide for the differences in the standards of safety and accommodation required for such varying circumstances, five categories of races are established, as follows

4.2 Category 0:
Trans-ocean races, where yachts must be completely self-sufficient for extended periods of time, capable of withstanding heavy storms and prepared to meet serious emergencies without the expectation of outside assistance.

4.3 Category 1:
Races of long distance and well offshore, where yachts must be completely self-sufficient for extended periods of time, capable of withstanding heavy storms and prepared to meet serious emergencies without the expectation of outside assistance.

4.4 Category 2:
Races of extended duration along or not far removed from shorelines or in large unprotected bays or lakes, where a high degree of self-sufficiency is required of the yachts but with the reasonable probability that outside assistance could be called upon for aid in the event of serious emergencies.

4.5 Category 3:

Races across open water, most of which is relatively protected or close to shorelines, including races for small yachts.

4.6 Category 4:

Short races close to shore normally held in daylight in relatively warm or protected waters.

In the following list for yachts not racing under the IOR, alternatives to the IOR terms are indicated in brackets.

5) BASIC REQUIREMENTS

Race Category

5.0 b) Weight jackets [IYRR 61.2] shall not be permitted.   0 1 2 3 4

5.1 All required equipment shall: 0 1 2 3 4
Function properly
Be readily accessible
Be of a type, size and capacity suitable
and adequate for the intended use and
size of yacht.

5.2 Yachts shall be self-righting (see IOR Part   0 1 2 3 4
XII). They shall be strongly built,
watertight and, particularly with regard
to hulls, decks and cabin trunks, capable
of withstanding solid water and
knockdowns. They must be properly
rigged and ballasted, be fully seaworthy,
and must meet the standards set forth
herein. "Properly rigged" means (inter
alia) that shrouds shall never be
disconnected.

Inboard engine installations shall be such
that when running can be securely
covered, and that the exhaust and fuel
supply systems are securely installed and
adequately protected from the effects
ofheavy weather. When an electric starter
is the only provision for starting the
engine, a separate battery shall be
carried, the primary purpose of which is
to start the engine.

0 1 2 3 4

Each yacht fitted with a propulsion
engine shall carry a minimum amount of
fuel in a permanently installed fuel tank.
This minimum amount of fuel may be
specified in the Notice of the Race, but if
not, shall be sufficient to be able to meet
charging requirements for the duration of
the race and to motor at $L(\sqrt{LWL})$ knots
for at least 8 hours.

0 1 2 3 4

Organizing clubs are recommended to
apply their own minimum fuel
requirements.

0

5.4 Ballast and Heavy Equipment. All
heavy items including inside ballast and
internal fittings (such as batteries, stoves,
gas bottles, tanks, engines, outboard
motors, etc.) and anchors and chains (se
8.31) and 8.32) shall be securely fastened
so as to remain in position should the
yacht be capsized 180 degrees.

0 1 2 3

5.5 Yacht equipment and fittings shall be
securely fastened.

4

	Race Category				
	0	1	2	3	4

5.6 Sail Numbers. This regulation applies to new sails delivered after 1st April 1988.

A yacht shall carry on all mainsails, all spinnakers, and all jibs with LPG greater than $1.3 \times J$ [longest perpendicular greater than $1.3 \times$ base or foretriangle]:

(a) A letter or letters showing her nationality except that national letters need not be carried in home waters, except in an international championship.
(b) A sail number allotted to her by her national or state authority.

National letters shall be placed in front of or above the sail numbers. When the national letters end in "I" [e.g., Italy, U.S. Virgin Islands], and are placed in front of the numbers, they shall be separated from them by a horizontal line approximately 50mm long. National letters need not be carried in home waters, except in an international championship.

The following specifications and minimum sizes of national letters and sail numbers shall apply: They shall be:
(i) Clearly visible, legible and of a single color that strongly contrasts with the sail, and
(ii) in Roman style (upright), without serifs, with arabic numerals and with lines that are continuous and of uniform thickness.

The minimum sizes for national letters and sail numbers shall be related to the yacht's length overall (LOA) and shall be as follows:

LOA	Height	Width excluding No. 1 and letter I	Thickness	Space between letters and numbers
under 3.5mm	230mm	150mm	30mm	45mm
3.5m–8.5m	300mm	200mm	40mm	60mm
8.5–11mm	375mm	250mm	50mm	75mm
Over 11mm	450mm	300mm	60mm	90mm

The sail numbers and letters of the size shown on the mainsail must be displayed by alternative means if none of the numbered sails is set. (See SR 10.52.)

6.0 STRUCTURAL FEATURES

Race Category

Yachts shall have been built in
accordance with ABS-approved plans
according to the ABS Guide for Building
and Classing Offshore Racing Yachts.
IOR Age or Series Date (whichever is
earlier) of 1/1986 or later.   0   1

IOR Age or Series Date (whichever is earlier)
of 1/1987 or later and rating of29.5 ft. and
above. (40 ft. LOA) and (12.19m LOA).   2

IOR Age or Series Date (whichever is earlier)
of 1/1988 or later and rating less than 29.5 ft.
(40 ft. LOA) and (12.19m LOA).   2

6.1. The **hull,** including deck, coach roof,
and all other parts, shall form an

Race Category

integral, essentially watertight, unit and   0   1   2   3   4
any openings in it shall be capable of
being immediately secured to maintain
this integrity (see 5.1). For example,
running rigging or control lines shall not
compromise this watertight unit.
Centerboard and daggerboard trunks shall
not open into the interior of the hull.

6.12 Hatches. No hatches forward of the   0   1   2   3   4
BMAX [maximum beam] station shall
open inwards except ports having an area
of less than 110 sq. in. (710sq.cm.).
Hatches shall be so arranged as to be
above the water when the hull is heeled
90 degrees. All hatches shall be
permanently fitted so that they can be
closed immediately and will remain
firmly shut in a 180–degree capsize. The
main companionway hatch shall be fitted
with a strong securing arrangement that
shall be operable from above and below.

6.13 Companionways. All blocking   0   1   2   3   4
arrangements, washboards, hatch boards,
etc.) shall be capable of being secured in
position with the hatch open or shut and
shall be secured to the yacht by lanyard
or other mechanical means to prevent
their being lost overboard.

6.14 Cockpit companionways, if extending   0   1   2   3   4
below main deck level, must be capable
of being blocked off to the level of the
main deck at the sheerline abreast the
opening. When such blocking
arrangements are in place, this

companionway (or hatch) shall continue
to give access to the interior of the hull.

6.21 Cockpits shall be structurall strong,   0   1   2   3   4
self-draining, and permanently
incorporated as an integral part of the
hull. They must be essentially
watertight—that is, all openings to the
hull must be capable of being strongly
and rigidly secured. Any bow, lateral,
central, or stern well will be considered
as a cockpit for the purposes of 6.21,
6.22, 6.23 and 6.31.

6.22 Cockpits opening aft to the sea. The   0   1   2   3   4
lower edge of the companionway shall
not be below main deck level as
measured above. The openings shall not
be less than 50% of maximum cockpit
width. The requirement in 6.31 that
cockpits must drain at all angles of heel
applies.

6.23 Cockpit Volume.

6.23.1 The maximum volume of all cockpits   0   1
below lowest coamings shall not exceed
6% $L \times B \times FA$ [6% loaded waterline $\times$
max. beam $\times$ freeboard abreast the
cockpit]. The cockpit sole must be at
least 2% L above LWL [2% length over
all above loaded waterline].

6.23.2 The maximum volume of all cockpits   2   3   4
below lowest coamings shall not exceed
9% $L \times B \times FA$ [9% loaded waterline $\times$
max. beam and freeboard abreast the

Race Category

cockpit]. The cockpit sole must be at
least 2%L above LWL [2% length overall
above loaded waterline].

6.31 Cockpit drains.

6.31.1 For yachts 21 ft. R (28 ft./8.53m   0   1   2   3   4
length overall and over). Cockpit
drainsadequate to drain cockpits quickly
but with a combined area (after
allowance for screens, if attached) of not
less than the equivalent of four ¾-in.
(19mm) diameter drains. Yachts built
before 1/72 must have drains with a
combined area (after allowance for
screens, if attached) of not less than the
equivalent of two 1-in. (25mm) drain.
Cockpits shall drain at all angles of heel.
Yachts built before 1/77 may conform to
6.31.2 for races in categories 3 and 4.

6.31.2 For yachts under 21 ft.R (28   0   1   2   3   4
ft./8.53m length overall). Cockpit drains
adequate to drain cockpits quickly but not
less in combined area (after allowance for
screens, if attached) than the equivalent
of two 1-in. (25mm) diameter drains.
Cockpits shall drain at all angles of heel.

6.4 Storm covering for all windows more   0   1   2   3   4
than 2 sq. ft. in area (1858sq.cm).

6.51 Seacocks or valves on all through-hull   0   1   2   3   4
openings below LWL, except integral
deck scuppers, shaft log, speed
indicators, depth finders, etc. However, a

means of closing such openings when
necessary, shall be provided. Does not
apply to category 4 races to yachts built
before 1/76.

6.52 Soft wood plugs, tapered and of the   0 1 2 3 4
correct size, to be attached to, or adjacent
to, the appropriate fitting.

6.53 Sheet winches shall be mounted in such   0 1 2 3 4
a way that no operator is required to be
substantially below deck.

6.54 Mast step. The heel of a keel-stepped   0 1 2 3 4
mast shall be securely fastened to the
mast step or adjoining structure.

6.55 Bulkhead. The hull shall have a watertight bulkhead.

6.6 Lifelines, Stanchions, Pulpits, and Jackstays

6.61
For all yachts.

6.61.1 Lifeline terminals and lifeline   0 1 2 3 4
material. Where wire lifelines are
required, they shall be multi-strand steel
wire (see also IYRR 62). A taut lanyard
of synthetic rope may be used to secure
lifelines, provided that when in position
its length not exceed 4 in. (100mm).

6.61.2 Stanchions shall not be angled at   0 1 2 3 4
more than 10 degrees from the vertical at
any point above 50mm from the deck;
nor within the first 50mm from the deck,
may they be displaced horizontally from

Race Category

the point at which they emerge from the
deck or base by more than 10mm. For
yachts with an Age Date of 1/88 or later,
stanchions shall be straight, except that
one bend is permitted in the first 50mm
above deck. For yachts with an Age Date
of 1/87 or later, stanchions, pulpits, and
lifelines shall not be made of carbon
fiber.

6.61.3 Overlapping pulpits. Lifelines need   0   1   2   3   4
not be affixed to the bow pulpit if they
terminate at, or pass through, adequately
braced stanchions 2 ft. (610mm) [18 in.
(457mm) for yachts under 21 ft. r] (28
ft./8.53m length overall) above
theworking deck, set inside and
overlapping the bow pulpit, provided that
the gap between the upper lifeline and
the bow pulpit does not exceed 6 in.
(152mm).

6.61.4 Pulpit and stanchion fixing. Pulpits   0   1   2   3   4
and stanchions shall be securely attached.
(a) When there are sockets or studs,
these shall be through-bolted, bonded, or
welded. The pulpit(s) and/or stanchions
fitted to these shall be mechanically
retained without the help of the lifelines.
(b) Without sockets or studs, pulpits
and/or stanchions shall be through-
bolted, bonded, or welded.

The bases of pulpits and stanchions shall
not be further inboard from the edge of
the working deck than 5% of BMAX
[maximum beam] or 6 in. (152mm),

whichever is greater. Stanchion bases
shall not be situated out board of the
working deck.

6.62 For yachts of 21 ft.R (28 ft./8.53m
length over all and over.

6.62.1 Taut double lifelines with upper
lifeline of wire at a height of not less
than 2 ft. (609mm) above the working
deck, to be permanently supported at
intervals of not more than 7 ft. (2.13m).
When the cockpit opens aft to the sea,
additional lifelines must be fitted so that
no opening is greater in height than 22
in. (560mm).

6.62.2 Pulpits. Fixed bow pulpit (forward of
headstay) and stern pulpit (unless lifelines
are arranged as to adequately
substitutefor a stern pulpit). Lower
lifelines need not extend through the bow
pulpit. Upper rails of pulpits shall be at
not less height above the working deck
than upper lifelines. Upper rails in bow
pulpits shall be securely closed while
racing. Any lifeline attachment point will
be considered as a stanchion in so far as
its base shall not be situated outboard of
the working deck.

6.63 For yachts under 21 ft. R (28 ft./8.53m
length overall).

6.63.1 Taut single wire lifelines, at a height   0   1   2   3   4
of not less than 1 in. (475mm) above the
working deck, to be permanently

Race Category

supported at intervals of not more than 7
ft. (2.13m). If the lifelines are at any
point more than 22 in. (560mm) above
the rail cap, a second intermediate
lifeline must be fitted. If the cockpit aft
to the sea additional lifelines must be
fitted so that no opening is greater in
height than 22 in. (560mm).

6.63.2 Pulpits. Fixed bow pulpit and stern   0   1   2   3   4
pulpit (unless lifelines are arranged to
adequately substitute for a stern pulpit).
Lower lifelines need not extend through
the bow pulpit. Upper rails of pulpits
must be at no less height above the
working deck than upper lifelines. Upper
rails in bow pulpits shall be securely
closed while racing. The bow pulpit may
be fitted abaft the forestay with its bases
secured at any points on deck, but a
point on its upper rail must be within 16
in. (406mm) of the forestay on which the
foremost headsail is handed. Any lifeline
attachment point will be considered as a
stanchion so far as its base shall not be
situated outboard of the working deck.

6.64 Toerails. A toerail of not less than 1 in.   0   1   2   3
(25mm) shall be permanently fitted
around the deck forward of the mast,
except in way of fittings. Location to be
not farther inboard from the edge of the
working deck than ⅓ of the local beam.

A third lifeline (or second for yachts
under 21 ft. R—(28 ft./8.53m length

overall) at a height of not less than 1 in.
(25mm) or more than 2 in. (50mm)
above the working deck will be accepted
in place of a toerail.

In yachts built before 1/81, a toerail of
¾-in. (19mm) will be accepted.

6.65 Jackstays

Wire jackstays must be fitted on deck, port   0   1   2
and starboard of the yacht's centerline to
provide secure attachments for safety
harnesses. Jackstays must be attached to
through-bolted or welded deck plates or other
suitable and strong attachment. The jackstays
must, if possible, be fitted in such a way that
a crew member, when clipped on, can move
from a cockpit to the forward or after end of
the main deck without unclipping the harness.
If the deck layout renders this impossible,
additional lines must be fitted so that a crew
member can move as described with a
minimum of clipping operations.
   A crew member must be able to clip on
before coming on deck, unclip after going
below and remain clipped on while moving
laterally across the yacht on the foredeck, the
afterdeck, and amidships. If necessary,
additional jackstays and/or through-bolted or
welded attachment points must be provided for
this purpose.
   Through-bolted or welded attachment
points, or other suitable and strongfastening
for safety harnesses must

Race Category

be provided adjacent to stations such as
the helm, sheet winches and masts,
where crew members work for long
periods. Jackstays should be positioned in
such a way that the safety harness
lanyard will be as short as possible.

7.0 ACCOMODATIONS

7.11 Toilet, securely installed	0	1	2	
7.12 Toilet, securely installed, or fitted bucket			3	4
7.2 Bunks, securely installed	0	1	2	3	4
7.3 Cooking stove, securely installed against a capsize with safe accessible fuel shutoff control capable of being safely operated in a seaway.	0	1	2	3
7.4 Galley facilities	0	1	2	3	4
7.51 Water tank(s), securely installed and capable of dividing the water supply into at least three compartments and discharging through a pump. The quantity of water to be taken aboard is left to the discretion of the organizing authority, but two gallons (9 liters) per person per 1,000 miles shall be taken as the absolute minimum.	0
7.52 Water tank(s), securely installed and capable of dividing the water supply into		1

Race Category

at least two compartments and
discharging through a pump.

7.53 At least one securely installed water   2   3
tank discharging through a pump.

8.0 GENERAL EQUIPMENT

8.1 Fire extinguishers, at least two, readily   0   1   2   3   4
accessible in suitable and different parts
of the boat.

8.21.1 Bilge pumps, at least two manually   0   1   2
operated, securely fitted to the yacht's
structure, one operable above, the other
below deck. Each pump shall be operable
wit hall cockpit seats, hatches and
companionways shut.

8.21.2 Each bilge pump shall be provided   0   1   2
with permanently fitted discharge pipe(s)
of sufficient capacity to accommodate
simultaneously both pumps.

8.21.3 No bilge pumps may discharge into a   0   1   2   3   4
cockpit unless that cockpit opens aft to
the sea. Bilge pumps shall not be
connected to cockpit drains.

8.21.4 Unless permanently fitted, each bilge   0   1   2   3   4
pump handle shall be provided wit ha
lanyard or catch or similar device to
prevent accidental loss.

8.22 One manual bilge pump operable with   3

Race Category

all cockpit seats, hatches and
companionways closed.

8.23 One manual bilge pump.   4

8.24 Two buckets of stout construction each
with at least 2 gallons (9 liters) capacity.
Each bucket to have a lanyard.

8.31 Anchors. Two with cables except yachts   0   1   2   3
rating under 21 ft. R (28 ft./8.53m
length overall), which shall carry at least
one anchor and cable. Anchors and any
chain shall be securely fastened in the
position recorded on the Rating
Certificate when not in use.

8.32 One anchor and cable. Anchors(s) and   4
any chain shall be securely fastened in
the position recorded on the Rating
Certificate when not in use.

8.41 Flashlights, one of which is suitable for   0   1   2   3
signaling, water-resistant, with spare
batteries and bulbs.

8.42 At least one flashlight, water-resistant,   4
with spare batteries and bulb.

8.5 First aid kit and manual.   0   1   2   3   4

8.6 Foghorn   0   1   2   3   4

8.7 Radar reflector. If a radar reflector is   0   1   2   3   4
octahedral it must have a minimum
diagonal measurement of 18 in.
(457mm), or if not octahedral, must have

Race Category

a documented "equivalent echoing area" of not less than 10 sq. m.

8.8 Set of **international code flags** and **international code book**.   0   1

8.9 Shutoff valves on all fuel tanks.   0   1   2   3   4

9.0 NAVIGATION EQUIPMENT

9.1 Compass, marine type, properly installed and adjusted.   0   1   2   3   4

9.2 Spare compass.   0   1   2   3

9.3 Charts, light list and **piloting equipment.**   0   1   2   3

9.4 Sextant, tables and accurate **time piece.**   0   1

9.5 Radio direction finder or an automatic position-fixing device.   0   1   2

9.6 Lead line or echo sounder   0   1   2   3   4

9.7 Speedometer or **distance-measuring instrument.**   0   1   2   3

9.8 Navigation lights, to be shown as required by the International Regulations for Preventing Collisions at Sea, mounted so that they will not be masked by sails or the heeling of the yacht.   0   1   2   3   4
Yachts under 7m LOA shall comply with the regulations for those between 12m and 7m LOA [i.e., they shall exhibit

sidelights and sternlight].

Navigation lights shall not be mounted below deck level. Spare bulbs for navigation lights shall be carried.

As a guide, minimum bulb wattage in navigation lights for yachts under sail should be as follows:

(a) Yachts less than 2m (39.6 ft.) LOA, 10 watts.

(b) Yachts of 12m (39.6 ft.) LOA and greater, 25 watts.

Attention is drawn to Part C and Technical Annex I of International Regulations for Preventing Collisions at Sea, 1972.

10.0 EMERGENCY EQUIPMENT

10.1 Emergency navigation lights 0 and power source. Emergency navigation lights shall have the same minimum specifications as the navigation lights in 9.8, and a power source and wiring separate from that used for the normal navigation lights. Emergency navigation lights shall not be used if the normal navigation lights (under Rule 9.8) are operable.

0 1 2 3

10.21 The following specifications for **mandatory sails** give maximum areas; smaller areas may well suit some yachts. Appropriate sheeting positions on deck shall be provided for these sails.

10.21.1 One storm trysail not larger than

0 1 2

Race Category

$0.175 \times P \times E$ in area. It shall be sheeted independently of the boom and shall have neither a headboard nor battens and be of suitable strength for the purpose. The yacht's sail number and letter(s) shall be placed on both sides of the trysail in as large a size as is practicable.

Aromatic polyamides, carbon fibers, and other high modulous fibers shall not be used in the storm trysail.

10.21.2 One storm jib of not more than $0.05 \times IG \times IG$ (5% height of the foretriangle squared) in area, the luff or

     0 1 2

which does not exceed $0.65 \times IG$ (65% height of the foretriangle), and of suitable strength for the purpose.

Aromatic polyamides, carbon fibers and other high modulous fibers shall not be used in the storm jib.

10.21.3 One heavy-weather jib of suitable strength for the purpose with area not greater than $0.135 \times IG \times IG$ (13.5% height of the foretriangle squared) and which does not contain reef points.

     0 1 2

10.22 One heavy-weather jib as in 10.21.3 (or heavy-weather sail in a boat with no forestay) and either:
(a) a storm trysail as in 10.21.1 or
(b) mainsail reefing capable of reducing effective luff to 60% P or less.

              3 4

10.23 Any storm or heavy-weather jib if designed for a seastay or luff-groove

     0 1 2 3 4

Race Category

device shall have an alternative method
of attachment to the stay.

10.24 No mast shall have less than two   0   1   2   3   4
halyards, each capable of hoisting a sail.

10.3 Emergency steering equipment

10.31 An emergency tiller capable of being   0   1   2   3
fitted to the rudder stock.

10.32 Crews must be aware of alternative   0   1   2   3   4
methods of steering the yacht in any sea
condition in the event of rudder failure.
An inspector may require that this
method be demonstrated.

10.4 Tools and spare parts, including   0   1   2   3   4
adequate means to disconnect or sever
the standing rigging from the hull in the
case of need.

10.5 Yacht's name on miscellaneous **buoyant** 0   1   2   3   4
equipment such as lifejackets, oars,
cushions, lifebuoys and lifeslings, etc.

10.51 Lifebuoys, lifeslings, liferafts and life- 0   1   2   3   4
jackets shall be fitted with **retro-
reflective material.**

10.52 Sail numbers, either portable or   0   1   2   3
displayed on each side of the hull and
meeting the requirements for mainsail
numbers.

10.61 Marine radio transmitter and   0   1   2
receiver. If the regular antenna depends

Race Category

upon the mast, an emergency antenna
must be provided.

Yachts fitted with VHF transceivers are
recommended to install VHF Channel 72
(156.625 MHZ Simplex). This is an
international ship-ship channel which, by
"common use," could become an
accepted yacht-yacht channel for all
ocean-racing yachts anywhere in the
world.

10.62 In addition to 10.61, a waterproof   0   1
hand-held VHF transceiver is
recommended.

10.63 Radio receiver capable of receiving   0   1   2   3   4
weather bulletins.

10.64 EPIRBS. Emergency indicator beacon   0   1
transmitting on 121.5, 243 or 406 MHz.

10.7 At least 2 gallons (9 liters) or **water** for   0   1   2   3
emergency use carried in one or more
containers.

11.0 SAFETY EQUIPMENT

11.1 Life jackets, one for each crew member.   0   2   3   4
In the absence of any specification, the
following definition of a life jacket is
recommended: "A life jacket should be of
a form which is capable of providing not
less than 16kg of buoyancy, arranged so
that an unconscious man will be securely
suspended face upwards at approximately
45 degrees to the water surface."

Race Category

11.2 Whistles attached to life jackets.   0   1   2   3

11.3 Safety belt* (harness type, one for each   0   1   2   3
crew member. Each yacht may be
required to demonstrate that ⅔ of the
crew can be adequately attached to strong
points on the yacht

11.4 Life raft(s)** capable of carrying the   0   1   2   3
entire crew and meeting the following
requirements:

A. Must be carried on the working deck
or in a special stowage opening
immediately to the working deck
containing the life raft(s) only.

B. For yachts built after 1–7–83:
Life raft(s) may only be stowed under the
working deck provided:
(a) the stowage compartment is
watertight or self-draining.
(b) if the stowage compartment is not

watertight, then the floor of the special
stowage is defined as the cockpit solely
for the purposes of rule 6.23.2.
(c) the cover of this compartment shall
be capable of being opened under water
pressure.

C. Life raft(s) packed in a valise and not
exceeding 40kg may be securely stowed
below deck adjacent to the
companionway.

D. Each raft shall be capable of being got

to the lifelines within 15 seconds.

E. Must have a valid annual certificate
from the manufacturer or an approved
servicing agent certifying that it has been
inspected, that it complies with the above
requirements and stating the official
capacity of the raft which shall not be
exceeded. The certificate, or a copy
thereof, to be carried on board the yacht.

* See Appendix I
** See Appendix II

11.51 Lifebuoy with a drogue, or lifesling,   0   1   2   3   4
   equipped with a self-igniting light within
   reach of the helmsman and ready for
   instant use.

11.52 In addition to 11.51. One lifebuoy,   0   1   2
   within reach of the helmsman and ready
   for instant use and equipped with a
   whistle, dye marker, drogue, a self-
   igniting light, and a pole and flag. The
   pole shall be either permanently extended
   or be capable of being fully automatically
   extended in less than 5 seconds. It
   shallbe attached to the lifebuoy with 10
   ft. (3.048m) of floatable line and is to be
   ofa length and so ballasted that the flag
   will fly at least 6 ft. (1.828m) off the
   water.

11.61 Distress signals conforming to the   0   1   2   3   4
   current International Convention for the
   Safety of Life at Sea (SOLAS)
   regulations (Chapter III, Visual Signals)

Race Category

to be stowed in a waterproof container or
containers, as indicated.

11.62 Twelve red parachute flares. (SOLAS reg. 35)	0	1			
11.63 Four red parachute flares. (SOLAS reg. 35)			2	3	
11.64 Four red hand flares. (SOLAS reg. 36)	0	1	2	3	4
11.65 Four white hand flares.	0	1	2	3	4

INDEX